Lecture Notes in Computer Science 8989

Commenced Publication in 1973
Founding and Former Series Editors:
Gerhard Goos, Juris Hartmanis, and Jan van Leeuwen

Editorial Board

More information about this series at http://www.springer.com/series/7584

Shigeru Chiba · Éric Tanter
Erik Ernst · Robert Hirschfeld (Eds.)

Transactions on Aspect-Oriented Software Development XII

 Springer

Editors-in-Chief

Shigeru Chiba
The University of Tokyo
Tokyo
Japan

Éric Tanter
University of Chile
Santiago
Chile

Guest Editors

Erik Ernst
Google Aarhus
Aarhus
Denmark

Robert Hirschfeld
Hasso Plattner Institute
Potsdam
Germany

ISSN 0302-9743   ISSN 1611-3349 (electronic)
Lecture Notes in Computer Science
ISBN 978-3-662-46733-6   ISBN 978-3-662-46734-3 (eBook)
DOI 10.1007/978-3-662-46734-3

Library of Congress Control Number: 2015934909

Springer Heidelberg New York Dordrecht London

Printed on acid-free paper

Springer-Verlag GmbH Berlin Heidelberg is part of Springer Science+Business Media
(www.springer.com)

Editorial

Welcome to Volume XII of the Transactions on Aspect-Oriented Software Development. This volume has one regular paper and a special section on selected papers from Modularity 2014. The regular paper "Modular Reasoning in Aspect-Oriented Languages from a Substitution Perspective" presents a new approach to modular reasoning of aspect-oriented programs. Modular reasoning in aspect-oriented languages like AspectJ has been leading interesting discussion in the research community and a number of papers have been published on this topic. This paper reports the latest result on this topic. In the paper, the authors propose their new language ContractAJ, in which programmers can describe contracts for modular reasoning. The special section following this paper is a collection of the papers selected from Modularity 2014 conference. The papers were guest edited by Erik Ernst, Research Results Program Chair, and Robert Hirschfeld, Modularity Visions Program Chair of the conference. Although the conference proceedings is already a collection of high-quality papers in this area, which are available from ACM digital library, this special section collected longer versions of the best papers presented at the conference.

We thank the guest editors for soliciting submissions, running review processes, and collecting final versions within such a short period. We are pleased to publish this special issue in a timely fashion. We also thank the editorial board members for their continued guidance and input on the policies of the journal, the reviewers for volunteering a significant amount of time despite their busy schedules, and the authors who submitted papers to the journal.

January 2015

Shigeru Chiba
Éric Tanter

Guest Editors' Foreword

Special Section of Selected Papers from Modularity 2014

This special section of TAOSD contains selected papers presented at Modularity 2014, the 13th conference in the conference series that started out under the name International Conference on Aspect-Oriented Software Development (AOSD). The papers were selected based on input from the Modularity 2014 Program Committees, for which we served as Program Committee Chairs. The authors of the selected papers were invited to submit a revised and extended version of their work. Each revised paper was reviewed both by a member of one of the two Program Committees who had been a reviewer of the original conference paper and by one other reviewer. Each paper underwent two revision steps, thus ensuring that the extensions were substantial and well integrated. As is common for this kind of section, we handled the reviewing process without the involvement of the Editors-in-Chief.

The result of the substantial efforts made by the authors and the careful feedback provided by the reviewers is this interesting snapshot of current state-of-the-art research on modularity. The topics covered include novel dynamic semantics through delegation proxies, modularity potential detection based on co-change clusters, improvements in reusability for components of semantic specifications of programming languages, and probabilistic model checking applied to dynamically generated members of a product line. We hope that you will enjoy reading this section!

January 2015

Erik Ernst
Robert Hirschfeld

Organization

Editorial Board

Contents

Regular Paper

Modular Reasoning in Aspect-Oriented Languages from a Substitution Perspective

Tim Molderez[(✉)] and Dirk Janssens

Ansymo (Antwerp Systems and Software Modelling),
University of Antwerp, Antwerp, Belgium
{tim.molderez,dirk.janssens}@uantwerp.be

Abstract. In object-oriented languages, a notion of behavioural subtyping is needed to enable modular reasoning. This is no longer sufficient when such languages are extended with aspects. In general, all aspects need to be inspected in order to understand the behaviour of a single method or proceed call, which complicates reasoning about aspect-oriented programs. In this paper, we present an approach to modular reasoning that consists of two parts. First, the advice substitution principle, based on behavioural subtyping, identifies when it is possible to remain unaware of an advice while preserving modular reasoning. Second, in cases where it is undesired or impossible to be unaware of an advice, a simple specification clause can be used to restore modular reasoning and to become aware of this advice. We show that our approach effectively enables modular reasoning about pre- and postconditions in a minimal aspect-oriented language called ContractAJ. To ensure the approach is used correctly, we also provide a runtime contract enforcement algorithm that is specified in ContractAJ, and implemented in AspectJ.

Keywords: Aspect-oriented programming languages · Modular reasoning · Behavioural subtyping · Contract enforcement · Design by contract

1 Introduction

Aspect-oriented programming (AOP) languages have introduced powerful mechanisms to modularize crosscutting concerns, as aspects allow for the modification of a program's behaviour in a quantifiable manner. However, aspects represent a double-edged sword: while powerful, the presence of aspects also complicates modular reasoning. Modular reasoning is mainly concerned with the ability to reason about a method call, based on the specifications of the receiver's static type. In an AOP language like AspectJ, modular reasoning is obstructed by the fact that aspects can implicitly alter the behaviour of method calls. In general, all aspects need to be inspected to determine whether or not a method call is affected by an aspect, which goes against modular reasoning.

Tim Molderez—Funded by a doctoral scholarship of the Research Foundation - Flanders (FWO).

© Springer-Verlag Berlin Heidelberg 2015
S. Chiba et al. (Eds.): Transactions on AOSD XII, LNCS 8989, pp. 3–59, 2015.
DOI: 10.1007/978-3-662-46734-3_1

In this paper, we present an approach to modular reasoning for aspect-oriented languages, without modifying the programming language itself. There are several languages that restrict AOP [2,33,39] in the sense that advice can only apply to join points that have been explicitly exposed by the developer, making it easy to distinguish which method calls may or may not be affected by advice. While this greatly helps in restoring modular reasoning, the advantages of the widely debated quantification and obliviousness [17] properties of AOP are lost to a certain extent.

If all usable join points need to be mentioned explicitly, it becomes less appealing to use aspects for crosscutting concerns where being unaware/oblivious of such concerns is unlikely to cause harm. This includes examples such as logging/tracing, caching, profiling, contract enforcement and various other concerns that provide additional functionality without interfering with the rest of the system. The extra effort needed to make join points explicit only grows as the aspects that implement such concerns rely more extensively on quantification, i.e. as they need to affect more and more locations in the source code. Given this observation, our goal is to enable modular reasoning in a manner that preserves obliviousness for those aspects where it is an advantage, and to become aware of those aspects where obliviousness is a disadvantage.

We will do this from a design by contract [30] perspective, based on a notion of substitution for advice. In object-oriented programming, the developer may not know the receiver's dynamic type when making method calls, so he/she can only take into account the specifications of the static type. Such specifications are defined in terms of preconditions, postconditions and invariants, also commonly referred to as contracts. To prevent any surprising behaviour when making method calls, subtypes should respect the contracts of their ancestors. In other words, they should adhere to a notion of behavioural subtyping [3,16,27]. This allows an instance of a subtype to substitute for any instance of an ancestor type. This paper uses a similar notion of substitution for advice: the advice substitution principle (ASP). This principle essentially states that an advice should comply with the contracts of the join points it advises. The ASP was first introduced informally by Wampler [41, Sect. 3.1.3] as one of several aspect-oriented design principles. We will present the ASP on a more formal level, as one of the two parts that form our approach to modular reasoning in AOP languages.

The second part of our approach focuses on advice that cannot satisfy the ASP. Unlike behavioural subtyping in OOP, we do not use the ASP as a strict rule that should hold for all advice. Instead, the ASP is used to distinguish between the advice that already preserve modular reasoning (e.g. logging, caching, profiling, ...), and the advice where extra effort is needed to restore modular reasoning (e.g. authentication, authorization, transaction management, ...). This extra effort comes in the form of a specification clause called @advisedBy. This clause explicitly indicates that a method may be advised by a given sequence of advice, such that this method and its clients become aware of these advice. This approach of using both the ASP and the @advisedBy clause forms the paper's main contribution. The approach is presented in the context of a representative, minimal aspect-oriented language called ContractAJ, which is based on Contract-Java [18], AspectJ and Eos-U [34]. Within this language, we will show that our approach is sound. That is, the approach effectively preserves modular reasoning of method and proceed calls in ContractAJ, even in the presence of shared join points, overriding advice, higher-order advice (advice that advises advice) and pointcuts depending on runtime information. In addition, we specify an algorithm that performs runtime contract enforcement in ContractAJ. It is able to assign the blame when a contract is broken, taking into account behavioural subtyping, the ASP and the @advisedBy clause. To demonstrate an instantiation of this algorithm in a full programming language, it is also implemented as a small design-by-contract library for AspectJ.

In summary, this paper makes the following contributions:

- We first present the syntax and operational semantics of the ContractAJ language (Sects. 2 and 3).
- We define and discuss the ASP (Sect. 4).
- For those advice where it is undesired or impossible to preserve obliviousness, we present the @advisedBy clause to restore modular reasoning (Sect. 5).
- We show that the approach preserves modular reasoning about pre- and post-conditions in method and proceed calls in ContractAJ (Sect. 6).
- Finally, we specify a runtime contract enforcement algorithm in ContractAJ. We also discuss its implementation in AspectJ (Sect. 7).

2   ContractAJ

Before delving into the specifics surrounding the ASP and @advisedBy clause, we first introduce the ContractAJ language, which is used throughout the paper to study modular reasoning in the context of aspects. This section presents the motivation behind ContractAJ, its syntax and its informal operational semantics.

2.1   Motivation

There are two main reasons for introducing the ContractAJ language. First, it is a minimal language, which makes it better suited to study modular reasoning at a more formal level. The ContractAJ language is based on the minimal ContractJava language introduced in Findler et al. [18], where it was used to specify a contract enforcement algorithm in an object-oriented setting. In its turn, ContractJava is an extension that adds contracts to the ClassicJava calculus [19].

The second reason to introduce ContractAJ is that we wish to explore AOP in a more flexible and unified form than is present in AspectJ. While AspectJ currently is the most established AOP language, some design decisions were made to achieve better performance or faster language adoption, resulting in a number of more specialised, less flexible language constructs. This includes the distinction between aspects and classes, limited control over instantiating aspects, anonymous advice and the restriction that an aspect cannot extend from a concrete (non-abstract) aspect. We prefer to keep ContractAJ a small and flexible language. Additionally, unifying aspect-oriented concepts with object-oriented ones also helps us to relate modular reasoning in AOP to modular reasoning in OOP. This type of unification is visible in several design choices:

- Like Eos-U [34] and CaesarJ [5], ContractAJ unifies aspects and classes. This means aspects are first-class, and aspects can freely extend other aspects. Pointcut-advice pairs are also named, such that they can be overridden.
- Before and after advice are treated as special cases of around advice, rather than viewing around advice as a combination of before and after advice. Around advice have the closest relation to overriding methods, in the sense that around advice also override the behaviour of methods, and that proceed calls behave in a similar fashion to super calls.
- The execution of advice is specified as an extension of the method lookup mechanism.
- When an advice is about to be executed, the same lookup mechanism is reused to allow for higher-order advice (advice that advises other advice).

2.2   Syntax

The syntax of ContractAJ is shown in Fig. 1. To illustrate most of the syntax's constructs, an example of a simple ContractAJ program is given in Fig. 2. It describes an aspect called `Security` with an around advice named `authenticate`, which is executed at each method call to `Account.withdraw`. What is immediately noticeable is the lack of an `aspect` keyword, indicating the unification of aspects and classes. Like the classpects in Eos-U or Caesar classes in CaesarJ, there is no separate module type dedicated to aspects. Instead, definitions of pointcuts and advice are allowed in regular classes, such that they can effectively serve as aspects. This allows for more flexibility, as the developer regains precise control over the instantiation of aspects by reusing the class instantiation mechanism. Once an aspect is instantiated with the `new` keyword, its pointcuts are active.

As pointcuts and advice are now regular class members, aspects can extend other aspects as well. Note that, for reasons of simplicity, pointcuts and advice are paired. Because these pointcut-advice pairs are named, this enables overriding. That is, if an aspect with an overriding pointcut-advice pair is instantiated, the overriding pointcut-advice pair is active, but the overridden one is not.

The pointcut language, shown in the *pcut* rule, provides most of the basic pointcut constructs: method and advice executions can be captured with `execution`. Method calls are captured with `call`. Like AspectJ, the receiver of method calls/advice executions can be bound to a variable using `this` or `target`. While there is no `args` construct to bind parameters as in AspectJ, method/advice arguments are bound directly in the `execution/call` pointcut. Note that our pointcut language also includes an `if` construct. Just like AspectJ, when an `if` construct is used, the pointcut can only match when the given if-condition is true at the current join point. We intentionally included this `if`

$$program ::= prec\ def^*\ \texttt{main}\{e\}$$
$$prec ::= \texttt{declare precedence}\ (c.a)^*;$$
$$def ::= \texttt{class}\ c\ \texttt{extends}\ c\ \{(field \mid method \mid adv)^*\}$$
$$field ::= t\ f$$
$$method ::= contract\ [\texttt{@advisedBy}\ (c.a)^*]\ t\ m\ (arg^*)\{e\}$$
$$adv ::= contract\ (\texttt{before} \mid \texttt{after} \mid \texttt{around})\ a:\ pcut\{e\}$$
$$contract ::= \texttt{@requires}\ e\ \texttt{@ensures}\ e$$
$$arg ::= t\ var$$
$$e ::= \texttt{new}\ c \mid var \mid bool \mid \texttt{null}$$
$$\mid e.f \mid e.f\texttt{=}e$$
$$\mid e.m(e^*) \mid \texttt{super}.m(e^*) \mid \texttt{proceed}(e^*)$$
$$\mid (t)\ e \mid e\ \texttt{instanceof}\ t$$
$$\mid \texttt{let}\{binding^*\}\ \texttt{in}\ \{e\}$$
$$\mid \texttt{if}(e)\{e\}\texttt{else}\{e\}$$
$$\mid \texttt{error}(e)$$
$$\mid \{e\ ;\ e\}$$
$$\mid \texttt{proc}$$
$$bool ::= \texttt{true} \mid \texttt{false}$$
$$binding ::= var\texttt{=}e$$
$$pcut ::= \texttt{execution}(t\ c.x(arg^*))\ \texttt{\&\&}\ \texttt{this}\ (var)[\texttt{\&\&}\ \texttt{if}\ (e)]$$
$$\mid \texttt{call}(t\ c.m(arg^*))\ \texttt{\&\&}\ \texttt{target}(var)[\texttt{\&\&}\ \texttt{if}\ (e)]$$
$$var ::= \text{a variable name or}\ \texttt{this}$$
$$c ::= \text{a class name (or}\ \texttt{Object})$$
$$f ::= \text{a field name}$$
$$m ::= \text{a method name}$$
$$a ::= \text{an advice name}$$
$$x ::= m \mid a$$
$$t ::= c \mid \texttt{boolean}$$

Fig. 1. ContractAJ syntax

construct to demonstrate that our approach to modular reasoning also takes into account pointcuts that can only be determined at runtime.

The *prec* rule contains the syntax of the advice precedence/composition mechanism; it determines in which order advice should be executed when multiple advice share the same join point. In the example of Fig. 2, the `declare precedence` statement specifies that the advice `Security.authenticate` has a higher precedence than `Logger.write` (not shown). ContractAJ's precedence mechanism is similar to that of AspectJ, apart from two small differences: ContractAJ's precedence statement is slightly more fine-grained, as it lists advice rather than aspects. ContractAJ programs also contain only one global declare precedence statement. While AspectJ does allow for multiple precedence declarations, note that they can always combined into one global statement. (Otherwise there would be a precedence conflict.)

The constructs needed to specify contracts are provided in the *contract* rule. Methods and advice can specify their preconditions and postconditions using the `@requires` and `@ensures` constructs. Note that our main focus is on pre- and postconditions, which is why there is no syntax for invariants, history constraints or frame properties. Additionally, the optional `@advisedBy` clause can be used

```
declare precedence Security.authenticate, Logger.write;

class Account extends Object {
    @requires  this.getAmount() >= m && m>0
    @ensures   this.getAmount() == old(this.getAmount()) - m
    @advisedBy Security.authenticate
    int withdraw(int m) {...} ... }

class Security extends Object {
    @requires proc
    @ensures if(isLoggedIn(acc.getOwner())){proc}else{true}
    around authenticate: call(int Account.withdraw(int m)) && target(acc) {
        if (isLoggedIn(acc.getOwner())) {
            proceed(acc,m);
        }
    } ... }
...
main {
    Security sec = new Security; Account acc = new Account;
    acc.withdraw(10); // advised by sec.authenticate
}
```

Fig. 2. An example ContractAJ program

by a method if it should become aware of one or more advice. We should also mention the `proc` keyword in the e rule, which serves as a placeholder for the contracts of any proceed calls. This keyword can only be used in the contracts of advice, to refer to the pre- or postcondition of the next advice we are aware of. The semantics of both `@advisedBy` and `proc` are detailed in Sect. 5.

Finally, note that we will use the symbols for a class (c), field (f), method (m), advice (a), method-or-advice (x) and type (t) as naming conventions throughout the entire paper.

2.3   Informal ContractAJ Semantics

The semantics of ContractAJ is an extension of the object-oriented Contract-Java [18] language. It is not a pure extension, in the sense that support for interfaces was removed in order to keep the language minimal. What is added semantics-wise can be found mainly in the language's join point model, pointcut language and the lookup procedure. This section describes ContractAJ's join point model, as well as informally explains ContractAJ's lookup procedure.

Join Point Model. The call and execution pointcuts of ContractAJ closely correspond to those of AspectJ: a call pointcut matches on method calls where the receiver's *static* type is, or is a subtype of, whichever type is specified in the pointcut. Similarly, an execution pointcut matches if the receiver's *dynamic* type is (a subtype of) the type specified in the pointcut.

However, what is different in ContractAJ is the join point model. In AspectJ, call pointcuts describe a set of call join points, where a call join point refers to the moment before method lookup. Likewise, execution pointcuts describe a set of execution join points, which refer to the moment after lookup.

In ContractAJ, there only are call join points. Both ContractAJ's call and execution pointcuts make use of this one kind of join point. This is possible as both the receiver's static and dynamic type are available at the moment before method lookup. We made this choice to simplify ContractAJ's semantics, while it still is representative for what is possible when using AspectJ's pointcuts.

Another difference between call and execution join points in AspectJ is that they are associated with different locations in the source code (i.e. join point shadows). However, this difference is only relevant when combining call/execution pointcuts with other pointcut constructs that match on join point shadows (e.g. AspectJ's `within` and `withincode`), which are not present in ContractAJ. Because of this, we argue that it is sufficient to support call join points only.

Lookup Semantics. The execution of advice in ContractAJ is expressed as an extension of the method lookup mechanism, which implies that advice execution is late-bound. Executing a method call $c.m$ in ContractAJ is done as follows:

1. For all instances of classes with pointcuts, try to match these pointcuts on the $c.m$ call join point. (If there are multiple instances of the same class, the pointcut is checked for each instance.) Note that, when looking for matching pointcuts, we do not yet consider any `if` pointcut constructs.
2. Given all matching pointcuts, the precedence mechanism will produce a composition/sequence $\langle c_1.a_1, c_2.a_2, \ldots, c_n.a_n, c.m \rangle$, where each $c_i.a_i$ represents the advice body associated with a matching pointcut. This composition determines the precedence order of the advice that advise $c.m$. Push this composition on a global stack.
3. Find the first advice in the composition where its corresponding pointcut either does not contain an `if` construct, or the `if` construct's condition evaluates to `true`.
   (a) If no such advice is found, pop the entire composition from the stack, perform method lookup on $c.m$ and execute the body that is found.
   (b) If an advice was found, remove this advice and all preceding advice from the composition, then *call* the advice that was found (as if it were a method call).

Note the emphasis on "call" in step 3.(b). This enables the use of higher-order advice, which are advice that match on other advice executions. A call to an advice is handled just like a method call, meaning that it reuses the same lookup mechanism.

Finally, the semantics of a proceed call is a simpler version of the above steps: As the desired composition already is on the stack whenever a proceed call is made, it only performs step 3. As this step includes testing `if` pointcut constructs, this implies that these tests are delayed until an advice body is about to be executed, which corresponds to AspectJ's semantics.

3   Formal ContractAJ Semantics

This section presents the operational semantics of the ContractAJ language in its entirety. The semantics follows a similar style as the ContractJava [18] language it is based on, making use of a contextual rewriting system [42].

3.1   Source Modifications

Before describing the semantics of ContractAJ, we will first perform three small, harmless transformations at the source code level, which make it easier to describe the operational semantics.

$$P, c \vdash a:\ \texttt{call(}t\ c'.m(t_1\ x_1\ \dots\ t_m\ x_m)\texttt{)}\ \texttt{\&\&}\ \texttt{target(}var\texttt{)}\ \dots\ \{e\}$$
$$\to_{\textsf{sep}}\ a:\ \texttt{call(}t\ c'.m(t_1\ x_1\ \dots\ t_m\ x_m)\texttt{)}\ \texttt{\&\&}\ \texttt{target(}var\texttt{)}\ \dots$$
$$t\ a(c'\ var, t_1\ x_1\ \dots\ t_m\ x_m)\{e\}$$

Fig. 3. Moving advice bodies to method bodies

$$\frac{m \in c''\ \text{and}\ c' \le c''}{\nexists c''' : m \in c'''\ \text{and}\ c'' < c'''}$$
$$P, c \vdash a:\ \texttt{execution(}t\ c'.x(t_1\ x_1\ \dots\ t_m\ x_m)\texttt{)}\ \texttt{\&\&}\ \texttt{this(}var\texttt{)}$$
$$\to_{\textsf{exec}}\ a:\ \texttt{call(}t\ c''.x(t_1\ x_1\ \dots\ t_m\ x_m)\texttt{)}\ \texttt{\&\&}\ \texttt{target(}var\texttt{)}\ \texttt{\&\&}\ \texttt{if(}var\ \texttt{instanceof}\ c'\texttt{)}$$

Fig. 4. Converting execution into call pointcuts

The first transformation, defined by the $\to_{\textsf{sep}}$ judgement[1] in Fig. 3, consists of removing the advice body from each pointcut-advice pair, and moving this body into a separate method declaration. This method declaration gets the same name and the same parameters as the corresponding pointcut-advice pair. If a pointcut now matches during program execution, ContractAJ's semantics can simply call the method that corresponds to the advice. After applying this transformation, ContractAJ essentially is a minimal version of the Eos-U [34] language, which unifies classes and aspects, and uses regular method bodies as advice bodies.

In the second transformation, we convert every[2] execution pointcut into an equivalent call pointcut. This transformation is defined by the $\to_{\textsf{exec}}$ judgement[3] in Fig. 4. ($<$ is the strict subtyping relation, such that $c < c'$ relates c to an ancestor class c'. $\in$ relates a method to its class.) As discussed in Sect. 2.3, the only difference between ContractAJ's call and execution pointcuts is that

---

[1] An analogous definition of $\to_{\textsf{sep}}$ can be given for advice with an execution pointcut.
[2] Note that execution pointcuts matching on advice executions are also converted into call pointcuts, which is accepted by ContractAJ's operational semantics as it reuses the dynamic type as static type in advice executions.
[3] An analogous definition of $\to_{\textsf{exec}}$ can be given in case an **if** construct is already present in the execution pointcut.

```
class Logger {
    before log: execution(void Duck.fly(int dist)) && this(duck) {...}}
```

After applying the $\rightarrow_{sep}$ and $\rightarrow_{exec}$ judgements:

```
class Logger {
    before log: call(void Bird.fly(int dist)) && target(duck)
        && if(duck instanceof Duck)
    void log(Duck duck, int dist) {...}}
```

Fig. 5. Example application of the first two transformations

the first matches on the receiver's static type whereas the latter matches on the dynamic type. When converting an execution pointcut into a call pointcut, $\rightarrow_{exec}$ ensures that the dynamic type still is taken into account by adding an if pointcut construct with a simple **instanceof** test. Note that, even though the call pointcut construct also tests the receiver's static type, we made sure that this test has no effect: The call construct tests that the receiver is an instance of the class where the desired method is first declared, which always is the case when the dynamic type test passes. An example application of both $\rightarrow_{exec}$ and $\rightarrow_{sep}$ can be found in Fig. 5 (where Bird declares method fly, and Duck is a subtype of Bird).

$$
\begin{aligned}
e ::= \quad & \dots \mid e{:}c.f \mid e{:}c.f{=}e \\
& \mid e{:}c.m(e^*) \\
& \mid \textsf{super} \equiv \textsf{this}{:}c.m(e^*) \mid \dots
\end{aligned}
$$

Fig. 6. Syntax modifications

In the third and final transformation, we will modify the syntax of method calls, super calls, field accesses and field assignments in such a way that the static type is always included explicitly, so we can easily refer to it when needed. For example, a method call $e.m(e*)$ now becomes $e{:}c.m(e*)$, where c is the static type of the receiver. We assume a type checker can be easily implemented which infers the static type for each of these statements. The altered syntax for these statements is shown in the e rule of Fig. 6.

3.2 Operational Semantics

The operational semantics of ContractAJ, like the ContractJava language, is expressed as a contextual rewriting system [42]. Our rewriting system operates on triples consisting of an expression, a store and a stack. That is, each evaluation rule has the following shape:

$$
P \vdash \langle e, \mathcal{S}, \mathcal{J} \rangle \hookrightarrow \langle e, \mathcal{S}, \mathcal{J} \rangle
$$

Such a rule can be read as: within program P, the left-hand-side (a triple with expression e, store $\mathcal{S}$ and join point stack $\mathcal{J}$) evaluates to the right-hand-side if the rule is applied. Each of the different data structures used in these triples is defined as follows:

P A program, as defined by the ContractAJ syntax.

e Each e is an expression, as defined by the syntax.

$$\mathcal{S} \quad \begin{aligned} \mathcal{S} &::= obj \mapsto \langle c, \mathcal{F} \rangle \\ \mathcal{F} &::= f \mapsto v \end{aligned}$$

The store $\mathcal{S}$ allows us to find the field values of each object: it is a mapping from objects to $\langle c, \mathcal{F} \rangle$ pairs, where each pair consists of a class c and a field record $\mathcal{F}$. A field record $\mathcal{F}$ contains the values for all fields in a particular object: it is a mapping from field names to field values.

$$\mathcal{J} \quad \begin{aligned} \mathcal{J} &::= \mathcal{A}; \mathcal{J} \mid \bullet \\ \mathcal{A} &::= \mathcal{E} + \mathcal{A} \mid \bullet \\ \mathcal{E} &::= \langle c, x, obj, bool \rangle \end{aligned}$$

The join point stack $\mathcal{J}$ keeps track of the sequence of advice/methods that should be executed at each join point that is encountered. The join point stack is a stack of $\mathcal{A}$ records. In turn, each $\mathcal{A}$ record is a stack[4] of $\mathcal{E}$ tuples $\langle c, x, obj, bool \rangle$. Such a tuple respectively describes a method/advice body $c.x$, the this object to be used and a boolean value that indicates whether $c.x$ is ready to be executed (true), or further lookup is needed (false). The ordering of $\mathcal{E}$ tuples within an $\mathcal{A}$ record will be determined by ContractAJ's precedence mechanism.

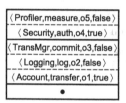

Fig. 7. Join point stack

The example in Fig. 7 gives a more visual idea of the join point stack's structure, in the context of a banking application: In this example, the stack contains three $\mathcal{A}$ records. The method Account.transfer was called at some point and Security.auth, TransMgr.commit and Logging.log respectively matched on this method call. The Security.auth advice was already moved into topmost $\mathcal{A}$ record to look for higher-order advice. One higher-order advice Profiler.measure was found. The boolean in its $\mathcal{E}$ tuple still is false, indicating that we are about to check whether any higher-order advice match on Profiler.measure.

In addition to the store and the join point stack, we also provide a number of predicates and functions in Fig. 8 that help define the operational semantics. Most of these are self-explanatory, but we will highlight the precedence and lookup mechanisms in more detail:

The $<^{\mathsf{prec}}$ predicate defines ContractAJ's precedence mechanism, which makes use of the global declare precedence statement to determine the ordering of advice when multiple pointcuts match at the same join point. The $<^{\mathsf{prec}}$ predicate is defined in terms of $precLook(c, a)$, which determines the element in the declare precedence statement that corresponds to a particular advice $c.a$,

---

[4] Note that we use two different concatenation symbols to avoid ambiguity. ";" concatenates records in $\mathcal{J}$ and "+" concatenates tuples in an $\mathcal{A}$ record.

Subtyping relations

$\prec$ $c \prec c' \Leftrightarrow$ class c extends $c'\{\ldots\}$ is in P

$\leq$ $\leq \equiv$ transitive, reflexive closure of $\prec$

$<$ $< \equiv$ transitive, irreflexive closure of $\prec$

Field f is a member of c

$\in$ $\langle c, f, t \rangle \in c \Leftrightarrow$ class $c\{\ldots t f \ldots\}$ is in P

Method/advice x is declared in class c

$\in$ $\langle x, (t_1, \ldots, t_n \to t), (var_1, \ldots, var_n), e \rangle \in c$
      $\Leftrightarrow$ class $c\{\ldots t\, x(t_1\ var_1 \ldots t_n\ var_n)\{e\}\ldots\}$ is in P

Advice $c.a$ is listed in the precedence statement as $c'.a$
               declare precedence$\ldots c'.a\ldots$ is in P

$precLook(c, a)$ $\dfrac{c \leq c' \text{ and } \langle a, \_, \_, \_ \rangle \in c'}{\nexists c": (c \leq c" < c' \text{ and declare precedence} \ldots c".a\ldots \text{ is in } P)}$
$$preclook(c, a) = c'$$

Advice precedence relation

$<^{\mathsf{prec}}$ $\langle c_a, a_a, \_, \_ \rangle <^{\mathsf{prec}} \langle c_b, a_b, \_, \_ \rangle$
      $\Leftrightarrow$ either $(precLook(c_a, a_a) = c'_a$ and $precLook(c_b, a_b) = c'_b$
      and declare precedence$\ldots c'_b.a_b \ldots c'_a.a_a \ldots$ is in $P)$
      or $(\nexists c'_a : precLook(c_a, a_a) = c'_a$ and $precLook(c_b, a_b) = c'_b)$

Test advice kind

$isBefore(c, a)$ class $c\ldots\{\ldots$ before $a:\ldots\}$ is in P

$isAfter(c, a)$ class $c\ldots\{\ldots$ after $a:\ldots\}$ is in P

$isAround(c, a)$ class $c\ldots\{\ldots$ around $a:\ldots\}$ is in P

$isMethod(c, m)$ $!isBefore(c, m)$ and $!isAfter(c, m)$ and $!isAround(c, m)$

Retrieve name of target binding

$target(c, a)$ $\dfrac{\text{class } c\ldots\{\ldots\ a\text{:call}(\ldots)\ \&\&\ \text{target}(var)\} \text{ is in } P}{target(c, a) = var}$

Retrieve the condition of an if pointcut construct

$ifPcut(c, a)$ $\dfrac{\text{class } c\ldots\{\ldots\ a:\ldots\ \&\&\ \text{if}(e)\ldots\} \text{ is in } P}{ifPcut(c, a) = e}$

$ifPcut(c, a)$ $\dfrac{\text{class } c\ldots\{\ldots\ a:\ldots\ \&\&\ \text{if}(e)\ldots\} \text{ is not in } P}{ifPcut(c, a) = \text{true}}$

Method lookup of m in the dynamic type c

$mlook(c, m)$ $\dfrac{c \leq c' \text{ and } \langle m, \_, \_, \_ \rangle \in c'}{\nexists c" : \langle m, \_, \_, \_ \rangle \in c" \text{ and } c \leq c" < c'}$
$$mlook(c, m) = c'$$

Body $c.x$ matches with call pointcut of advice $c'.a$

$call(c, x, c', a)$ $\dfrac{\text{class } c'\ldots\{\ldots a\text{:call}(t\, c_{pcut}.x(\ldots))\ldots\} \text{ is in } P}{\text{where } c \leq c_{pcut} \text{ and } \exists c'_{pcut} : c'_{pcut} = mlook(c_{pcut}, x)}$

Find the sequence of advice matching on $c.x$
      $\mathcal{A}$ is a sequence of distinct $\mathcal{E}$-tuples such that:
   $\forall \mathcal{E}_i \in \mathcal{A} : (\mathcal{E}_i = \langle c_i, a_i, o_i, \text{false} \rangle$ and $call(c, x, c_i, a_i))$

$alook(c, x, \mathcal{S})$ $\dfrac{\text{and } \mathcal{S}(o_i) = \langle c'_i, \_ \rangle \text{ and } c_i = mlook(c'_i, a) \quad \forall \mathcal{E}_i, \mathcal{E}_{i+1} \in \mathcal{A} : \mathcal{E}_i <^{\mathsf{prec}} \mathcal{E}_{i+1}}{alook(c, x, \mathcal{S}) = \mathcal{A}}$

Fig. 8. Helper predicates and functions

either directly or as a subtype. (The well-formedness rules in Sect. 3.4 ensures this element can always be uniquely determined.) Note that $<^{\text{prec}}$ is undefined when neither of the two advice being compared are mentioned in the `declare precedence` statement. In case only one advice is mentioned, it gets the higher precedence.

The core of ContractAJ's lookup mechanism is defined by *mlook*, *call* and *alook*. The $mlook(c, m)$ function performs regular method lookup. Predicate $call(c, x, c, a')$ tests whether a particular method/advice $c.x$ matches with the `call` pointcut construct in advice $c'.a$, either directly or as a subtype. Finally, the *alook* function determines the sequence of advice whose `call` pointcut construct matched on $c.x$. More specifically, the *alook* function produces a list of $\mathcal{E}$ tuples, ordered by the precedence mechanism, where each tuple describes which advice body matched, the corresponding aspect instance o_i and a `false` value to indicate that we have not checked for higher-order advice yet. Regarding the aspect instance o_i, we also specify that the matching advice $c_i.a_i$ does not always have to be part of the type of o_i directly, but may also be inherited.

After discussing the helper predicates and functions, we can now present the rules that compose ContractAJ's operational semantics, shown in Fig. 9. First, note that the syntax of expressions (e) is extended with two new statements: `return` and `jpop`. These two statements are not available to the developer writing ContractAJ programs, but are only used internally by the semantics. The `jpop` statement is used whenever an $\mathcal{A}$ record needs to be popped from the join point stack. The only purpose of the `return` statement is to serve as a marker in the theorems of Sect. 6, such that we can easily refer to any configuration where the execution of a method/advice body is about to finish. Next, the definition of evaluation context E specifies the order in which subexpressions should be evaluated for each type of compound expression, which ensures there can only be one possible sequence of rule applications to evaluate a ContractAJ program. Finally, we can discuss the evaluation rules themselves in Fig. 9. The more interesting rules are those that specify the behaviour of method and proceed calls: [**call**], [**before**], [**after**], [**around**], [**call**$_{\text{around}}$], [**exec**] and [**jpop**]:

[**call**] - This rule matches on method calls $obj:c.x$. This method call is replaced with a proceed call (wrapped in a `jpop` expression). While it may seem peculiar to replace every method call with a proceed call, they both share the same intuition: Try to execute the next matching advice; otherwise do regular method lookup. The only difference is that a method call has the additional task of looking for the matching advice, which is exactly what this [**call**] rule does with the help of the *alook* function. This function produces a list of $\mathcal{E}$ tuples that each represent an advice whose `call` pointcut construct matched on $c.x$. The $\langle c, x, obj, \texttt{true} \rangle$ tuple, representing the method call, is appended to the result of *alook* to complete the $\mathcal{A}$ record that is then pushed onto the join point stack. After an application of the [**call**] rule, the proceed call it produced must be evaluated next. The semantics of proceed calls is defined by the [**before**], [**after**], [**around**] and [**exec**] rules.

$$\dots \mid obj \qquad\qquad \mathsf{E} = [] \mid \mathsf{E} : c.f \mid \mathsf{E} : c.f{=}e \mid v{:}c.f = \mathsf{E}$$
$$e = \mid \mathtt{jpop}\{e\} \qquad\quad \mid \mathsf{E}.m(e\dots) \mid v.m(v\dots\mathsf{E}\,e\dots)$$
$$\quad\mid \mathtt{return}{:}c\{e\} \qquad \mid \mathtt{super} \equiv v{:}c.m(v\dots\mathsf{E}\,e\dots)$$
$$\quad\quad\qquad\qquad\qquad \mid (t)\,\mathsf{E} \mid \mathsf{E}\ \mathtt{instanceof}\ t \mid \mathtt{if}(\mathsf{E})\{e\}\mathtt{else}\{e\}$$
$$v = \begin{array}{l} obj \mid \mathtt{null} \\ \mid \mathtt{true} \mid \mathtt{false} \end{array} \qquad \begin{array}{l} \mid \{\mathsf{E};e\} \mid \mathtt{let}\{var{=}v\dots var{=}\mathsf{E}\dots var{=}e\dots\}\mathtt{in}\{e\} \\ \mid \mathtt{return}{:}c\{\mathsf{E}\} \mid \mathtt{jpop}\{\mathsf{E}\} \end{array}$$

[call] $P \vdash \langle \mathsf{E}[obj{:}c.x(v_1 \dots v_n)], \mathcal{S}, \mathcal{J} \rangle$
$\hookrightarrow \langle \mathsf{E}[\mathtt{jpop}\{\mathtt{proceed}(obj\,v_1 \dots v_n)\}], \mathcal{S}, \mathcal{A}; \mathcal{J} \rangle$
where $\mathcal{A} = alook(c, x, \mathcal{S}) + \langle c, x, obj, \mathtt{true} \rangle$ and $!isAround(c, x)$

[before] $P \vdash \langle \mathsf{E}[\mathtt{proceed}(obj\,v_1 \dots v_n)], \mathcal{S}, \mathcal{A}; \mathcal{J} \rangle$
$\hookrightarrow \langle \mathsf{E}[\mathtt{if}(e')\{obj_{asp}{:}c.a(obj\,v_1 \dots v_n)\}; \mathtt{proceed}(obj\,v_1 \dots v_n)], \mathcal{S}, \mathcal{A}'; \mathcal{J} \rangle$
where $\mathcal{A} = \langle c, a, obj_{asp}, \mathtt{false} \rangle + \mathcal{A}'$ and $\langle a, (t_1, \dots, t_n \to t), (var_1, \dots, var_n, e) \rangle \in c$
and $isBefore(c, a)$ and $var_{tgt} = target(c, a)$ and $e = ifPcut(c, a)$
and $e' = e[obj_{asp}/\mathtt{this}, obj/var_{tgt}, v_1/var_1, \dots, v_n/var_n]$

[after] $P \vdash \langle \mathsf{E}[\mathtt{proceed}(obj\,v_1 \dots v_n)], \mathcal{S}, \mathcal{A}; \mathcal{J} \rangle$
$\hookrightarrow \langle \mathsf{E}[\mathtt{proceed}(obj\,v_1 \dots v_n); \mathtt{if}(e')\{obj_{asp}{:}c.a(obj\,v_1 \dots v_n)\}], \mathcal{S}, \mathcal{A}'; \mathcal{J} \rangle$
(same constraints as **[before]**, except that $isBefore(c, a)$ becomes $isAfter(c, a)$)

[around] $P \vdash \langle \mathsf{E}[\mathtt{proceed}(obj\,v_1 \dots v_n)], \mathcal{S}, \mathcal{A}; \mathcal{J} \rangle$
$\hookrightarrow \langle \mathsf{E}[\mathtt{if}(e')\{obj_{asp}{:}c.a(obj\,v_1 \dots v_n)\}\mathtt{else}\{\mathtt{proceed}(obj\,v_1 \dots v_n)\}], \mathcal{S}, \mathcal{A}'; \mathcal{J} \rangle$
(same constraints as **[before]**, except that $isBefore(c, a)$ becomes $isAround(c, a)$)

[call$_{around}$] $P \vdash \langle \mathsf{E}[obj_{asp}{:}c.a(v_1 \dots v_n)], \mathcal{S}, \mathcal{A}; \mathcal{J} \rangle$
$\hookrightarrow \langle \mathsf{E}[\mathtt{proceed}(obj_{asp}\,v_1 \dots v_n)], \mathcal{S}, \mathcal{A}' + \mathcal{A}; \mathcal{J} \rangle$
where $\mathcal{A}' = alook(c, a, \mathcal{S}) + \langle c, a, obj_{asp}, \mathtt{true} \rangle$ and $isAround(c, a)$

[exec] $P \vdash \langle \mathsf{E}[\mathtt{proceed}(obj\,v_1 \dots v_n)], \mathcal{S}, \mathcal{A}; \mathcal{J} \rangle$
$\hookrightarrow \langle \mathsf{E}[\mathtt{return}{:}c\{e[obj_{this}/\mathtt{this}, v_1/var_1, \dots, v_n/var_n]\}], \mathcal{S}, \mathcal{A}'; \mathcal{J} \rangle$
where $\mathcal{A} = \langle c, x, obj', \mathtt{true} \rangle + \mathcal{A}'$
and if $isMethod(c, x)$ then $(obj_{this} = obj)$ else $(obj_{this} = obj')$
and $\mathcal{S}(obj_{this}) = \langle c', \dots \rangle$ and $c'' = mlook(c', x)$
and $\langle x, (t_1, \dots, t_n \to t), (var_1, \dots, var_n, e) \rangle \in c''$

[jpop] $P \vdash \langle \mathsf{E}[\mathtt{jpop}\{v\}], \mathcal{S}, \mathcal{A}; \mathcal{J} \rangle \hookrightarrow \langle \mathsf{E}[v], \mathcal{S}, \mathcal{J} \rangle$

[super] $P \vdash \langle \mathsf{E}[\mathtt{super} \equiv obj{:}c.m(v_1 \dots v_n)], \mathcal{S}, \mathcal{J} \rangle$
$\hookrightarrow \langle \mathsf{E}[e[obj/\mathtt{this}, v_1/var_1, \dots, v_n/var_n], \mathcal{S}, \mathcal{J} \rangle$
where $\langle m, (t_1, \dots, t_n \to t), (var_1, \dots, var_n, e) \rangle \in c$

[return] $P \vdash \langle \mathsf{E}[\mathtt{return}{:}c\{e\}], \mathcal{S}, \mathcal{J} \rangle \hookrightarrow \langle \mathsf{E}[e], \mathcal{S}, \mathcal{J} \rangle$

[new] $P \vdash \langle \mathsf{E}[\mathtt{new}\ c], \mathcal{S}, \mathcal{J} \rangle \hookrightarrow \langle \mathsf{E}[obj], \mathcal{S}[obj \mapsto \langle c, \mathcal{F} \rangle], \mathcal{J} \rangle$
where $obj \notin dom(\mathcal{S})$ and $\mathcal{F} = \{c'.f \mapsto \mathtt{null} \mid c \leq c' \text{ and } \exists t : \langle c', f, t \rangle \in c'\}$

[get] $P \vdash \langle \mathsf{E}[obj{:}c'.f], \mathcal{S}, \mathcal{J} \rangle \hookrightarrow \langle \mathsf{E}[v], \mathcal{S}, \mathcal{J} \rangle$
where $\mathcal{S}(obj) = \langle c, \mathcal{F} \rangle$ and $\mathcal{F}(c'.f) = v$

[set] $P \vdash \langle \mathsf{E}[obj{:}c'.f{=}v], \mathcal{S}, \mathcal{J} \rangle \hookrightarrow \langle \mathsf{E}[v], \mathcal{S}[obj \mapsto \langle c, \mathcal{F}[c'.f \mapsto v] \rangle], \mathcal{J} \rangle$
where $\mathcal{S}(obj) = \langle c, \mathcal{F} \rangle$

[cast] $P \vdash \langle \mathsf{E}[(t)\ obj], \mathcal{S}, \mathcal{J} \rangle \hookrightarrow \langle \mathsf{E}[obj], \mathcal{S}, \mathcal{J} \rangle$
where $\mathcal{S}(obj) = \langle c, \mathcal{F} \rangle$ and $c \leq t$

[inst$_{true}$] $P \vdash \langle \mathsf{E}[obj\ \mathtt{instanceof}\ t], \mathcal{S}, \mathcal{J} \rangle \hookrightarrow \langle \mathsf{E}[\mathtt{true}], \mathcal{S}, \mathcal{J} \rangle$
where $\mathcal{S}(obj) = \langle c, \mathcal{F} \rangle$ and $c \leq t$

[inst$_{false}$] $P \vdash \langle \mathsf{E}[obj\ \mathtt{instanceof}\ t], \mathcal{S}, \mathcal{J} \rangle \hookrightarrow \langle \mathsf{E}[\mathtt{false}], \mathcal{S}, \mathcal{J} \rangle$
where $\mathcal{S}(obj) = \langle c, \mathcal{F} \rangle$ and $c \nleq t$

[let] $P \vdash \langle \mathsf{E}[\mathtt{let}\ \{var_1{=}v_1 \dots var_n{=}v_n\}\ \mathtt{in}\ \{e\}], \mathcal{S}, \mathcal{J} \rangle \hookrightarrow \langle \mathsf{E}[e[v_1/var_1, \dots, v_n/var_n]], \mathcal{S}, \mathcal{J} \rangle$

[if$_{true}$] $P \vdash \langle \mathsf{E}[\mathtt{if}(\mathtt{true})\{e_1\}\mathtt{else}\{e_2\}], \mathcal{S}, \mathcal{J} \rangle \hookrightarrow \langle \mathsf{E}[e_1], \mathcal{S}, \mathcal{J} \rangle$

[if$_{false}$] $P \vdash \langle \mathsf{E}[\mathtt{if}(\mathtt{false})\{e_1\}\mathtt{else}\{e_2\}], \mathcal{S}, \mathcal{J} \rangle \hookrightarrow \langle \mathsf{E}[e_2], \mathcal{S}, \mathcal{J} \rangle$

[seq] $P \vdash \langle \mathsf{E}[\{v;e\}], \mathcal{S}, \mathcal{J} \rangle \hookrightarrow \langle \mathsf{E}[e], \mathcal{S}, \mathcal{J} \rangle$

[error] $P \vdash \langle \mathsf{E}[\mathtt{error}(msg)], \mathcal{S}, \mathcal{J} \rangle \hookrightarrow \langle \mathtt{error}:\ msg, \mathcal{S}, \mathcal{J} \rangle$

Fig. 9. Operational semantics of ContractAJ

[**before**] - This rule matches if there is a before advice $c.a$ in the tuple at the top of the join point stack. This tuple is popped and the `proceed` expression is replaced with an explicit method call to the advice body, followed by the implicit `proceed` call. Note that this explicit call to the advice body will only be executed if the advice's `if` pointcut construct succeeds. Because we are using an explicit method call, this will cause the [**call**] rule to match, which will then look for any higher-order advice that match on $c.a$. An infinite regression cannot occur when this before advice reappears at a later point in the evaluation; this is due to the boolean value in each $\mathcal{E}$ tuple. It indicates whether we have already processed this advice or not. More specifically, the [**before**] rule will only match if the boolean in the join point stack's top entry is `false`. Once the [**call**] rule has processed the explicit call to the before advice, that boolean will be set to `true`.

[**after**] - This rule is analogous to [**before**], except that the implicit proceed call comes before explicitly calling the advice.

[**around**] - This rule is analogous to [**before**] as well. If the `if` pointcut construct evaluates to true, an explicit call is made to the around advice. Otherwise, the advice is skipped by only making a `proceed` call to the next advice.

[**call$_{around}$**] - This rule is a variant of the [**call**] rule; it only handles explicit calls to around advice. Whereas [**call**] will push a new record onto the join point stack, [**call$_{around}$**] will extend the existing record that is currently at the top of the stack. The reason for this difference is to support higher-order around advice that do *not* make a proceed call. If an around advice $c.a$ does not proceed, this means that any remaining advice in the current advice composition, and the method/advice body being advised will no longer be executed. Additionally, it is possible that the body being advised is another around advice: in this case all remaining advice in the composition of that around advice and the body it advises will not be executed either, and so on. To achieve this behaviour, [**call$_{around}$**] extends the record at the top of the stack: all of the bodies that should no longer be executed are now grouped into one record, such that they will be removed from the stack once the execution of $c.a$ is finished.

[**exec**] - This rule matches once we are ready to execute the $\mathcal{E}$ tuple at the top of the join point stack, as indicated by the `true` value in this tuple. The *mlook* function is first used to perform regular method lookup using dynamic type c and method/advice x, resulting in lookup result c'. The receiver object obj_{this} is determined in one of two ways: If x represents an advice, it is retrieved from the top tuple in the stack. Otherwise, we use the first argument of the proceed call (obj), which represents the binding of the `target` pointcut construct. This adds support for receiver substitution, as the value of obj can be chosen by the developer (if the proceed call is part of an around advice).

We can then replace the `proceed` expression with e, the body of $c'.x$. Formal parameters and the *this* object are also bound to their values. A `return` wrapper is also added to the e expression, which ensures the [**return**] rule will match once the evaluation of e is finished. Finally, the $\mathcal{E}$ tuple at the top of the stack is removed, as it is no longer needed[5].

[**jpop**] - This rule pops the top $\mathcal{A}$ record from the join point stack. This top record typically already is empty at this point, unless there were around advice that did not make a proceed call. Note that jpop expressions are only created by the [**call**] rule, not by [**call**$_{around}$]. This is because there should only be one jpop expression per record, and [**call**$_{around}$] only extends an existing record instead of adding a new one.

[**super**] - This rule handles super calls. In order to keep the semantics simple, we chose not to support advice on super calls. As such, the rule can immediately replace the call with the corresponding method body.

[**return**] - As mentioned earlier, return expressions only serve as markers that indicate the end of a body's execution. These expressions are created by the [**exec**] rule at the start of a body's execution.

3.3 Lookup Sequences

To provide a more high-level view on ContractAJ's lookup mechanism, Fig. 10 represents all possible sequences of rule applications that can be taken starting from a configuration with a method/proceed call, and ending with the configuration where we have determined which body will be executed. A few example sequences are also given in Fig. 11.

$$
\begin{aligned}
mcall &::= [\textbf{call}] \; lookup*|skip* \; [\textbf{exec}] \\
pcall &::= lookup* \mid skip* \; [\textbf{exec}] \\
lookup &::= skip* \; match \\
match &::= ([\textbf{before}] \ldots [\textbf{if}_{\textbf{true}}] \; [\textbf{call}]) \mid ([\textbf{around}] \ldots [\textbf{if}_{\textbf{true}}] \; [\textbf{call}_{\textbf{around}}]) \\
skip &::= ([\textbf{after}] \ldots [\textbf{if}_{\textbf{false}}] \mid [\textbf{if}_{\textbf{true}}]) \mid ([\textbf{before}] \mid [\textbf{around}] \ldots [\textbf{if}_{\textbf{false}}])
\end{aligned}
$$

Fig. 10. All possible lookup sequences

mcall/pcall - *mcall* represents all possible sequences of rule applications for method calls, whereas *pcall* represents proceed calls. Note that the only difference between the two is that *mcall* initially applies the [**call**] rule. A method call starts in a configuration $\langle e, \mathcal{S}, \mathcal{J} \rangle$, where e decomposes into the method call to be executed. The [**call**] rule then replaces this method call in e with a proceed call, such that the lookup mechanism for proceed calls can be reused.

lookup - The *lookup* sequence may be applied multiple times in *mcall* and *pcall*. It searches for the first before/around advice that must be executed. (After advice will be discussed later as a separate case, due to the preceding implicit proceed call.) If *lookup* does not match in *mcall/pcall*, the subsequent application of [**exec**] must initiate the execution of a method body, as there is a

---

[5] The tuple might still be needed in case an around advice makes multiple proceed calls. This is however not supported, as it is an uncommon scenario and would unnecessarily complicate the semantics.

Method call leading to the execution of a method body (no matching advice):
  [call] [exec]

Method call where the first advice to be executed is an around advice:
(The call pointcut of an after advice did match first, but its if construct failed.)
  [call] [after] ... [if$_{false}$] [around] ... [if$_{true}$] [call$_{around}$] [exec]

Method call advised by a before advice, which is advised by an around advice:
  [call] [before] ... [if$_{true}$] [call] [around] ... [if$_{true}$] [call$_{around}$] [exec]

Fig. 11. A few example lookup sequences

method body at the top of $\mathcal{J}$. If *lookup* matches exactly once, [exec] will initiate a non-higher-order before/around advice. If *lookup* matches more than once, a higher-order before/around advice will be initiated.

skip - The *skip* sequence represents an advice that initially matches, but will not be executed. This can happen for one of two reasons: The call pointcut construct of an advice matches, but its if construct does not. In this case, either [before],[after] or [around] is applied first, which will insert a runtime test for the if pointcut construct. The subsequent rule applications (indicated with an ellipsis) represent the evaluation of this if condition. If it fails, [if$_{false}$] matches and this advice will not be executed. The second reason for not (immediately) executing an advice is because it is an after advice. Because there is an preceding implicit proceed call which must be evaluated first, a method/proceed call cannot directly result in the execution of an after advice body.

match - The *match* sequence represents a matching before/around advice. In this case, the advice's if pointcut construct does succeed, as indicated by the application of [if$_{true}$]. We will now explicitly call the matching advice (to look for any higher-order advice), as indicated by the application of [call]/[call$_{around}$].

Finally, we should still discuss the execution of after advice bodies: Due to the presence of the implicit proceed call, an after advice body can only be initiated once this implicit proceed call finishes, resulting in the "[return] *mcall*" rule sequence. The application of [return] represents the end of the after advice's implicit proceed call, which is then followed by an explicit call to the after advice body.

3.4   Well-Formedness Rules

To wrap up the definition of ContractAJ's semantics, Fig. 12 presents the constraints that must be satisfied by every ContractAJ program in order to be well-formed. Most constraints were carried over from the object-oriented ClassicJava [19] language. The constraints specific to ContractAJ are mostly self-explanatory. Only the *AdvByOK* constraint should be discussed in some more detail: This constraint is defined in terms of the *advBy*(c, m) helper function, which retrieves the complete @advisedBy clause of $c.m$, including the part inherited from its super class. An @advisedBy clause specifies a list of advice that a method is expecting to be advised by, in the given order. At runtime, this

	Each class is defined only once.
$UniqClasses$	$\forall c, c'$ class c ... class c' ... is in $P \implies c \neq c'$
	Each member is defined only once per class.
$UniqFields$	$\forall f, f'$ class ... { ... f ... f' ... } is in $P \implies f \neq f'$
$UniqMethods$	$\forall m, m'$ class ... { ... $m(...)\{...\}...m'(...)\{...\}...$ } is in $P \implies m \neq m'$
$UniqAdvice$	$\forall a, a'$ class ... { ... a : ... { ... } ... a' : ... { ... } ... } is in $P \implies a \neq a'$
	The superclass of each class is defined.
$CompleteClasses$	$rng(\prec) \subseteq dom(\prec) \cup \{\texttt{Object}\}$
	Class hierarchy is an order.
$WellFoundedClasses$	$\leq$ is antisymmetric
	Method overriding preserves the type.
$ClassMethodsOK$	$\forall c, c', e, e', m, T, T', V, V' (\langle m, T, V, e \rangle \in c$ and $\langle m, T', V', e' \rangle \in c')$
	$\implies (T = T'$ or $c \leq c')$
	No duplicate entries in the precedence declaration.
$PrecedenceOK$	$\forall c, a, c', a'$ declare precedence $...c.a...c'.a'...$ is in $P \implies \langle c, a \rangle \neq \langle c', a' \rangle$
	Proceed calls may not be used in methods.
$ProceedInAdvice$	$\nexists m$: class ... { ... $m(...)\{...$ proceed $...\}...$ } is in P
	The proc keyword may only be used in specifications.
$ProcInSpecs$	$\nexists x$: class ... { ... $x(...)\{...$ proc $...\}...$ } is in P
	Retrieve the complete @advisedBy clause of a method
	class $c...\{...$ @advisedBy $c_1.a_1,...,c_n.a_n; ...m...\}$ is in P
	$A = advBy(c', m)$ if $(\exists c' : c' = mlook(c, m)$ and $c \neq c')$
$advBy(c, m)$	$A = \emptyset$ otherwise
	$\overline{advBy(c, m) = (c_1, a_1, ..., c_n, a_n) \circ A}$
	Advice in an @advisedBy clause may not override each other
	and should respect the precedence order.
$AdvByOK$	$\forall c, m, A \ \langle m, \_, \_, \_ \rangle \in c$ and $A = advBy(c, m) = (c_1, a_1, ..., c_n, a_n)$
	$\implies ((c_i \leq c_j \implies a_i \neq a_j)$ where $i \neq j)$ and $(c_i <^{\text{prec}} c_j$ where $i < j)$

Fig. 12. Static constraints on ContractAJ programs

expectation may also be fulfilled by an overriding advice. To prevent ambiguities when determining which element in an @advisedBy clause corresponds to a particular advice, the $AdvByOK$ constraint requires that these elements may not override each other. Additionally, the constraint requires that the elements of the @advisedBy clause are ordered such that they respect the precedence declaration.

4 The Advice Substitution Principle

After defining the ContractAJ language, we can use it to present our approach to modular reasoning in AOP languages. This approach can be divided into two parts: the advice substitution principle (ASP) and the @advisedBy clause. This section will focus on the first part, the ASP. If an advice complies with this principle, modular reasoning is possible even while remaining oblivious of this advice. That is, the advice will not cause any surprising behaviour whenever a method call (or proceed call) is made. The purpose of the ASP is similar to the notion of observers, spectators, spectative and harmless advice [11,15,21,37]. However, the key difference between these notions and the ASP is that the ASP is a property of an advice's specification rather than its implementation. This allows for two advantages: First, our approach to modular reasoning should be familiar to OOP developers, as it is a natural extension of modular reasoning in OOP, which is typically also defined in terms of a program's specifications. Second, because a program's specifications describe the expected behaviour of each module, it also is clear what constitutes unexpected/surprising behaviour. This is what allows the ASP to be weaker/less conservative than observers, spectators, spectative and harmless advice. These notions only rely on the program implementation, where it is far from trivial to deduce what constitutes unexpected behaviour.

The ASP is based on the notion of behavioural subtyping in object-oriented languages [3, 16, 24, 27]. The ASP presented in this paper is however slightly different than the ASP first introduced by Wampler [41], which is an adaptation of Liskov and Wing's constraint-based behavioural subtyping [27, Fig.4]. Our version of the ASP is based on Dhara and Leavens' strong behavioural subtyping (SBS) [16, Def. 4.1and 4.2], as it has a postcondition rule that is more flexible than Liskov and Wing's. We paraphrase the rules on preconditions, postconditions and invariants of the SBS definition as follows:

Strong behavioural subtyping (SBS). *Type t is a strong behavioural subtype of type u, if and only if $t < u$ and:*

- *For all objects of type t, and for all common methods m in t and u:*
  - *The precondition of $t.m$ must be equal to or weaker than the precondition of $u.m$.*
  - *The postcondition of $t.m$ must be equal to or stronger than the postcondition of $u.m$, if the precondition of $u.m$ held in the pre-state.*
- *For all objects of type t:*
  - *The invariant of u should be preserved in t.*

To adapt the SBS rules to an aspect-oriented setting, the basic idea is to view the execution of an advice as a form of substitution. This is quite easy to understand when all advice are viewed as around advice. This is not a simplification, as a before advice can be seen as an around advice where the proceed call at the end is implicit. Likewise, an after advice corresponds to an around advice where the implicit proceed call is at the beginning. If the pointcut associated with an around advice matches on a certain join point, then that join point essentially is replaced with the execution of that advice. In other words, the join point representing a method call is *substituted* with the execution of an advice. In order to perform a method call, while remaining unaware of the advice that substitutes for it, an advice's contracts should comply with the contracts of those join points it advises.

4.1   Around Advice

From the point of view that executing advice can be seen as a form of substitution, the SBS rules can be adapted as follows to an advice substitution principle for around advice:

ASP for around advice. *Consider an around advice a in type t that is applied to join point u.x, representing a method call or an advice execution. If x is a method, u is the static type of the receiver. If x is an advice, u is the class containing x. The around advice satisfies the ASP if and only if, for all objects of type t:*

- *The precondition of t.a must be equal to or weaker than the precondition of u.x.*
- *The postcondition of t.a must be equal to or stronger than the postcondition of u.x, if the precondition of u.x held in the pre-state.*
- *The invariant of u should be preserved in t.*

What is important to note is that we defined the ASP in terms of a single advice applying at a particular join point. Stating that "aspect t complies with the ASP" means that each advice in t must take into account the contracts of *all* the join points it advises. Each of these join points can have its own contracts, which means that an advice may need to take into account several different contracts, depending on the advice's pointcut. While the exact set of join points in a pointcut can only be determined at runtime, the developer only needs to take into account all join point shadows, i.e. the mapping of each join point to its location in the source code. These join point shadows can be determined statically by examining the advice's pointcut.

4.2   Before and After Advice

As mentioned earlier, before/after advice can be interpreted as special cases of around advice. It is important to note however that it would be unintuitive to include the effects of the implicit proceed call in the contracts of a before/after advice, such that these contracts would effectively be the same as an equivalent around advice. It is unintuitive for the simple reason that the developer does not need to be aware of any implicit proceed calls. Moreover, even if the developer knows there is an implicit proceed call, he/she may not consider it to be part of the advice body. Consequently, the ASP needs to be adjusted for before/advice to take this into account.

In a before advice, its postcondition refers to the moment *before* executing the implicit proceed call at the end of the advice body. In order for the composition of the before advice body $(t.a)$ and the implicit proceed call to be substitutable for the advised join point $(u.x)$, the **ASP for before advice** becomes:

- *The precondition of t.a must be equal to or weaker than the precondition of u.x.*
- *If the precondition of u.x held before executing the advice, it should still hold after the advice (at the implicit proceed call). This implies the postcondition of t.a may not invalidate u.x's precondition.*
- *The invariant of u should be preserved in t.*

Similarly, an after advice's precondition refers to the moment *after* executing the implicit proceed call in the beginning of the advice body. The **ASP for after advice** is as follows, for an after advice body $t.a$ advising join point $u.x$:

- *The precondition of $t.a$ must be equal to or weaker than the **post**condition of $u.x$.*
- *If the postcondition of $u.x$ held before executing the advice, it should still hold after the advice.' This implies the postcondition of $t.a$ may not invalidate $u.x$'s postcondition.*
- *The invariant of u should be preserved in t.*

4.3   Relating the Principle to Quantification

As pointcuts are a quantification mechanism, a pointcut may potentially describe a large set of join point shadows. For example, a call/execution pointcut not only matches with the given type, but also its subtypes. Likewise, a pointcut (in AspectJ) could make use of wildcards to match with a large amount of shadows. If an advice now wants to comply with the ASP, it is important to consider that the number of reasoning tasks grows with the number of join point shadows it advises. While this paper does not aim to tackle this scaling problem, as it is separate from modular reasoning about method calls, the problem can be mitigated in a number of ways. First, examining only the advice body itself can sometimes already reveal whether it is ASP-compliant or not. For example, an advice that only modifies its own state, often classified as observer, spectator or spectative advice [11, 21, 37], most likely is ASP-compliant. Second, the developer can rely on tool support like the runtime contract enforcement algorithm of Sect. 7 to test whether an advice complies with the ASP. Finally, this scaling problem is also closely related to the fragile pointcut problem [22], which is about pointcuts (typically in AspectJ) relying on the names of types and methods to determine the set of matching join points, which is quite sensitive to changes. The various methods to tackle this fragility problem may also mitigate the scaling problem, as pointcuts can only get more fragile when they intend to match with a larger set of join point shadows.

4.4   Call and Execution Pointcuts

The ASP essentially states that advice should take into account the contracts of the join points they advise. There are however two subtleties to `call` and `execution` pointcuts when trying to determine this set of join points.

First, there is the fact that the specified type in `execution` pointcuts refers to the *dynamic* type of method calls, whereas the ASP is defined in terms of the contracts in the *static* type. It would be much easier if developers who write advice with an `execution` pointcut could ensure the ASP by only looking at the type specified directly in the pointcut. Fortunately, this is possible, as long as those specified types satisfy the SBS rules. For example, consider a method `User.toString()`. If `User` is a strong behavioural subtype, it may substitute for

any of its ancestor classes. By extension, if an advice with pointcut `execution(*`
`User.toString())` only takes into account the contracts of `User.toString`, the
advice may substitute for any call to `toString` where the static type is `User`,
or an ancestor. In other words, the ASP also is satisfied if an advice takes into
account the dynamic type of its join points, assuming those types are behavioural
subtypes.

The second subtlety involving `call` and `execution` pointcuts is that these
pointcuts not only match if the static/dynamic type equals the pointcut's specified type, but they also match on subtypes. Complying with the ASP then
means that the developer should be aware of *all subtypes* of the pointcut's specified type, which goes against the grain of modular reasoning. Unfortunately, in
this case the ASP is not automatically guaranteed if we only take into account
the specified types, even if all of their subtypes comply with the SBS rules. This
can be demonstrated with the counterexample shown in Fig. 13.

```
class A {
    @requires x > 0
    void foo(int x) {...}}

class B extends A {
    @requires x > -10 // Weaker than A's precondition
    void foo(int x) {...}}

class C {
    @requires x > -5  // Weaker than A's precondition
    around anAdvice: execution(void A.foo(int x)) {...}}

main {
    A inst = new B;
    inst.foo(5);      // No contract violations
    B inst2 = new B;
    inst2.foo(-8);}   // Contract violation in C
```

Fig. 13. Contract violation caused by C only taking into account A

The advice in C is written such that it takes the contracts of `A.foo` into
account. However, the developer of C may not take into account subclass B,
which overrides `A.foo`. Note that `B.foo` complies with the SBS rules, but its
preconditions happen to be stronger than the advice in C. The advice could now
inadvertently cause a contract violation whenever B is the static type in a method
call. It is possible that the problem illustrated in Fig. 13 hardly ever occurs in
practice, as it seems quite unlikely to accidentally create a situation where an
advice does not comply with a subtype, but does comply with the specified type.
Nonetheless, a practical approach to solve the problem is that the developers of
aspects initially only take into account the types specified directly in a pointcut,
but then also use tool support (like the contract enforcement algorithm of Sect. 7)
to monitor whether any subtypes are causing ASP violations.

4.5   The proc Keyword

Because an advice may need to comply with the contracts of several different join points, a mechanism is needed to keep advice contracts reasonably compact, and to prevent any unnecessary coupling with the contracts of each join point. After all, aspects are meant to implement *crosscutting* concerns, which indicates that they are typically loosely coupled to the functionality implemented by the advised join point.

ContractAJ provides a "specification inheritance" mechanism in the form of the proc keyword. When proc is used in the pre/postcondition of an advice that complies with the ASP, it refers to the pre/postcondition of the join point being advised. For example, consider the caching aspect in Fig. 14. If Cache.store is advising a call to List.set, its precondition is i>=0 && i<this1.getLength(). The postcondition is this1.get(i)==val && this2.isCached(i,val). Note that we numbered each this keyword to avoid naming conflicts, as one refers to the instance of List and the other to the Cache instance.

```
class List{
    @requires i>=0 && i<this.getLength()
    @ensures this.get(i)==val
    void set(int i, Object val) {...} ...}

class Cache {
    @requires proc
    @ensures proc && this.isCached(i,val)
    around store: call(void List.set(int i, Object val)) {...} ...}
```

Fig. 14. Example of using the proc keyword

The proc keyword is somewhat similar to e.g. the also keyword used in JML [23, Sect. 2.3] to inherit the specifications of an overridden method. The main difference is that the proc keyword can be used anywhere in the pre- or postcondition, whereas the use of also is constrained such that behavioural subtyping is always enforced by construction. We do not impose such constraints on proc, and hence make it possible for preconditions to be too strong, and postconditions too weak. This is needed to allow for aspects that cannot comply with the ASP, which is explained in Sect. 5.

4.6   Effective Specifications

To make our notion of modular reasoning precise, we need to define which pre- and postconditions need to be ensured whenever a method or proceed call is made. We refer to these specifications as the "effective pre/postcondition" of a particular method call or proceed call. These effective pre/postconditions should allow for modular reasoning, in the sense that a developer who wants to make a call within a certain class, only needs to consider the specifications of that class itself, or anything explicitly referenced by that class.

$$pre(c, x) \quad \frac{\texttt{class } c \ldots \texttt{\{@requires } e \ldots t\, x \ldots\texttt{\}} \text{ is in } P}{pre(c, x) = e}$$

$$\textit{eff}_{pre}(c, m) = pre(c, m)$$

$$\textit{effProc}_{pre}(c, m) = pre(c, m)$$

$$\textit{effProc}_{pre}(c, a) = pre(c, a)[\texttt{proc} \mapsto \textit{effProc}_{pre}(c', x)]$$
$$\text{where } c.a \text{ advises } c'.x \text{ and } !isMethod(c, a)$$

Fig. 15. Defining the effective precondition of method/proceed calls

The definition[6] of effective preconditions can be found in Fig. 15. The $pre(c, x)$ function simply retrieves the precondition of a body $c.x$ from the program's code. The $\textit{eff}_{pre}(c, m)$ function defines the effective precondition of a method call $obj : c.m$. Note that we use the method call notation (defined in Fig. 6 of Sect. 3.1) of ContractAJ's semantics to emphasize that c stands for the static type of the receiver (obj). Because the developer does not need to be aware of any ASP-compliant advice, the effective precondition simply is $pre(c, m)$, which is no different from modular reasoning in object-oriented languages.

The $\textit{effProc}_{pre}(c, m)$ function defines the effective precondition of a proceed call, where the proceed call is located in an advice that advises a method call $obj : c.m$. Because an ASP-compliant advice does not have to be aware of any other advice, the effective precondition of a proceed call also is $pre(c, m)$. However, keep in mind that $\textit{effProc}_{pre}$ is defined in terms of a single method body $c.m$, and that an advice can apply to multiple different method bodies. As the ASP requires that an advice takes into account all of its advised join points, the developer should also take into account the multiple applicable versions of $\textit{effProc}_{pre}$ when making a proceed call.

Finally, $\textit{effProc}_{pre}$ also is defined for proceed calls that occur in higher-order advice. That is, $\textit{effProc}_{pre}(c, a)$ defines the effective precondition of a proceed call, if this proceed call occurs within an advice that advises $c.a$. In this case, the effective precondition is $pre(c, a)$, but because $c.a$ might make use of the `proc` keyword, we should also evaluate the keyword to its concrete value. The `proc` keyword is replaced with the effective precondition of any proceed calls inside $c.a$, which is $\textit{effProc}_{pre}(c', x)$, considering that $c.a$ advises $c'.x$.

Next to the definitions of effective preconditions, one can also give definitions of effective postconditions in $\textit{eff}_{post}$ and $\textit{effProc}_{post}$, which are identical to $\textit{eff}_{pre}$ and $\textit{effProc}_{pre}$ apart from replacing every occurrence of "pre" with "post".

4.7   Frame Conditions

To allow for formal verification, methods and advice should also have a frame condition [8], which specifies what does *not* change after executing a method/advice.

---

[6] This definition only applies if all advice are ASP-compliant; it will be extended later in Sect. 5.5 to take into account non-ASP-compliant advice as well.

While the paper does not focus in particular on formal verification with program specifications, we should briefly discuss the relation between the ASP and frame conditions, as they also play a role in modular reasoning.

In a specification language such as JML, a frame condition is specified by an @assignable clause, which lists what *might* change after executing a method. This implies that everything that is not listed will not change. Because frame conditions are considered part of postconditions, this means they may not be weakened according to the ASP. That is, the frame condition of an advice may not modify *more* variables/fields than the frame conditions of the advised join points. With a strict interpretation of frame conditions, this means an aspect is not allowed to modify its own fields. This would exclude several aspects that are otherwise ASP-compliant, such as aspects that implement logging, caching or contract enforcement. However, the base system can safely remain unaware of such aspects, despite the fact that they modify their own (private) fields. Given this observation, it seems reasonable that the frame properties of a method may ignore any modifications to private fields of aspects, as these modifications are irrelevant to the behaviour of the base system. This should cause no harm, as long as the values of these fields cannot be accessed outside the corresponding aspect's control flow. Perhaps a more precise idea can be formed of what can safely be considered irrelevant to the frame condition of a method, in order to give ASP-compliant advice more freedom to modify locations. However, we should then consider systems like data groups [25] or ownership types [9,14], which goes beyond the scope of this paper.

5   The @advisedBy Clause

The ASP ensures that, if an advice complies with this principle, that advice can safely substitute for the join points it advises without causing any surprising behaviour. While several kinds of crosscutting concerns (e.g. logging, profiling, caching, monitoring, ...) can be implemented in an ASP-compliant manner, there also are several others that inherently cannot comply with the ASP. That is, they must alter the specifications of their advised join points in some way. For example, consider the Security.authenticate advice in Fig. 16. If the user is currently logged in, the advice will ensure the same postcondition as its advised join points, which is okay with the ASP in this instance. However, if the user is not logged in, the advice will block the execution of the advised method and ensures nothing at all (i.e. true). In this case, the postcondition clearly is weaker than the advised join point, which violates the ASP. It is also clear that this advice cannot be rewritten in an ASP-compliant way, as its very purpose is to ensure that the requested operation is blocked when the user is not authenticated.

Even if only a single advice in the system would violate the ASP, it seems that we should revert back to global reasoning, which would defeat the purpose of the ASP. To deal with such non-ASP-compliant advice (or "non-ASP advice" for short), one option is to simply avoid non-ASP advice altogether and implement their functionality using plain method calls instead. While this certainly is a valid option, it also sacrifices AOP's benefits. In particular, there no longer is a notion of quantification: Rather than using one pointcut to indicate all the join points where a block of code should be executed, several method calls have to be added instead, possibly including additional residual logic if these calls should only be executed on certain (run-time) conditions.

Rather than going back to square one, we propose a simple clause called "@advisedBy" that preserves modular reasoning, quantification, allows pointcuts that can only be determined at runtime, and allows ASP-advice to share join points with non-ASP advice. The starting observation is that, if an advice cannot comply with the ASP, it must be doing something surprising that was not expected by the caller of the advised method. To prevent such surprises, the caller should be made aware of any non-ASP advice that apply to this method, which is done by adding an @advisedBy clause to the method's specifications.

An example usage of the @advisedBy clause is shown in Fig. 16. The clause is used in Account.withdraw, which specifies that this method expects to be advised by Security.authenticate and Security.authorize, in that order. Note that the deposit method is also advised by Logger.log, which does not need to be mentioned in the @advisedBy clause as it is ASP-compliant.

```
class Account {
    @requires  this.getAmount() >= m && m>0
    @ensures   this.getAmount() == old(this.getAmount()) - m
    @advisedBy Security.authenticate, Security.authorize
    int withdraw(int m) {...} ...}

class Security {
    @requires proc
    @ensures if(isLoggedIn()){proc}else{true}
    around authenticate: call(void Account.withdraw(int m)) {...}

    @requires proc
    @ensures if(isAuthorised()){proc}else{true}
    around authorize: call(void Account.withdraw(int m))
        && if(isEnabled()) {...} ...}

class Logger {
    @requires true
    @ensures old(getLogEntries())+1==getLogEntries()
    before log: execution(void Account.withdraw(int m)) {...} ...}
```

Fig. 16. Using the @advisedBy clause

In general, the @advisedBy clause indicates that a method is expecting to be advised by the listed advice. Consequently, any client that wants to call this method will notice its @advisedBy clause and should take into account the listed advice. From the perspective of an advice, if it is mentioned in an @advisedBy clause and it makes a proceed call, that advice should now be aware of the next element executed in the clause. In the example of Fig. 16, when authenticate makes a proceed call, it should be aware that this will execute the authorize advice. Likewise, the proc keyword mentioned in authenticate's specifications will refer to the pre/postcondition of `authorize`. Because the `log` advice is not mentioned explicitly in the `@advisedBy` clause, the `proc` keyword in `authorize` refers directly to the specifications in `Account.deposit`, as discussed in Sect. 4.5.

Finally, note that the `@advisedBy` clause can only be added to methods, which implies that all higher-order advice should be ASP-compliant. Conceptually it is possible to add an `@advisedBy` clause to an advice, to indicate that it is aware of the listed higher-order advice. However, constructing effective pre/postconditions is complicated by a combination of two factors: First, when advising a before/after advice, only the advice body is advised, not the implicit proceed call. Second, all before/after advice should take into account the effects of their implicit proceed call (even if they are non-ASP-compliant). These two factors complicate the definition of effective pre/postconditions in method/proceed calls, which is why we decided to leave support for non-ASP-compliant higher-order advice as future work.

5.1   Relating the `@advisedBy` Clause to Quantification

At this point, the reader may wonder how the `@advisedBy` clause still preserves · AOP's notion of quantification. After all, for every method call $obj:c.m$ that may be advised by a non-ASP advice, there should be an `@advisedBy` clause in $c.m$ that mentions this advice. At first glance, all the extra effort required to add all of these `@advisedBy` clauses seems to cancel out the benefits of having pointcuts as a quantification mechanism. However, it is possible to provide tool support that automatically inserts all `@advisedBy` clauses in the right places of the source code, and removes the need to write each clause manually. Given such tool support, we consider that the `@advisedBy` clause does not inhibit the quantification property of AOP.

Generating `@advisedBy` clauses in AspectJ is quite straightforward, where it is sufficient to inspect the pointcut of every advice. In a nutshell: If a pointcut makes use of a `call` construct, an `@advisedBy` clause should only be added to the method bodies specified directly in the `call` construct. In case a pointcut makes use of an `execution` construct, which only matches if the dynamic type is a certain (sub)type, the `@advisedBy` clause should be added into the types that declare the specified method bodies.

To take into account the fact that `call/execution` constructs also include subtypes, `@advisedBy` clauses are implicitly inherited by subtypes. In this manner, an `@advisedBy` clause will mention the desired advice when examining the static type of any method call that may be advised by that advice. Tool support that could generate `@advisedBy` clauses is actually already largely present in the AspectJ Development Tools [10], as it is quite similar to the markers that indicate each join point shadow.

In case of ContractAJ, some additional information is required to generate `@advisedBy` clauses in the right places. This is because it is possible to override advice, and an advice may be mentioned either directly or as a subtype in an `@advisedBy` clause, which allows for additional expressivity. Nonetheless, we assume ContractAJ can be easily extended with a simple construct to describe in which locations an @advisedBy clause should be added. For example, a class might contain the following "declare @advisedBy" statement:

```
declare @advisedBy Authentication.authenticate: Bank.set*(*);
```

Tool support can then make use of this information to insert @advisedBy clauses that list Authentication.authenticate in every method body that matches Bank.set*(*). Finally, if multiple such statements want to add an @advisedBy clause to the same method, the program's precedence declaration is used to ensure that the advice listed in the @advisedBy clause are ordered correctly.

5.2   Interaction with ASP-Compliant Advice

Using the @advisedBy clause allows advice to alter the contracts of the join points they advise. However, what does this mean when such advice shares join points with an ASP-compliant advice (that is not mentioned in the @advisedBy clause)? An ASP-compliant advice only needs to take into account the advised join points' pre- and postconditions, but it can ignore any @advisedBy clauses. As a consequence, if both an ASP- and a non-ASP advice advise the same join point, the ASP-advice should get a lower precedence. That is, it should come after the non-ASP advice in an advice composition. While it is possible that the ASP-advice may never cause surprising behaviour if it had a higher precedence, this is not automatically ensured by the ASP. Aside from this constraint, the benefits of ASP-advice remain: An ASP-advice can be positioned anywhere after the non-ASP advice in advice compositions, while the remainder of the system does not have to be aware of this advice. In case it is required for an ASP-advice to be executed at a higher precedence, it always is possible to explicitly mention it in @advisedBy clauses.

5.3   Overriding Advice

Because each advice in ContractAJ has a name, it becomes possible to override advice. Analogous to method overriding, when an advice in one aspect has the same name as an advice in one of its ancestor aspects, that advice is said to be overriding. However, overriding only has a purpose when the developer is *expecting* one advice body to be executed, but at runtime an overridden version might substitute for it. There are no such expectations if advice execution is implicit, which is the case for ASP-compliant advice.

The introduction of the @advisedBy clause gives purpose to overriding advice. When a method uses an @advisedBy clause, it is *expecting* those listed advice. These expectations, which can be determined statically, do not have to be fulfilled per se by exactly those listed advice. They might as well be implemented by a subaspect with an overriding advice. As can be seen in the example of Fig. 17, Account.withdraw is expecting to be advised by Security.authenticate. At runtime, this expectation could be filled in by a subaspect RemoteSecurity, which overrides the authenticate advice to e.g. implement a different authentication system. A similarly useful scenario could be that Security only is an

```
class Security {
    around authenticate: call(int Account.withdraw(int i)) {...}}

class RemoteSecurity extends Security {
    around authenticate: call(int Account.withdraw(int i)) {...}}

class Account {
    @advisedBy Security.authenticate
    void withdraw(int i) {...}}

main {
    Security sec = new RemoteSecurity;
    Account acc = new Account(30);
    account.withdraw(10);}
// The @advisedBy clause in Account.withdraw lists Security
// , but is actually advised at runtime by RemoteSecurity.
```

Fig. 17. Example of overriding advice

abstract aspect, and the overriding advice in `RemoteSecurity` provides a concrete implementation. This notion of overriding advice implies that, similar to overriding methods in classes, overriding advice leave aspects "open for extension, but closed for modification" (the open/closed principle [29]). That is, an aspect's behaviour can be modified by defining a subaspect, without the need to modify any `@advisedBy` clauses.

As the use of overriding advice is similar to overriding methods, the SBS rules can be reused to ensure that aspects with overriding advice can substitute for any ancestor aspect without causing surprising behaviour. We only need to make a minor extension to the SBS such that the pre- and postcondition rules apply to both methods and advice:

Strong behavioural subtyping, extended (SBS'). *Type t is a strong behavioural subtype of type u, if and only if $t < u$ and:*

- *For all objects of type t, and for all common methods **and advice** x in t and u:*
  - *The precondition of $t.x$ must be equal to or weaker than the precondition of $u.x$.*
  - *The postcondition of $t.x$ must only be equal to or stronger than the postcondition of $u.m$, if the precondition of $u.m$ held in the pre-state.*
- *The invariant of u should be preserved in t.*

Note that ensuring the SBS' rules for an advice is independent from the join points it advises, even if the `proc` keyword is used. While the actual value of the `proc` keyword does depend on which join point is advised, we know that this value will be the same for the pre/postcondition of both $t.x$ and $u.x$. Consequently, it is not necessary to know `proc`'s value to determine whether one advice's pre/postcondition is stronger or weaker than another. However, while the SBS' rules can be satisfied without considering the value of the `proc` keyword, an advice's implementation should of course correspond to its specifications. By simply using `proc` in the precondition of an advice (without knowing which contracts it refers to), we can ascertain that the right precondition is satisfied to make a proceed call at the very beginning of the advice body. However, if a proceed call is made at a later point in time, we need to make sure that this precondition is preserved. Because of this, we may still need to determine which contracts proc refers to. Likewise, we may need these contracts to ensure that the postcondition of a proceed call is preserved at the end of the advice.

5.4   Constraints on the @advisedBy Clause

To avoid ambiguities when executing a call with an @advisedBy clause, there may not be multiple aspect instances that correspond to the same element in the @advisedBy clause. Moreover, if an advice is mentioned in the @advisedBy clause of a method, it is expected that this advice, or an overriding version, *will* be executed when that method is called (unless the advice's if pointcut construct failed). If the developer is free to instantiate aspects at any time, which is the case in ContractAJ, these two constraints cannot be enforced statically. The easiest solution would be to throw a runtime exception whenever the constraints are broken, which is also done by ContractAJ's contract enforcement algorithm in Sect. 7. Another approach would be to use AspectJ's more constrained instantiation mechanism, which ensures by construction there cannot be more than one instance of the same aspect at a given join point. While this approach avoids runtime exceptions, we still opted to give the developer full control over aspect instantiation in ContractAJ, as it would be difficult to combine AspectJ's instantiation mechanism with the notion of overriding advice in an intuitive/useful manner. We give preference to supporting overriding advice, because it leaves aspects open for extension in the presence of non-ASP advice.

5.5   Extending the Effective Specifications

Due to the introduction of the @advisedBy clause, applications may now contain both ASP- and non-ASP-compliant advice. However, this also requires some modifications to our definitions of effective specifications in Sect. 4.6. These new definitions can be found in Fig. 18. The eff_{pre} and $\mathit{effProc}_{pre}$ functions still have the same intuition behind them: eff_{pre} defines the effective precondition of method calls and $\mathit{effProc}_{pre}$ defines the effective precondition of proceed calls. However, note that $\mathit{effProc}_{pre}(c, m, i)$ has now gained a third parameter i, which indicates a certain position within the @advisedBy clause of $c.m$. More specifically, $\mathit{effProc}_{pre}(c, m, i)$ describes the effective precondition of any proceed calls within an advice mentioned at position i of $c.m$'s @advisedBy clause. This effective precondition essentially states that the advice at position i should become aware of all subsequent advice in the @advisedBy clause. Let us now take a closer look at each of the functions in Fig. 18:

[eff_{pre}] - The effective precondition of method calls $\mathit{eff}_{pre}(c, m)$, corresponds to $\mathit{effProc}_{pre}(c, m, 0)$. Because the first advice of the @advisedBy clause only has index 1, setting i to 0 intuitively means that we should become aware of all advice in the @advisedBy clause when making a method call, which indeed is

$$\textit{eff}_{pre}(c, m) = \textit{effProc}_{pre}(c, m, 0)$$

$$\textit{effProc}_{pre}(c, m, i) = \begin{cases} \texttt{if}(\textit{ifPcut}(c_{i+1}, a_{i+1}))\{\textit{adv}_{pre}(c_{i+1}, a_{i+1}, c, m, i+1)\} \\ \texttt{else if}(\textit{ifPcut}(c_{i+2}, a_{i+2}))\{\textit{adv}_{pre}(c_{i+2}, a_{i+2}, c, m, i+2)\} \\ \ldots \\ \texttt{else if}(\textit{ifPcut}(c_n, a_n))\{\textit{adv}_{pre}(c_n, a_n, c, m, n)\} \\ \texttt{else}\{\textit{pre}(c, m)\} \end{cases}$$
$$\text{where } \textit{isMethod}(c, m) \text{ and } \textit{advBy}(c, m) = \langle c_1, a_1, \ldots, c_n, a_n \rangle \text{ and } 0 \le i < n$$

$$\textit{effProc}_{pre}(c, m, i) = \textit{pre}(c, m)$$
$$\text{where } \textit{isMethod}(c, m) \text{ and } |\textit{advBy}(c, m)| = 0$$

$$\textit{effProc}_{pre}(c, a, i) = \textit{pre}(c, a)[\texttt{proc} \mapsto \textit{effProc}(c', x, j)]$$
$$\text{where } c.a \text{ advises } c'.x \text{ and } !\textit{isMethod}(c, a)$$
$$\text{and } c.a \text{ is mentioned at position } j \text{ of the } \texttt{@advisedBy} \text{ clause of } c'.x$$

$$\textit{adv}_{pre}(c, a, c', x, i) = \textit{iPre}(c, a)[\texttt{proc} \mapsto \textit{effProc}_{pre}(c', x, i+1)]$$
$$\text{where } c.a \text{ advises } c'.x$$

$$\textit{iPre}(c, a) = \begin{array}{ll} \textit{pre}(c, a) & \text{if } \textit{isAround}(c, a) \\ \textit{pre}(c, a) \ \texttt{\&\&} \ \texttt{proc} \text{ if } \textit{isBefore}(c, a) \text{ or } \textit{isAfter}(c, a) \end{array}$$

Fig. 18. Defining the effective precondition of method/proceed calls

the desired definition. An example of the effective precondition of a method call to Bank.createAccount is also given in Fig. 19.

[$\textit{effProc}_{pre}$] - The effective precondition of proceed calls is split up into three different cases. The second and third case are straightforward, as they correspond to the old definition of $\textit{effProc}_{pre}$ in Sect. 4.6. The first case however is new: it describes the effective precondition of proceed calls where the advised method has a non-empty @advisedBy clause. Given i, the effective precondition that is produced consists of an if statement that iterates over all succeeding advice (from $i + 1$ to n) in the @advisedBy clause of $c.m$. What may be surprising is that we test the if pointcut construct for each of these advice (using the $\textit{ifPcut}$ function defined in Fig. 8). This is necessary because, if we allow the advice mentioned in the @advisedBy clause to modify the expected behaviour of a method/proceed call, we must know which advice will be executed next. Because the if constructs are the only[7] part of a ContractAJ pointcut that (in general) cannot be determined statically, they are included in the effective precondition itself.

[$\textit{adv}_{pre}$] - Once we have determined which advice will be executed next, the $\textit{adv}_{pre}$ function is used to retrieve that advice's precondition. Additionally, $\textit{adv}_{pre}$ replaces any occurrences of the proc keyword with the effective precondition of any proceed calls in its advice body using $\textit{effProc}_{pre}$, meaning that we recursively iterate through the remainder of the @advisedBy clause. This continues until we eventually reach the else branch in $\textit{effProc}_{pre}$, which ends with the precondition of the advised method.

---

[7] An execution pointcut can only be determined dynamically, but we assume that it has already been converted into a call pointcut conjoined with an if construct, as described in Fig. 4 of Sect. 3.1.

```
class Bank {
    @requires u.getBank()==this
    @ensures result!=null && result.getOwner()==u
    @advisedBy Security.authenticate, Security.authorize
    Account createAccount(User u) {...}}

class Security {
    @requires proc
    @ensures if(isLoggedIn(u)){proc}else{true}
    around authenticate: call(Account Bank.createAccount(User u))
        && target(b) {...}

    @requires isLoggedIn(u) && proc
    @ensures if(isAuthorized(u)){proc}else{true}
    around authorize: call(Account Bank.createAccount(User u))
        && target(b) && if(isEnabled()) {...}}

main {
    Bank b = new Bank;
    b.createAccount(new User);}
// Effective precondition of Bank.createAccount:
//   if(isEnabled()) {
//       isLoggedIn(u) && u.getBank()==this
//   } else {
//       u.getBank()==this
//   }
```

Fig. 19. Example of an effective precondition

[*iPre*] - What is important to note about adv_{pre} is that we do not directly retrieve the precondition of an advice with the *pre* function, but we make use of $iPre(c, a)$ instead. In case $c.a$ is an around advice body, $iPre(c, a) = pre(c, a)$. However, if $c.a$ is a before or after advice, the **proc** keyword will also be conjoined. This is necessary because otherwise the effects of the implicit proceed call would not be included into the effective precondition. In other words, *iPre* makes the implicit proceed call of a before/after advice explicit, such that we obtain that advice's precondition as if it were an around advice. This also holds for the analogous *iPost* function, which conjoins **proc** to a before/after advice's postcondition. In general, we are not allowed to simply conjoin the **proc** keyword, e.g. because a before advice body might not preserve the precondition of its proceed call. However, this is remedied by the rules that will be defined in Sect. 5.6 and ensure that all before/after advice take into account their implicit proceed call.

This covers each function used to define the effective preconditions of method and proceed calls. The definitions for effective postconditions are analogous, as each occurrence of "pre" is simply replaced with "post".

We should note that, in general, the entire effective specification of a method/proceed call can become quite large and complex. However, the functions of Fig. 18 do take into account the worst case where every pointcut effectively makes use of an **if** construct (that can only be determined at runtime). However, as indicated in Apel et al. [4], typically only a small fraction of aspect code makes use of such advanced features. In the best (and more common) case, each pointcut in an @advisedBy clause can be determined statically, drastically simplifying the entire effective precondition of a method call to the following:

$$eff_{pre}(c,m) = \begin{array}{l} iPre(c_1, a_1)[\texttt{proc} \mapsto \\ \quad iPre(c_2, a_2)[\texttt{proc} \mapsto \\ \quad\quad \ldots \\ \quad\quad\quad iPre(c_n, a_n)[\texttt{proc} \mapsto pre(c,m)] \ldots]] \end{array}$$
$$\text{where } isMethod(c,m) \text{ and } advBy(c,m) = \langle c_1, a_1, \ldots, c_n, a_n \rangle$$

That is, $c.m$ would use the precondition of the first advice in the @advisedBy clause, and each advice's proc keyword would be replaced with the precondition of the next advice in the clause.

5.6   Before and After Advice

The $iPre$ function in Fig. 18 includes the effects of the implicit proceed call in before/after advice by simply conjoining the proc keyword to its pre- and postcondition. However, in order for this to be correct, there are some rules that must be satisfied. These rules, which are a weaker version of the ASP for before/after advice, are referred to as the "implicit proceed rules" (IPR):

IPR for before advice. *Consider a before advice* t.a *that is applied to join point* u.x. *If* t.a *is mentioned in the* @advisedBy *clause of* u.x, *it is mentioned at position* i. *If* t.a *is not mentioned in the* @advisedBy *clause (or such a clause is not present) then* $i = 0$. *The before advice satisfies the IPR if and only if, for all objects of type* t:

- *If* $effProc_{pre}(u, x, i)$ *held before executing the advice, it should still hold after the advice.*
- *If* $post(t, a)$ *holds after the advice, it should still hold after the implicit proceed call.*
- *The invariant of* u *should be preserved in* t.

Likewise, the **IPR for after advice** are defined as:

- *If* $effProc_{post}(u, x, i)$ *held before executing the advice, it should still hold after the advice.*
- *If* $pre(t, a)$ *held before the implicit proceed call, it should still hold after the implicit proceed call.*
- *The invariant of* u *should be preserved in* t.

Note that the second rule in the IPR of both before- and after advice requires that the implicit proceed call should preserve a certain condition. As the advice body has no control over what the proceed call may or may not preserve, we can only rely on what we can determine to be preserved. If we are conservative, we can only ascertain that the proceed call will preserve anything that is equal to or weaker than its postcondition. However, a weaker notion of preservation is possible when frame conditions are available: In addition to preserving the proceed call's own postcondition, we know that it will preserve conditions that depend only on variables/fields that are *not* modified by the proceed call.

5.7   Modular Reasoning in ContractAJ

To summarize Sects. 4 and 5, modular reasoning about method/proceed calls in ContractAJ can be achieved as follows:

- All classes should take into account the SBS' rules (Sect. 5.3). That is, a subtype should take into account the contracts of its supertype. This also holds for overriding advice.
- To remain oblivious of an advice, it should comply with the ASP (Sects. 4.1 and 4.2). That is, the advice should comply with the contracts of all join points it advises. If an ASP-compliant advice shares join points with advice mentioned in an @advisedBy clause, the ASP-compliant advice should have a lower precedence. (Sect. 5.2)
- If it is not possible or undesired to be oblivious of an advice $c.a$, it should be mentioned by an @advisedBy clause in all method bodies $c'.m$, where c' is the static type in any method calls to m that are advised by $c.a$. Advice $c.a$ may either be mentioned directly in an @advisedBy clause, or indirectly as an overridden advice. If $c.a$ is a before/after advice, it should comply with the IPR (Sect. 5.6) in order to take into account the effects of its implicit proceed call. Finally, the constraints of Sect. 5.4 should be taken into account as well.

In using this approach, there is little that changes from the perspective of an OOP developer who writes classes (without advice). This is especially important when considering that the bulk of a typical aspect-oriented application consists of regular classes and only a fraction of the code is made up of aspects [4]. When making a method call that only has ASP-compliant advice applied to it, nothing changes. When calling a method that has an @advisedBy clause, the listed advice need to be taken into account. This arguably does not add much complexity compared to reasoning about OOP applications: In OOP applications, the contracts of a method not only reflect the concern that it implements, but the contracts of any crosscutting concerns would have to be included as well. In AOP, these two are now separated, though the @advisedBy clause provides an explicit link needed to construct the effective specification. Moreover, the developer does not even have to construct this specification by him/herself, as it should be straightforward to build a tool that statically determines the effective pre- and postcondition of all method and proceed calls.

As for the developers writing advice, ensuring that the rules for either ASP or non-ASP advice hold can be done quite easily for advice that advise only a small number of join point shadows. As discussed in Sect. 4.3, the number of reasoning tasks grows with the number of advised join point shadows. In this case, the contracts of an advice can be written without rigorously inspecting each join point shadow, but tools like the contract enforcement algorithm of Sect. 7 should be used to help verify whether the advice satisfies the approach.

Finally, in case an advice is non-ASP-compliant, the right methods should mention the advice in an @advisedBy clause. As discussed in Sect. 5.1, tool support can be provided to generate these clauses. Because the use of an @advisedBy affects the effective specification of method calls, deciding on which @advisedBy clauses go where should be done as early as possible. Keep in mind that crosscutting concerns also form part of a system's design and aspects should therefore not be added as an afterthought. Nonetheless, using @advisedBy clauses still leaves the system open for extension, as the listed advice may also be implemented by subaspects.

6   Soundness of the Approach

In Sects. 4 and 5 we presented our approach to modular reasoning in aspect-oriented languages. We now want to show that this approach is sound. That is, if a ContractAJ program is written such that it takes into account the SBS' rules, the ASP, IPR and the constraints on @advisedBy clauses, then all pre- and postconditions encountered in any program execution are satisfied. Note that we do not consider invariants: In OOP, the precondition and postcondition rules of SBS are known to be sound, but the invariant rule is not [24]. For example, because a subclass may strengthen its invariant, and because an invariant can be considered a part of each method's pre- and postcondition, it is possible to create conflicts with the precondition rule. Such problems with the invariant rule are carried over to the ASP as well. While achieving soundness in invariants could be done by only allowing an invariant to depend on certain parts of the program state, or by placing restrictions on ownership [26,31,32], we consider this to go beyond the paper's scope.

Aside from focusing only on pre- and postconditions, we do consider the various complex ways in which advice can be composed: Multiple advice can apply to the same join point; advice can depend on pointcuts that can only be determined at runtime; advice can be overridden, and higher-order advice (advice that advise other advice executions) are allowed. We will first define what constitutes a valid advice composition. Once this is done, we can show that our approach preserves modular reasoning in a number of theorems: Initially programs with only ASP-compliant advice are considered. We then add support for advice mentioned in an @advisedBy clause and finally allow for higher-order advice.

6.1   Valid Advice Compositions

In Sect. 5.4 we discussed two dynamic constraints that should hold for each advice composition, in order to avoid ambiguities in @advisedBy clauses. To show that our approach to modular reasoning is sound, we should first make these constraints precise by defining what constitutes a valid advice composition. An advice composition is a sequence $\langle c_1.a_1, \ldots, c_n.a_n, c.x \rangle$, where each $c_i.a_i$ represents an advice body that will be executed, in the given precedence order, and $c.x$ represents the body advised by each $c_i.a_i$. We can now define a *valid* advice composition (for method call join points) as follows:

Valid advice composition *(for method calls). During the evaluation of program P, consider a join point that represents a method call $obj:c.m$.*

The method call corresponds to an advice composition $\langle c_1.a_1, \ldots, c_n.a_n, c.m \rangle$.
Method body $c.m$ has the following valid @advisedBy clause: @advisedBy
$d_1.b_1, \ldots, d_k.b_k$, where $k \geq 0$. The advice composition is valid if and only if
there exists an index j, $0 \leq j \leq k$ such that:

- *There is an order-preserving, injective function f from $(c_1.a_1, \ldots, c_j.a_j)$ to*
  $(d_1.b_1, \ldots, d_k.b_k)$ such that, for each i, either $c_i.a_i = f(c_i.a_i)$ or $c_i.a_i$ over-
  rides $f(c_i.a_i)$.
- *For each $d_i.b_i$ in $(d_1.b_1, \ldots, d_1.b_k)$ the pointcut of $d_i.b_i$ matches on $obj:c.m$*
  if and only if $d_i.b_i \in \{f(c_1.a_1), \ldots, f(c_j.a_j)\}$.

This definition states that a valid advice composition can be divided into two
parts: $(c_1.a_1, \ldots, c_j.a_j)$ represents the advice mentioned in the @advisedBy
clause and $(c_{j+1}.a_{j+1}, \ldots, c_n.a_n)$ represents the ASP-compliant advice, which
have a lower precedence. The function f is order-preserving to ensure that each
advice mentioned in the @advisedBy clause respects the precedence order specified by the @advisedBy clause. (This is already ensured statically by the constraints in Sect. 3.4) The function is injective to prevent that two advice in
the composition could be mentioned by the same element in the @advisedBy
clause. Finally, we require that the pointcut of each advice in the @advisedBy
clause is respected, such that it matches the expectations created by the effective pre- and postconditions of $c.m$. This constraint only is needed because an
overriding advice might use a different pointcut than the advice it overrides.

The definition of valid advice compositions for advice execution join points
is trivial: Because advice cannot have an @advisedBy clause, all advice compositions on advice executions are valid.

6.2   Shared Join Points

We will now show that our approach is sound when multiple advice can share
the same join points. That is, the developer can assume that all effective pre-/
postconditions of any method/proceed calls and all pre/postconditions of method
and advice bodies during program execution will hold, on the condition that our
approach is taken into account and that he/she ensures that the implementation of each advice/method body correctly implements its own specifications. In
doing so the developer is allowed to assume modular reasoning at any method
call. To make these conditions more precise, we first define what it means when
"modular reasoning about a method call is possible":

Definition 1. *Modular reasoning about a method call $obj:c.m$ during an exe-*
cution of a program P is possible if the following holds: Let $\langle e, \mathcal{S}, \mathcal{J} \rangle$ be a con-
figuration in P, where e decomposes to a context with method call $obj:c.m$. If
$\mathit{eff}_{pre}(c, m)$ is satisfied in this configuration, then $\mathit{eff}_{post}(c, m)$ is satisfied in the
configuration that represents the end of the method call.

An analogous definition can be given for proceed calls. Intuitively, the developer
should ensure the preconditions of the next advice that this proceed call will execute. However this developer can, and should, only determine which advice comes

next based on the @advisedBy clauses where the current advice is mentioned, which can be statically determined using the *effProc* functions of Sect. 5.5.

Definition 2. *Modular reasoning about a proceed call during an execution of a program P is possible if the following holds: Let $\langle e, \mathcal{S}, \mathcal{J} \rangle$ be a configuration in P, where e decomposes to a context with a proceed call. Let this proceed call be part of the execution of an advice body $c'.a$ that advises method c.m and assume that either $c'.a$ satisfies the ASP or it is mentioned at position i of c.m's* @advisedBy *clause. If $effProc_{pre}(c, m, i)$ is satisfied in this configuration, $effProc_{post}(c, m, i)$ is satisfied in the configuration that represents the end of the proceed call.*

Next, we can define what it means for an advice/method body to correctly implement its own specifications; we refer to this property as "local correctness":

Definition 3. *An advice/method body x in class c is locally correct in a program P if the following holds:*

- *If, at a method/proceed call in any execution of body c.x in P: (1) $pre(c, x)$ was satisfied at the beginning of executing c.x. (2) Modular reasoning is possible for all prior method/proceed calls in the execution of c.x.*
  Then: the effective precondition of that method/proceed call is satisfied.
- *If, in any execution of body c.x in P: (1) $pre(c, x)$ was satisfied at the beginning of executing c.x. (2) Modular reasoning is possible for all method/proceed calls in the execution of c.x.*
  Then: $post(c, x)$ is satisfied when the execution of c.x finishes.

In Theorem 1, we start by considering the execution of ContractAJ programs that only contain ASP-compliant advice, no @advisedBy clauses and no higher-order advice. Theorem 2 then extends the first theorem with the use of the @advisedBy clause. We assume that all pre- and postconditions are free from side-effects and always terminate. Likewise, we also assume that the conditions in any if pointcut constructs are free from side-effects and always terminate, as they should only be used to determine whether an advice matches, rather than altering the program's state.

Theorem 1. *Let P be a program without any* @advisedBy *clauses or higher-order advice. The effective pre/postcondition of each method/proceed call (including implicit proceed calls) and the pre/postcondition of each method/advice body during the evaluation of P will be satisfied if: (1) All advice in P satisfy the ASP rules. (2) All classes in P satisfy the SBS' rules. (3) All method/advice bodies in P are locally correct. (4) The initial precondition of P is satisfied at the start of the program.*

We only need to focus on those points during the execution where a method/advice body is about to start or about to end. It is only at those points that we need to check whether the pre/postcondition of a method/advice body is satisfied, as well as the effective pre/postcondition of the method/proceed call that initiated the body's execution. Any other point in the execution of P is irrelevant, as there are no method/advice contracts to be considered.

The proof proceeds by induction on the length of the reduction sequence leading to such relevant points, with a case analysis on the last steps. In the base case, 0 steps, P's initial precondition is satisfied by (4). In the inductive step, consider the start of a method/advice body. The "start of a body" does not refer to just one particular configuration in the evaluation of a program, but rather to the entire sequence of configurations that decomposes a method/proceed call into the body that will be executed. These sequences are precisely described by Fig. 10 in Sect. 3.3, which specifies all possible sequences of rule applications during the lookup process. During the entirety of such a sequence, both the effective precondition of the method/proceed call and the precondition of the body to be executed must hold. Note that it is sufficient to show this for any one configuration in this sequence, because none[8] of the rules in Fig. 10 can modify the program's store.

(A) Body initiated via method call - Consider the case where the execution of a body is initiated by a method call, as described by the *mcall* sequence in Fig. 10. Let $\langle e, \mathcal{S}, \mathcal{J} \rangle$ be a configuration in P where e decomposes into a method call $obj\!:\!c.m$. (Keep in mind that c represents the receiver's static type.)

(A.1) We first show that $pre(c, m)$ is satisfied in this configuration, using (3) and induction on the length of the execution: Let $c'.x$ be the body that contains the method call $obj\!:\!c.m$. By (3), we know $c'.x$ is locally correct. By induction, the pre/postconditions in all configurations prior to $\langle e, \mathcal{S}, \mathcal{J} \rangle$ were satisfied. This implies that $pre(c', x)$ was satisfied at the start of $c'.x$, and moreover modular reasoning is possible for all method/proceed calls in the execution of $c'.x$, prior to the call $obj\!:\!c.m$. Now local correctness of $c'.x$ indeed ensures that $pre(c, m)$ holds at $\langle e, \mathcal{S}, \mathcal{J} \rangle$. (We will reuse this reasoning a few times; we will use "by (3)+induction" as a shorthand for it.) Because there are no @advisedBy clauses in P, $\mathit{eff}_{pre}(c, m) = pre(c, m)$, and hence the effective precondition of method call $obj\!:\!c.m$ holds.

(A.2) The *mcall* sequence of Fig. 10 always leads to the execution of either a method, before advice or around advice body. It remains to be shown that the precondition of this body holds when its execution starts. Consider configuration $\langle e', \mathcal{S}, \mathcal{J}' \rangle$, in which the [exec] rule at the end of *mcall* is applied:

- **Method body** - Let $c''.m$ be the method body that is executed by our method call $obj\!:\!c.m$. Because $pre(c, m)$ holds, and because SBS' ensures that $pre(c'', m)$ cannot be stronger than $pre(c, m)$ (2), the precondition of the method body $pre(c'', m)$ is satisfied.
- **Before/around advice body** - Let $c''.a$ be the before/around advice initiated by $obj\!:\!c.m$. Because $pre(c, m)$ holds, and because the ASP (1) ensures that $pre(c'', a)$ cannot be stronger than $pre(c, m)$, the precondition of the advice body $pre(c'', a)$ is satisfied.

---

[8] The evaluation of the condition in **if** pointcut constructs might involve store-altering rule applications. However, this is harmless as we assume that these conditions are free from side effects and always terminate.

(B) Body initiated via proceed call - Now consider the case where the execution of a body is initiated by a proceed call, as described in the *pcall* sequence of Fig. 10. Let $\langle e, \mathcal{S}, \mathcal{J} \rangle$ be a configuration where e decomposes into a proceed call (i.e. a `proceed` not produced by the [**call**] rule, as this corresponds to the *mcall* sequence). Let $c.m$ be the method that is being advised by $c'.a$, the advice that initiated this proceed call. If $c'.a$ is an around advice or an after advice, the effective precondition of this proceed call $effProc_{pre}(c, m)$ holds by (3)+induction. If $c'.a$ is a before advice, we only know by (3)+induction that $effProc_{pre}(c, m)$ is satisfied when the execution of $c'.a$ starts. However, because the ASP (1) requires that before advice preserve this effective precondition, $effProc_{pre}(c, m)$ still holds at $\langle e, \mathcal{S}, \mathcal{J} \rangle$. We now know $effProc_{pre}(c, m)$ always holds at $\langle e, \mathcal{S}, \mathcal{J} \rangle$. As there are no @advisedBy clauses, $effProc_{pre}(c, m) = pre(c, m)$. Because $effProc_{pre}(c, m)$ holds, and because the *pcall* expression is identical to *mcall* (apart from the initial application of [**call**]), we can reuse the reasoning of (A.2) to conclude that the precondition of the body to be executed is satisfied in this case as well.

(C) Initiating after advice bodies - As the execution of an after advice body cannot be initiated directly by a method/proceed call, it is treated as a separate case. For the same reason, we only need to show that the after advice body's precondition holds; there is no effective precondition that needs to hold. As discussed in Sect. 3.3, the execution of an after advice body corresponds to the rule sequence "[**return**] *mcall*" where [**return**] indicates the end of the implicit proceed call. Let $\langle e, \mathcal{S}, \mathcal{J} \rangle$ be the configuration where we are about to apply the [**call**] rule in *mcall*. In this configuration, e decomposes to $obj\!:\!c.a$, representing a "call" to the after advice to be executed. (Keep in mind that the operational semantics internally uses method calls to execute advice bodies.) Let $c'.m$ be the method advised by $c.a$. In case the implicit proceed call preceding $c.a$ ended with another after advice body, we know $effProc_{post}(c', m)$ held at the beginning of executing this body, by (3)+induction. By the ASP (1), we know that $effProc_{post}(c', m)$ still holds at $\langle e, \mathcal{S}, \mathcal{J} \rangle$, as after advice are required to preserve the effective postcondition. In any other case, the preceding implicit proceed call directly ensures $effProc_{post}(c', m)$ at $\langle e, \mathcal{S}, \mathcal{J} \rangle$ by (3)+induction. As there are no @advisedBy clauses, $effProc_{post}(c', m) = post(c', m)$. Because the ASP (1) requires that $pre(c.a)$ may not be stronger than $post(c', m)$, the precondition of the after advice body $pre(c, a)$ holds.

(D) Returning from a body - After covering every possible way to initiate the execution of a body, we still need to do the analogue for the end of executing a body. In short: We now only need to consider the [**return**] rule, as it always represents the end of a body's execution. Let $\langle e, \mathcal{S}, \mathcal{J} \rangle$ be a configuration where e decomposes into a `return` expression. By (3)+induction, the body's postcondition holds. In case of method, after advice and around advice bodies, we still need to show that the effective postcondition holds of the method/proceed call that initiated the execution of this body. For method bodies, this is ensured by SBS' (2). For around/after advice bodies, this is ensured by the ASP (1). In case of a before advice body, there is no effective postcondition to be shown at $\langle e, \mathcal{S}, \mathcal{J} \rangle$, due to the presence of the implicit proceed call that follows.   □

Theorem 2. *Let P be a program without any higher-order advice. The effective pre/postcondition of each method/proceed call (including implicit proceed calls) and the pre/postcondition of each method/advice body during the evaluation of P will be satisfied if: (1) All advice in P that are not mentioned in any @advisedBy clauses satisfy the ASP rules. (2) All classes in P satisfy the SBS' rules. (3) All method/advice bodies in P are locally correct. (4) The initial precondition of P is satisfied at the start of the program. (5) Each advice composition is valid. (6) All before/after advice satisfy the IPR rules. (7) Advice mentioned in an @advisedBy clause have a higher precedence than advice not mentioned in any @advisedBy clauses.*

This proof is an extension of Theorem 1's proof; the main difference is that we now have a distinction between those advice that are mentioned in an @advisedBy clause, and those that are not.

Body initiated via method call - Let $\langle e, \mathcal{S}, \mathcal{J} \rangle$ be a configuration where e decomposes to a method call $obj : c.m$. By (3)+induction, the effective precondition of the method call, $\mathit{eff}_{pre}(c, m) = \mathit{effProc}_{pre}(c, m, 0)$, is ensured at $\langle e, \mathcal{S}, \mathcal{J} \rangle$. Let $c'.a$ be the body to be executed.

- In case $c'.a$ is an ASP-compliant around/before advice or a method body, then either $c.m$ does not have an @advisedBy clause, or the if pointcut constructs of each advice in the @advisedBy clause must have evaluated to false (because each advice composition must be valid (5)). In both cases, we know that $\mathit{effProc}_{pre}(c, m, 0) = \mathit{pre}(c, m)$, which corresponds to the situation after (A.1) in the proof of Theorem 1. Consequently, we may conclude that the precondition of the method/ASP-compliant body to be executed is satisfied.
- If $c'.a$ is an around/before advice mentioned at position i of the @advisedBy clause of $c.m$, then it follows from (5) that all preceding if pointcut constructs have evaluated to false. We now know that $\mathit{effProc}_{pre}(c, m, 0) = \mathit{adv}_{pre}(c_i.a_i, c, m, i)$, where $c_i.a_i$ is the ith advice in the @advisedBy clause of $c.m$ and $c'.a \leq c_i.a_i$. Because $c'.a$ satisfies SBS' (2) and its precondition may not be stronger than $\mathit{adv}_{pre}(c_i.a_i, c, m, i)$, $\mathit{adv}_{pre}(c'.a, c, m, i)$ is satisfied as well, which is the precondition of $c'.a$ (with the proc keyword adjusted to the current join point).

Body initiated via proceed call - Let $\langle e, \mathcal{S}, \mathcal{J} \rangle$ be a configuration where e decomposes to a proceed call which executes body $c.a$. Consider that this proceed call is located in $c'.a'$, which advises $c''.m$. Method $c''.m$ has an @advisedBy clause with n elements, where $n \geqslant 0$.

- If $c'.a'$ is an ASP-compliant advice, $\mathit{pre}(c'', m)$ is satisfied. If it is mentioned as the last advice in the @advisedBy clause of $c''.m$, $\mathit{effProc}_{pre}(c'', m, n) = \mathit{pre}(c'', m)$ is satisfied. Both cases correspond to the situation after (A.1) in the proof of Theorem 1, and we know the body to be executed must be either ASP-compliant or a method body, due to (7). We conclude that the body's precondition holds as well.

– If $c'.a'$ is mentioned at position i of the @advisedBy clause, where $i \neq n$, then by (3)+induction (and the IPR if $c'.a'$ is a before advice), $effProc_{pre}(c'', m, i)$ is satisfied. Let the body to be executed at $\langle e, \mathcal{S}, \mathcal{J} \rangle$ be located at position j, where $i < j \leq n$. Due to (5), all if constructs between i and j must have evaluated to false, so $effProc_{pre}(c'', m, i) = adv_{pre}(c_j, a_j, c'', m, j)$. Because $c.a \leq c_j.a_j$ and due to SBS', $adv_{pre}(c, a, c'', m, j)$ is satisfied as well.

Initiating after advice bodies - Let $\langle e, \mathcal{S}, \mathcal{J} \rangle$ be a configuration where e decomposes to $obj{:}c.a$, representing the "call" to an after advice body. By (3)+induction (and the IPR if the preceding proceed call ended with another after advice), $effProc_{post}(c', m, i)$ is ensured by the preceding proceed call. Due to the IPR rules, $pre(c, a)$ holds.

Returning from a body - Let $\langle e, \mathcal{S}, \mathcal{J} \rangle$ be a configuration where e decomposes to a return expression, where the execution of a body $c.x$ is about to finish. By (3)+induction, its postcondition holds. If $c.x$ is a method body, the SBS' ensures the effective postcondition of the method/proceed call that initiated $c.x$. If $c.x$ is an after/around advice not mentioned in the @advisedBy clause, this is ensured by the ASP. Finally, if $c.x$ is an after/around advice mentioned at position i of the @advisedBy clause of $c'.m$, then SBS' implies that $adv_{post}(c_i, a_i, c', m, i)$ holds. Due to (5), the if condition of $c.a$ must have been the first to evaluate to true at the method/proceed call initiating the execution of $c.a$. In case of a method call, we know that $adv_{post}(c_i, a_i, c', m, i) = effProc_{post}(c', m, 0) = eff_{post}(c', m)$. In case of a proceed call, $adv_{post}(c_i, a_i, c', m, i) = effProc_{post}(c', m, j)$, where $0 < j < i$. □

6.3   Higher-Order Advice

As ContractAJ's pointcuts can also match on the execution of advice, it is possible to create higher-order advice: advice with pointcuts that match on other advice executions. For example, it is possible that an advice myAdvice intercepts executions of myMethod, and there is another advice myMetaAdvice which intercepts executions of myAdvice. We will refer to myAdvice as a first-order advice and myMetaAdvice as a second-order advice. There also is no restriction on the number of orders, so there may be a third-order myMetaMetaAdvice which advises myMetaAdvice, and so on. Note that "the order of an advice" is not a fixed number; it can change per join point, as the same pointcut can match on advice executions of different orders.

Note that all higher-order advice must be ASP-compliant, which is a consequence of the fact that we only allow @advisedBy clauses to be specified for method bodies, not for advice bodies. This implies that a higher-order advice cannot be mentioned in an @advisedBy clause.

We can now show once more that, if our approach to modular reasoning is used, the effective pre/postconditions of each method/proceed call and the pre/postconditions of each method/advice body will be satisfied. While we allow the use of higher-order advice, we do make the assumption that the order of an advice must be a finite number. This is necessary to avoid situations where an advice (directly or indirectly) advises itself and creates an infinite recursion. In this case, we of course cannot show that the advice's postcondition would ever hold, as the program no longer terminates.

Theorem 3. *Let P be program where higher-order advice (of finite order) are allowed. The effective pre/postcondition of each method/proceed call (including implicit proceed calls) and the pre/postcondition of each method/advice body during the evaluation of P will be satisfied if: (1) All advice in P that are not mentioned in any @advisedBy clauses satisfy the ASP rules. (2) All classes in P satisfy the SBS' rules. (3) All method/advice bodies in P are locally correct. (4) The initial precondition of P is satisfied at the start of the program. (5) Each advice composition is valid. (6) All before/after advice satisfy the IPR rules. (7) Advice mentioned in an @advisedBy clause have a higher precedence than advice not mentioned in any @advisedBy clauses.*

The proof extends that of Theorem 2. In this previous theorem, *lookup* could only match at most once within the *mcall* and *pcall* rules of Fig. 10. Because higher-order advice are now allowed, *lookup* may now match multiple times.

Body initiated via method call - Consider a configuration $\langle e, \mathcal{S}, \mathcal{J} \rangle$ in the evaluation of P. Let e decompose into a context where we are about to execute a method call $obj\!:\!c.m$. By (3)+induction, $\mathit{eff}_{pre}(c, m)$ is satisfied. In case the body to be executed is either a method body or a first-order before/around advice body, this corresponds to cases covered by Theorem 2. If the body to be executed is an nth-order before/around advice $c_n.a_n$, it can be shown that its precondition will be satisfied by transitively applying the ASP: In order for the lookup procedure to reach this n^{th}-order advice body, there must have been $n - 1$ lower-order advice $(c_1.a_1, \ldots, c_{n-1}.a_{n-1})$ that matched first. That is, $c_n.a_n$ advises $c_{n-1}.a_{n-1}$, which in turn advises $c_{n-2}.a_{n-2}$, and so on, until we end up at $c_1.a_1$ which advises the $obj\!:\!c.m$ call. Due to the ASP (1), $pre(c_1, a_1)$ may not be stronger than $pre(c, m)$. In turn, $pre(c_2, a_2)$ may not be stronger than $pre(c_1, a_1)$, and so on. Because of this, we can conclude that $pre(c_n, a_n)$ is satisfied, as it cannot be stronger than $pre(c, m)$.

Body initiated via proceed call - Let $\langle e, \mathcal{S}, \mathcal{J} \rangle$ be a configuration, where e decomposes into a context with a proceed call. Let this proceed call be located in an nth-order advice body $c_n.a_n, n \geq 1$. The effective precondition of this proceed call is ensured by (3)+induction (and the ASP if $c_n.a_n$ is a before advice). The execution of the proceed call at $\langle e, \mathcal{S}, \mathcal{J} \rangle$ can lead to either another n^{th}-order advice body (the next advice in the composition), an advice with an order greater than n (if the next n^{th}-order advice that would otherwise be executed is being advised) or an $n - 1^{th}$-order body (if we are executing the last element of the composition). Knowing that the order of the body to be executed is at least $n - 1$, showing that its precondition holds can be divided into three cases:

- If $c_n.a_n$ is a first-order advice and its proceed call leads to a method body or a first-order advice body, this situation corresponds to Theorem 2.

- If $c_n.a_n$ is a first-order advice and its proceed call leads to a higher-order advice body, we can apply the reasoning of Theorem 2 and conclude that the precondition holds of the first-order advice that would normally be executed, in the absence of any matching higher-order advice. Knowing that this precondition holds, the ASP can be applied transitively to conclude that the precondition holds of the higher-order advice that is actually executed.
- Finally, if $c_n.a_n$ is a higher-order advice, the effective precondition of its proceed call takes into account the precondition of $c_{n-1}.a_{n-1}$. By transitively applying the ASP, we know the precondition of the body to be executed holds, as its order must be $n-1$ or greater.

Initiating after advice bodies - Let $\langle e, \mathcal{S}, \mathcal{J} \rangle$ be a configuration, where e decomposes into a context where an nth-order after advice is about to be executed. If it is a first-order advice, this corresponds to Theorem 2. By (3)+induction (and the ASP if the preceding proceed call ended with another after advice), the effective postcondition of the preceding implicit proceed call holds. Consequently, $pre(c_n.m_n)$ holds by the ASP.

Returning from a body - Let $\langle e, \mathcal{S}, \mathcal{J} \rangle$ be a configuration where e decomposes to a `return` expression, where the execution of a body $c.x$ is about to finish. By (3)+induction, $post(c, x)$ holds. In case $c.x$ is a method body or a first-order advice body, which is initiated by a method call, or a proceed call in a first-order advice, these cases correspond to Theorem 2. In any other case, the ASP can be applied transitively to show that the effective postcondition holds of the call that initiated $c.x$.   □

7   Runtime Contract Enforcement

To enforce correct usage of our approach to modular reasoning, this section presents a runtime contract enforcement algorithm for the ContractAJ language. This algorithm produces an error whenever a contract is broken, and determines which type is to blame. Because the contract enforcement algorithm needs access to some additional join point information, we will first define a few extensions to expose this information. The contract enforcement algorithm is then specified by means of a transformation that adds contract enforcement aspects to a given ContractAJ program. Finally, we also discuss the algorithm's implementation in AspectJ, to demonstrate that it can also be applied to a full-fledged aspect-oriented programming language.

7.1   ContractAJ Extensions

In this section, a few extensions are made the ContractAJ language so that we can retrieve additional information about each advised join point, similar to the notion of the `thisJoinPoint` variable in AspectJ. This runtime information is needed to be able determine which contracts need to be checked.

Additional run-time information is also needed in case a higher-order around advice makes use of the `proc` keyword. To evaluate the `proc` keyword within an nth-order around advice, we should be able to determine which $n\text{-}1^{th}$-order advice it advises. In turn, if this $n\text{-}1^{th}$-order advice uses `proc`, we need to determine the $n\text{-}2^{th}$-order it advises, and so on.

To make this information available, we will first extend the $\mathcal{E}$ tuples used in the join point stack with a fifth element:

$$\mathcal{E} ::= \langle c, x, obj, bool, \mathcal{E} | \bullet \rangle$$

When considering an $\mathcal{E}$ tuple that represents a particular advice execution, this fifth element is used as a pointer to the $\mathcal{E}$ tuple of its advised join point. We will refer to this pointer as the AP (advised join point pointer). For example, consider the execution of an advice $c.a$ that advises method $c'.m$. This results in the following tuple for $c.a$:

$$\langle c, a, \_, \_, \mathcal{E}_{AP} \rangle \text{ where } \mathcal{E}_{AP} = \langle c', m, \_, \_, \bullet \rangle$$

The AP in the tuple of $c.a$ refers to the tuple of $c'.m$. In turn, the AP in the tuple of $c'.m$ is empty, as it represents a method. We can now use this AP to navigate from an nth-order advice to all lower-order advice it advises (i.e. with an order smaller than n). To ensure that the AP is filled in correctly, the [call], [around] and [call$_{around}$] rules of the operational semantics are modified accordingly in Fig. 20. The [epop] rule is added as well, and ContractAJ's syntax is extended with the epop expression:

[call] $P \vdash \langle E[obj:c.x(v_1 \ldots v_n)], \mathcal{S}, \mathcal{J} \rangle$
$\hookrightarrow \langle E[\text{jpop}\{\text{proceed}(obj\ v_1 \ \ldots\ v_n)\}], \mathcal{S}, \mathcal{A}; \mathcal{J} \rangle$
where $\mathcal{A} = alook(c, x, \mathcal{S}, \mathcal{E}) + \mathcal{E}$ and $\mathcal{E} = \langle c, x, obj, \text{true}, \bullet \rangle$ and $!isAround(c, x)$

[around] $P \vdash \langle E[\text{proceed}(obj\ v_1 \ \ldots\ v_n)], \mathcal{S}, \mathcal{A}; \mathcal{J} \rangle$
$\hookrightarrow \langle E[\text{if}(e')\{obj_{asp}:c.a(obj\ v_1 \ldots v_n)\}\text{else}\{\text{epop}();\text{proceed}(obj\ v_1 \ldots v_n)\}], \mathcal{S}, \mathcal{A}; \mathcal{J} \rangle$
where $\mathcal{A} = \langle c, a, obj_{asp}, \text{false}, \mathcal{E} \rangle + \ldots$
and $isAround(c, a)$ and $var_{tgt} = target(c, a)$ and $e = ifPcut(c, a)$
and $e' = e[obj_{asp}/\text{this}, obj/var_{tgt}, v_1/var_1, \ldots, v_n/var_n]$

[call$_{around}$] $P \vdash \langle E[obj_{asp}:c.a(v_1 \ \ldots\ v_n)], \mathcal{S}, \mathcal{E} + \mathcal{A}; \mathcal{J} \rangle$
$\hookrightarrow \langle E[\text{proceed}(obj_{asp}\ v_1 \ \ldots\ v_n)], \mathcal{S}, \mathcal{A}' + \mathcal{A}; \mathcal{J} \rangle$
where $\mathcal{A}' = alook(c, a, \mathcal{S}, \mathcal{E}'') + \mathcal{E}''$ and $isAround(c, a)$
and $\mathcal{E} = \langle c, a, obj_{asp}, \text{false}, \mathcal{E}' \rangle$ and $\mathcal{E}'' = \langle c, a, obj_{asp}, \text{true}, \mathcal{E}' \rangle$

[epop] $P \vdash \langle E[\text{epop}()], \mathcal{S}, \mathcal{E} + \mathcal{A}; \mathcal{J} \rangle \hookrightarrow \langle E[\text{true}], \mathcal{S}, \mathcal{A}; \mathcal{J} \rangle$

Fig. 20. Adding support for the AP

[call] - In case of the [call] rule, which handles method calls, the AP of the tuple that represents the method ($\mathcal{E}$) is empty. The *alook* function (not shown here) can be easily extended such that the AP of the tuples for all matching

advice is set to $\mathcal{E}$. Note that the execution of a before/after advice body is also handled via the [**call**] rule, meaning that their AP is also set to •. This is not a problem, as we only use the AP to resolve the value of the `proc` keyword, which can only be used in the pre/postcondition of around advice.

[**around**] - The main modification made to this rule, which processes around advice, is that it no longer pops the around advice's tuple from the stack. This is done because we still need its AP if e' evaluates to `true` and the $obj_{asp}{:}c.a$ call is processed by [**call**$_{\mathbf{around}}$]. However, if e' evaluates to `false` the tuple is not needed and should be removed, which is done by the `epop()` statement.

[**call**$_{\mathbf{around}}$] - When looking for higher-order advice matching on an around advice, the tuples of these matching advice will get $\mathcal{E}''$ as their AP, representing the around advice. In turn, the AP of $\mathcal{E}''$, which is $\mathcal{E}'$, can be found in the tuple that was left on the stack by the application of [**around**].

[**epop**] - This rule simply pops the top tuple from the join point stack.

After introducing the AP, we can use it to define the helper functions in Fig. 21: The $jpElem(\mathcal{J},i,j)$ function is used to retrieve a particular $\mathcal{E}$ tuple from the join point stack, relative to the tuple at the top of the stack. Given that this top $\mathcal{E}$ tuple is an nth-order advice, we make use of $jpElem(\mathcal{J},\mathcal{E},i,j)$ to navigate to the $\mathcal{E}$ tuple of the n-ith-order advice. If this tuple is the kth element in the $\mathcal{A}$ record that contains it, the k+jth element is finally returned.

The two $advBy$ functions relate to the `@advisedBy` clause of a method: One determines the position at which an advice is mentioned in an `@advisedBy` clause, whereas the other retrieves an advice's class at a certain position in the clause. Both make use of the $advBy(c,m)$ function (defined in Fig. 12 of Sect. 3.4) to retrieve the complete `@advisedBy` clause of a method, which includes the clause inherited from the super class.

$jpElem(\mathcal{J},i,j)$

Retrieve the jth element in an $(n-i)^{th}$-order composition, with an nth-order element at the top of $\mathcal{J}$

$$\frac{\mathcal{J}=\mathcal{A};\ \ldots \text{ and } \mathcal{A}=\mathcal{E}+\ldots \text{ and } \mathcal{E}'=jpElem(\mathcal{J},\mathcal{E},i,j)}{jpElem(\mathcal{J},i,j)=\mathcal{E}'}$$

$jpElem(\mathcal{J},\mathcal{E},i,j)$

$$\frac{i=0 \text{ and } (\mathcal{J}=\langle\ldots,\langle\mathcal{E}_1,\ldots,\mathcal{E}_k,\ldots,\mathcal{E}_{k+j},\ldots\rangle,\ldots\rangle) \text{ and } \mathcal{E}_k=\mathcal{E} \text{ and } \mathcal{E}_j=\mathcal{E}'}{jpElem'(\mathcal{J},\mathcal{E},i,j)=\mathcal{E}'}$$

$$\frac{i>0 \text{ and } \mathcal{E}=\langle\_,\_,\_,\_,\mathcal{E}''\rangle \text{ and } \mathcal{E}'=jpElem'(\mathcal{J},\mathcal{E}'',i-1,j)}{jpElem'(\mathcal{J},\mathcal{E},i,j)=\mathcal{E}'}$$

$advBy(c,a,c',m)$

Determine at which position $c.a$ is mentioned in the `@advisedBy` clause of $c'.m$

$$advBy(c',m)=(c_1,a_1,\ldots,c_n,a_n)$$
$$\frac{\text{where } a=a_i \text{ and } c\le c_i \text{ and } \nexists c_j:j\ne i \text{ and } c\le c_j<c_i)}{\text{otherwise } i=-1}$$
$$advBy(c,a,c',m)=i$$

$advBy(c,m,i)$

Retrieve the class at position i in the `@advisedBy` clause of $c.m$

$$\frac{advBy(c,m)=(c_1,a_1,\ldots,c_i,a_i,\ldots,c_n,a_n)}{advBy(c,m,i)=c_i}$$

Fig. 21. Helper functions

Finally, using *jpElem* and *advBy*, we can extend the ContractAJ language with the following new keywords that will be used to define the contract enforcement algorithm: `advBy`, `jpStatic`, `jpThis`, `pre`, `iPre`, `effProcPre` and `advPre`. Their semantics is defined in Fig. 22:

[advBy]
$$\begin{array}{l} P \vdash \langle \mathsf{E}[\mathtt{advBy(}c,a,c',m\mathtt{)}],\mathcal{S},\mathcal{J}\rangle \hookrightarrow \langle \mathsf{E}[i],\mathcal{S},\mathcal{J}\rangle \\ \text{where } i = \mathit{advBy}(c,a,c',m) \end{array}$$

[jpStatic]
$$\begin{array}{l} P \vdash \langle \mathsf{E}[\mathtt{jpStatic(}i\mathtt{)}],\mathcal{S},\mathcal{J}\rangle \hookrightarrow \langle \mathsf{E}[c],\mathcal{S},\mathcal{J}\rangle \\ \text{where } \mathcal{E} = \mathit{jpElem}(\mathcal{J},i,1) \text{ and } \mathcal{E} = \langle c,_,_,_,_\rangle \end{array}$$

[jpThis]
$$\begin{array}{l} P \vdash \langle \mathsf{E}[\mathtt{jpThis(}i\mathtt{)}],\mathcal{S},\mathcal{J}\rangle \hookrightarrow \langle \mathsf{E}[\mathit{obj}],\mathcal{S},\mathcal{J}\rangle \\ \text{where } \mathcal{E} = \mathit{jpElem}(\mathcal{J},i,1) \text{ and } \mathcal{E} = \langle _,_,\mathit{obj},_,_\rangle \end{array}$$

[pre]
$$\begin{array}{l} P \vdash \langle \mathsf{E}[\mathtt{pre(}c,x,\mathit{obj},\mathit{obj}',\mathit{proc},v_1 \ldots v_n\mathtt{)}],\mathcal{S},\mathcal{J}\rangle \\ \hookrightarrow \langle \mathsf{E}[e[\mathit{obj}/\mathtt{this},\mathit{obj}'/\mathit{tgt},\mathit{proc}/\mathtt{proc},v_1/\mathit{var}_1,\ldots,v_n/\mathit{var}_n],\mathcal{S},\mathcal{J}\rangle \\ \text{and } \mathtt{class}\ c\mathtt{\{\ldots @requires}\ e\ \ldots\ t\ x\mathtt{(}\mathit{var}_1,\ldots,\mathit{var}_n\mathtt{)\ldots\}} \text{ is in } P \\ \text{and } \mathit{tgt} = \mathit{target}(c,x) \end{array}$$

[effProc$_{\mathbf{pre}}$]
$$\begin{array}{l} P \vdash \langle \mathsf{E}[\mathtt{effProcPre(}i,j,k,v_1 \ldots v_n\mathtt{)}],\mathcal{S},\mathcal{J}\rangle \\ \hookrightarrow \langle \mathsf{E}[\mathtt{if(}\mathit{ifCond}[\mathit{obj}/\mathtt{this},\mathit{obj}'/\mathit{tgt},v_1/\mathit{var}_1,\ldots,v_n/\mathit{var}_n]\mathtt{)\{} \\ \quad\quad \mathtt{advPre(}i,j,k,v_1 \ldots v_n\mathtt{)} \\ \quad \mathtt{\}\ else\ \{effProcPre(}i,j,k+1,v_1 \ldots v_n\mathtt{)\}},\mathcal{S},\mathcal{J}\rangle \\ \text{where } \mathit{jpElem}(\mathcal{J},i,j) = \langle c,a,\mathit{obj},_,\mathcal{E}\rangle \text{ and } \mathcal{E} = \langle c',m,\mathit{obj}',_,_\rangle \\ \text{and } \mathit{advBy}(c,a,c',m) \neq -1 \text{ and } c \leqslant \mathit{advBy}(c',m,k) \\ \text{and } \langle a,(t_1,\ldots,t_n \rightarrow t),(\mathit{var}_1,\ldots,\mathit{var}_n,e)\rangle \in c \\ \text{and } \mathit{ifCond} = \mathit{ifPcut}(c,a) \text{ and } \mathit{tgt} = \mathit{target}(c,a) \end{array}$$

[effProc$_{\mathbf{pre}}$]
$$\begin{array}{l} P \vdash \langle \mathsf{E}[\mathtt{effProcPre(}i,j,k,v_1 \ldots v_n\mathtt{)}],\mathcal{S},\mathcal{J}\rangle \\ \hookrightarrow \langle \mathsf{E}[\mathtt{pre(}c',m',\mathit{obj}',\mathit{obj}'',\mathit{proc},v_1 \ldots v_n\mathtt{))}],\mathcal{S},\mathcal{J}\rangle \\ \text{where } \mathit{jpElem}(\mathcal{J},i,j) = \langle c,m,\mathit{obj},_,\mathcal{E}\rangle \text{ and } \mathcal{E} = \langle c',m',\mathit{obj}',_,\mathcal{E}''\rangle \\ \text{and } \mathit{advBy}(c,m,c',m') = -1 \\ \text{and if } \mathit{isMethod}(c',m') \text{ then } (\mathit{proc} = \mathtt{true} \text{ and } \mathit{obj}'' = \mathtt{null}) \\ \text{else } (\mathit{proc} = \mathtt{effProcPre(}i+1,1,\mathit{advBy}(c',m',c'',m''),v_1 \ldots v_n\mathtt{)} \\ \text{and } \mathcal{E}'' = \big\langle c'',m'',\mathit{obj}'',_,_\big\rangle) \end{array}$$

[effProc$_{\mathbf{pre}}$]
$$\begin{array}{l} P \vdash \langle \mathsf{E}[\mathtt{effProcPre(}i,j,k,v_1 \ldots v_n\mathtt{)}],\mathcal{S},\mathcal{J}\rangle \\ \hookrightarrow \langle \mathsf{E}[\mathtt{error("@advisedBy\ mismatch,\ expected\ instance\ of\ }c'\mathtt{")}],\mathcal{S},\mathcal{J}\rangle \\ \text{where } \mathit{jpElem}(\mathcal{J},i,j) = \langle c,_,_,_,\mathcal{E}\rangle \text{ and } \mathcal{E} = \langle c',m',_,_,_\rangle \\ \text{and } c'' = \mathit{advBy}(c',m',k) \text{ and } c \nleqslant c'' \end{array}$$

[adv$_{\mathbf{pre}}$]
$$\begin{array}{l} P \vdash \langle \mathsf{E}[\mathtt{advPre(}i,j,k,v_1 \ldots v_n\mathtt{)}],\mathcal{S},\mathcal{J}\rangle \\ \hookrightarrow \langle \mathsf{E}[\mathtt{iPre(}c,a,\mathit{obj},\mathit{obj}',\mathtt{effProcPre(}i,j+1,k+1,v_1 \ldots v_n\mathtt{)},v_1 \ldots v_n\mathtt{))}],\mathcal{S},\mathcal{J}\rangle \\ \text{where } \mathit{jpElem}(\mathcal{J},i,j) = \langle c,a,\mathit{obj},_,\mathcal{E}\rangle \text{ and } \mathcal{E} = \langle _,_,\mathit{obj}',_,_\rangle \end{array}$$

Fig. 22. Semantics of contract enforcement expressions

[advBy] - The `advBy(`c, a, c', m`)` expression directly uses the *advBy* function to retrieve the position in which advice c`.`a is mentioned in the `@advisedBy` clause of c'`.`m.

[jpStatic] - If the $\mathcal{E}$ tuple at the top of $\mathcal{J}$ is an nth-order advice, the `jpStatic(`i`)` expression uses *jpElem* to retrieve the type of the n-i^{th}-order body being advised.

[jpThis] - This expression is similar to `jpStatic`, but it retrieves the instance corresponding to the n-i^{th}-order body being advised.

[**pre**] - The $\mathtt{pre}(c, x, obj, obj', proc, v_1 \ldots v_n)$ expression retrieves the precondition e of body $c.x$, as well as binds all variables in e to their values. These variables respectively constitute of the $\mathtt{this}$ object, the $\mathtt{target}$ binding, the $\mathtt{proc}$ keyword and the arguments of $c.x$.

[**effProc$_{\mathbf{pre}}$**] - The $\mathtt{effProcPre}(i,j,k,v_1 \ldots v_n)$ expression is the runtime equivalent of $\mathit{effProc_{pre}}$ in Fig. 18 of Sect. 5.5, which defines the effective precondition of a proceed call. Parameters i and j are used to describe which advice contains the proceed call in question, as determined by $jpElem(\mathcal{J}, i, j)$. Parameter k indicates the position of the advice within the $\mathtt{@advisedBy}$ clause (if any) of its advised join point. The $\mathtt{effProcPre}$ expression is defined as three cases: The first describes the effective precondition if there is an $\mathtt{@advisedBy}$ clause, whereas the second describes the effective precondition in the absence of an $\mathtt{@advisedBy}$ clause. The third case detects invalid advice compositions, as defined in Sect. 6.1. If $jpElem(\mathcal{J}, i, j)$ is not mentioned as the kth element in the $\mathtt{@advisedBy}$ clause, a runtime error is produced, as it is no longer possible to evaluate the effective precondition in an unambiguous manner.

[**adv$_{\mathbf{pre}}$**] - Finally, the $\mathtt{advPre}(i,j,k,v_1 \ldots v_n)$ expression is the runtime equivalent of the static adv_{pre} function defined in Fig. 18 of Sect. 5.5. It retrieves the precondition of an advice body using $\mathtt{iPre}$ and determines the value of its $\mathtt{proc}$ keyword. Note that $\mathtt{iPre}$ of course is the runtime equivalent of the $iPre$ function of Fig. 18. Its semantics are not shown here, as the rule is nearly identical to [**pre**].

7.2   Contract Enforcement in ContractAJ

After defining the extensions to the ContractAJ language, we can make use of them to present our contract enforcement algorithm. This algorithm has been implemented as a number of judgements, based on the algorithm for the object-oriented ContractJava language of Findler et al. [18]. Applying these judgements will transform a ContractAJ program into a new version of the program where support for contract enforcement is added. What is different from Findler et al. [18] is that, because contract enforcement is a crosscutting concern, we can implement it by adding a number of aspects. The judgements that form the contract enforcement transformation have the following shape:

$$context \vdash lhs \rightharpoonup rhs$$

This can be read as: "Within $context$, an occurrence of lhs in the source code produces the code in rhs". The most important judgements describing the contract enforcement algorithm are shown in Fig. 23:

[**def**] - This rule specifies the $\rightharpoonup_{\mathsf{def}}$ judgement, which describes the entire transformation at a high level: the transformation is initiated by applying this judgement to every class in the program. As a result, a contract-checking class ($\mathtt{Contract\_c}$) will be generated for each existing class (c). An example is given in Fig. 24 where the contract checking class $\mathtt{Contract\_Security}$ is generated for class $\mathtt{Security}$.

x_j is a method or an advice $\qquad\qquad for\ j \in [1, m]$

$P, c \vdash x_j \rightarrow_{\mathsf{adv}} xcheck_j$ if $\not\exists c'' : x_j \in c''$ and $c < c''$

$P, c \vdash x_j \rightarrow_{\mathsf{pre}} xpre_j \quad P, c \vdash x_j \rightarrow_{\mathsf{post}} xpost_j$

[def] ——

$P \vdash$ `declare precedence ...; ... class c extends` c' `{`$x_1 \ldots x_m$`}...main{...}` $\rightarrow_{\mathsf{def}}$
`declare precedence ...,Contract_c.`$xcheck_1$`,...,Contract_c.`$xcheck_m$`; ...`
`class Contract_c extends Object {`$xcheck_1 \ldots xcheck_m$`}`
`class c extends` c' `{`$x_1 \ldots x_m$ $xpre_1 \ldots xpre_m$ $xpost_1 \ldots xpost_m$`}`
`...main{Contract_c c_c = new Contract_c; ...}`

$P, c \vdash t\ m(t_1\ x_1, \ldots, t_n\ x_n)) \rightarrow_{\mathsf{adv}}$
`around` m`: call(`$t\ c.m(t_1\ x_1, \ldots, t_n\ x_n)$`) && target(`$dyn$`) {`
    `if(pre(jpStatic(0),`m, dyn`,null,true,`$x_1 \ldots x_n$`)) {`
      $dyn.m$`_SbsPreCheck(`$x_1 \ldots x_n$`)`
    `} else {error("Precondition violation: getStackTrace[1]")}`

[adv$^{\mathbf{m}}$]   `let {`$returnVal$`=proceed(`$dyn, x_1 \ldots x_n$`)} in {`
        `if(post(jpStatic(0),`$m, returnVal, dyn$`,null,true,`$x_1 \ldots x_n$`)) {`
          $dyn.m$`_SbsPostCheck(`$returnVal, x_1 \ldots x_n$`)`
        `} else {error("Postcondition violation:"` dyn`)};`
      $returnVal$`}}`

$P, c \vdash$ `around` a`: call|execution(`$t\ c'.x(t_1\ x_1 \ldots t_n\ x_n)$ $\rightarrow_{\mathsf{adv}}$
`around` a`: execution(`$t\ c.a(t_1\ x_1 \ldots t_n\ x_n)$`) && this(`$dyn$`) {`
  `let {`i `= advBy(jpStatic(0),`a`,jpStatic(1),`x`)} in {`
  `if(`i `==-1) { // If the user-advice is not mentioned in @advisedBy`
    `let {`$jpPre$ `= effProcPre(0,1,-1,`$x_1 \ldots x_n$`)`
      $advPre$ `= pre(jpStatic(0),`a, dyn`,jpThis(1),`$jpPre\ x_1 \ldots x_n$`)} in {`
      `if(`$jpPre$`) {`
        `if(!`$advPre$`) {error("ASP violation, precondition too strong:"` dyn`)}`
      `} else {error ("Precondition violation: getStackTrace[1]")}}`
    `let {`$returnVal$`=proceed(`$dyn, x_1 \ldots x_n$`)`
      $jpPost$ `= effProcPost(0,1,-1,`$x_1 \ldots x_n$`)`
      $advPost$ `= post(jpStatic(0),`$a, returnVal, dyn$`,jpThis(1),`$jpPost, x_1 \ldots x_n$`)} in {`
      `if(`$jpPost$`) {`

[adv$^{\mathbf{ar}}$]   `if(!`$advPost$`) {error("ASP violation, postcondition too weak:"` dyn`)}`
      `} else {error("Postcondition violation:"` dyn`)};`
      $returnVal$`}`
  `} else { // If the user-advice is mentioned in @advisedBy`
    `let {`$proc$ `= effProcPre(0,2,`$i + 1, x_1 \ldots x_n$`)`
      pre `= pre(jpStatic(0),`a, dyn`,jpThis(1),`$proc, x_1 \ldots x_n$`)} in {`
      `if(`pre`) {`$dyn.a$`_SbsPreCheck(jpThis(1),`$proc, x_1 \ldots x_n$`)`
      `} else {error("Precondition violation: getStackTrace[1]")}}`
    `let {`$returnVal$`=proceed(`$dyn, x_1 \ldots x_n$`)`
      $proc$ `= effProcPost(0,2,`$i + 1, x_1 \ldots x_n$`)`
      $post$ `= post(jpStatic(0),`$a\ dyn$`,jpThis(1),`$proc, x_1 \ldots x_n$`)} in {`
      `if(`$post$`) {`$dyn.a$`_SbsPostCheck(jpThis(1),`$proc, returnVal, x_1 \ldots x_n$`)`
      `} else {error("Postcondition violation:"` dyn`)};`
      $returnVal$`}}}`

$P, c \vdash t\ m(t_1\ x_1,\ \ldots,\ t_n\ x_n)\ \{e\} \rightarrow_{\mathsf{pre}}$
`boolean` m`_SbsPreCheck(`$t_1\ x_1,\ \ldots,\ t_n\ x_n$`) {`
`let{`$next$`=(`$\exists^?$`super.`m`_SbsPreCheck(`$x_1 \ldots x_n$`)`

[pre$^{\mathbf{m}}$] res`=pre(`c, m`,this,null,true,`$x_1 \ldots x_n$`)} in {`
    `if (!`$next$ `||` res`) {`
      res
    `} else {error("SBS' violation, precondition too strong:"` $this$`)}}`

Fig. 23. Contract enforcement judgements

First, the `declare precedence` statement is extended to ensure that every advice in `Contract_c` has a lower precedence than all other advice. This is necessary to make sure that the existing advice will not interfere with contract enforcement advice at shared join points. Next, we can examine the definition of `Contract_c` itself: For each method/advice x_j in c, an advice $xcheck_j$ is added to `Contract_c`. This around advice is executed whenever x_j is called and will then perform contract enforcement. To avoid confusion, henceforth we will call the contract enforcement advice "contract-advice". Normal advice defined in the original program will be called "user-advice". Note that the $xcheck_j$ contract-advice are only created for non-overriding methods/advice. It would be redundant to add them to overriding members due to the use of a call pointcut, which also matches on subtypes. The code of each contract-advice is produced by the $\rightarrow_{adv}$ judgement, defined in the [**adv**] rules (only [**adv^m**] and [**adv^{ar}**] are shown). Next, $xpre_j$ and $xpost_j$ are two helper methods that are added to the existing c class; they check whether the SBS' pre- and postcondition rules hold. These two methods are specified by the [**pre**] and [**post**] rules (only [**pre^m**] is shown). Finally, the program's main expression is extended such that `Contract_c` is instantiated.

```
declare precedence Security.authenticate, contract_Security.authenticate;

class Bank {
  @requires u.getBank()==this
  @ensures result!=null && result.getOwner()==u
  @advisedBy Security.authenticate
  Account createAccount(User u) {...}}

class Security {
  @requires proc
  @ensures if(isLoggedIn(u)){proc}else{true}
  around authenticate: call(Account Bank.createAccount(User u)) && target(b) {...}
  boolean authenticate_SbsPreCheck(Bank b,boolean proc,User u) { ... }
  boolean authenticate_SbsPostCheck(Bank b,boolean proc,Account returnVal,User u) {...}}

class Contract_Security {
  around authenticate: execution(Account Security.authenticate(User u)) && this(dyn) {
    let{i=advBy(Security,authenticate,Bank,createAccount)} in {
    if(i==-1) { ...
    } else {
      let{proc="u.getBank()==this"
        pre="u.getBank()==this"} in {
        if(pre) {dyn.authenticate_SbsPreCheck(jpThis(1),proc,u)
        } else {error("Precondition violation: getStackTrace[1]")}}
      let{returnVal=proceed(dyn,u)
        proc="result!=null && result.getOwner()==u"
        post="if(isLoggedIn(u)){result!=null && result.getOwner()==u}else{true}"} in {
        if(post) {dyn.authenticate_SbsPostCheck(jpThis(1),proc,returnVal,u)
        } else {error("Postcondition violation:" dyn)};
        returnVal}}}

main {
  Contract_Security c_security = new Contract_Security; ...}
```

Fig. 24. Example of a contract enforcement aspect

[**adv^m**] - This rule specifies the contract-advice that enforces contracts of methods. An around contract-advice is used for this purpose, associated with a call pointcut that matches whenever $c.m$ is called, where c is (a subtype of) the static type of the call.

In the contract-advice's body, the precondition of m is first checked, in class jpStatic(0), which corresponds to the receiver's static type in the $c.m$ call. If this precondition check fails, we state that "getStackTrace[1]" is to be blamed. In most cases, this simply means that the caller of the method is to be blamed. However, if one or more user-advice are present at this method, the previous user-advice in the composition is to be blamed. We can only blame this previous advice; otherwise an error would have been generated earlier by the contract-advice that check each user-advice. After pre(jpStatic(0),m,...) is checked, we invoke $dyn.m\_SbsPreCheck$, the SBS'-checking helper method, which is specified in rule [$\mathbf{pre^m}$]. After this SBS'-check has passed for the preconditions, we can make a proceed call to execute the method that we are checking. Once this is done, the postconditions are checked, which is analogous to checking the preconditions.

[$\mathbf{adv^{ar}}$] - This lengthy rule specifies the contract-advice that checks all around user-advice. The reason for its length is the fact that it handles both ASP-compliant advice and advice mentioned in an @advisedBy clause. First, we try to determine the position (i) of the user-advice within the @advisedBy clause of its advised join point using advBy. If it returns -1, this indicates the user-advice is not mentioned in the @advisedBy clause (if there was one), which implies the user-advice is ASP-compliant:

ASP-compliant advice - We first determine the precondition of the advised join point in $jpPre$. This precondition corresponds to the effective precondition of the user-advice's proceed call, which is why effProcPre(0,1,...) is used. The precondition of the user-advice itself is stored in $advPre$ (with $jpPre$ as the value of the proc keyword). Next, $jpPre$ is checked: Similar to [$\mathbf{adv^m}$], "getStackTrace[1]" is to be blamed if the test fails. If the test passes, $advPre$ is tested next: If checking the user-advice's precondition fails, we know it is too strong and the ASP is broken. If this check passes, we can proceed with executing the user-advice, do the analogous checks for postconditions and finally return the user-advice's return value.

Advice mentioned in an @advisedBy clause - In case the user-advice is mentioned in an @advisedBy clause, we will first determine the value of the proc keyword using effProcPre(0,2,$i + 1$,...). The pre variable then contains the user advice's precondition. The contract enforcement procedure itself is quite similar to [$\mathbf{adv^m}$]: The precondition is first tested. If this test passes, $dyn.a\_SbsPreCheck$ should be tested, as the elements in an @advisedBy clause can also match with subtypes. Once this test passes, the proceed call is made and the analogous postcondition tests are done. Figure 24 presents an example of a contract-advice, such that the contracts that will be checked are visible. These concrete contracts are only shown to improve the example's clarity. The actual source code of Contract_Security.authenticate would show pre, effProcPre, post and effProcPost expressions instead, as this contract-advice should also be able to enforce the contracts of any user-advice that override `Security.authenticate`.

[**pre^m**] - This rule checks that the precondition of a particular method is not stronger than any of its ancestors. This is done by recursively traversing up the subtype hierarchy tree with a `super.m_SbsPreCheck` call. (The $\exists^?$ symbol before `super.m_SbsPreCheck` means: if `m_SbsPreCheck` does not exist in `super`, the call is left out.) There is also a similar [**pre**] variant of this rule (not shown) for advice: The only difference is that this helper method contains two extra parameters: the value of the `target` binding and the value of the `proc` keyword.

To finish up the contract enforcement algorithm, we should still discuss the [**adv**] rules that are not shown in Fig. 23. The [**adv^{ar}**] rule that was discussed here is focused on around user-advice. We should also specify separate variants for before and after user-advice, which are mostly similar to [**adv^{ar}**]. In case of before advice, the postcondition checks are replaced by only checking the postcondition of the advice itself, i.e. without testing the ASP or SBS'. If this check fails, the advice itself is to blame. If the before advice interferes with the next element in the composition, this will be detected by that element's precondition check, which will correctly blame `getStackTrace[1]`. The after advice is treated similarly, precondition checks are replaced by only checking the precondition of the advice itself.

7.3   AspectJ Implementation

To demonstrate an instantiation of our contract enforcement algorithm in a full programming language, we have implemented it as a lightweight design by contract library for AspectJ, which is available for download[9]. The library itself is written completely using the constructs provided by AspectJ itself. As the library consists of aspects, and aspects are implicitly instantiated in AspectJ, contract enforcement is automatically enabled as soon as the library is included on a project's build path. Contracts are specified as strings in Java annotations (`@ensures`, `@requires`, `@invariant`); they are evaluated at runtime by a scripting engine. To keep the library small and simple, we make the assumption that the developer will not produce any side effects in the program's contracts, rather than build a fleshed-out behavioural interface specification language like JML. Contracts have access to the necessary information to implement basic design by contract support in AspectJ: the `this` object, parameters, the return value (in case of postconditions) and the `old()` function to evaluate expressions in the pre-state of a method/advice execution and retrieve the result in the post-state.

Regarding the implementation of the enforcement algorithm, most of the algorithm can be translated fairly directly from ContractAJ to AspectJ. Rather than creating a contract enforcement aspect per class/aspect, the implementation only has two contract enforcement aspects that handle all method/advice executions. The extensions made in Sect. 7.1 can be reproduced in AspectJ using reflection and the `thisJoinPoint` variable. The AspectJ counterpart of

---

[9] The library and source code are available at: https://github.com/timmolderez/adbc.

the AP (the fifth element in each $\mathcal{E}$ tuple) is also available in higher-order advice as the last argument of `thisJoinPoint.getArgs()`, which points to the `thisJoinPoint` variable[10] of the advised join point.

One subtle difference between the algorithm and the implementation is concerned with making sure that a contract-advice always is the very last advice to be executed in an advice composition, which requires using an execution pointcut. This is due to the fact that, in AspectJ, an advice matching at a call join point is always executed before an advice that matches at the corresponding execution join point. This is not the case for ContractAJ, due to its simpler join point model discussed in Sect. 2.3. Using an execution pointcut creates a new problem, as AspectJ only provides access to the dynamic type of the advised method call. We also need to know the static type to be able to determine which contracts need to be enforced. Luckily, we can work around this problem by introducing a helper advice that matches on any call join point, and temporarily stores the static type in a stack, until contract enforcement is performed at the corresponding execution join point.

8 Related Work

Observers and assistants - There are several related papers in the field of modular reasoning for aspects. Most closely related is the work on observers and assistants by Clifton and Leavens [11–13]. Their work focuses on modular reasoning in AspectJ, using JML as the specification language. On the surface, our work looks quite similar to theirs, as our distinction between ASP-advice and non-ASP advice is akin to the distinction between observers and assistants. As mentioned in Sect. 4, the main difference between ASP-compliant advice and observers is that the ASP is defined in terms of the advice's specification rather than its implementation. This allows the ASP to be more permissive than the notion of observers: An observer can only modify the state it owns, as well as global state. In Clifton's thesis [13], observers (also called spectators) are further restricted since around advice must make exactly one proceed call. ASP-advice is not subjected to these restrictions: In addition to the state it owns and global state, ASP-advice may also modify any state that is being modified by the join points it advises, as long as the specifications of its advised join points are taken into account. Likewise, ASP-compliant advice may make as many proceed calls (including zero) as desired. To give a few examples that distinguish ASP-compliant advice from observers: Consider a caching aspect for e.g. a database. Whenever a query is made, an advice would test the cache. This advice would be ASP-compliant, as it does not alter the database's behaviour. It is however not an observer, since the advice does not make a proceed call on a cache hit. Another kind of example, closely related to context-oriented programming [20], would be an advice that acts like an overriding method (i.e. a body of code that extends the behaviour of an existing method), but one that is only active within

---

[10] One caveat is that an advice body should make use of its `thisJoinPoint` variable in order for it to be available for higher-order advice.

a certain context, e.g. a particular control flow. Such an advice should be ASP-compliant, just like overriding methods should be SBS-compliant. However, if this advice modifies a field in the receiver of the advised method calls, it cannot be an observer, as this field is not owned by the corresponding aspect.

Moreover, ASP-compliant advice are guaranteed to preserve modular reasoning, on the assumption that each module correctly implements its own specifications. Ensuring that an advice is ASP-compliant can be done statically by the developer, given the advice's specifications and those of its join point shadows. On the other hand, it is undecidable in general to statically ensure that an observer will only modify its own/global state and will make one proceed call in any control flow path. Granted, in case of ASP-compliant advice, the undecidability problems have been delegated to the assumption that each module correctly implements its own specifications. Nonetheless, this problem is well-known and the vast amount of work that strives to approximate a solution can be readily leveraged.

Clifton and Leavens' notion of assistants is closely related to the use of @advisedBy clauses. Restoring modular reasoning for assistants is done by explicitly mentioning these aspects in an **accepts** statement in a module, to indicate that any join points in this module may be advised by the mentioned advice. Using an @advisedBy clause has a similar purpose, but it is more fine-grained: An @advisedBy clause is associated with a method and mentions a number of advice, which makes it straightforward to tell which advice are expected at a particular method call. Constructing the effective specification of an advice is also done very differently: In case of assistants, a graph is constructed that contains the possible advice compositions per join point shadow. The specification of each path in the graph is then constructed by composing the specification of each node on the path and eliminating all intermediate states, which can be a demanding process. It also does not prevent interference between the advice, as before/after advice are not constrained such that they take into account their implicit proceed call. In case of non-ASP advice, the effective specification is arguably much simpler to construct, the IPR of Sect. 5.6 prevents interference and the specification leaves room for extension using overriding advice or higher-order advice. Finally, Clifton and Leavens' work also approaches around advice quite differently: There is no equivalent of a **proc** keyword. Instead, the specification of an around advice is split up into a before and an after part. The before part refers to all code up until a proceed call is made, and the after part refers to the code after a proceed call is made. This becomes more complex/verbose once proceed calls appear in control statements (e.g. in an authentication or authorization advice). Multiple specification cases are needed, as there now are multiple possible before-and after parts. While the **proc** keyword does not expose when/whether a proceed call will be made, it also is simpler to use.

Translucid contracts - The work on translucid contracts for the Ptolemy language [6] is closely related as well. The Ptolemy language requires all advisable join points to be announced explicitly as events, including which information is exposed to event handlers (similar to advice). Each event is associated with its own specifications called translucid contracts. The modules that announce events are aware of these contracts, and event handlers have to comply with the contracts in order not to cause any surprising effects. While this approach is flexible in the sense that the event announcer can be oblivious of which, how many or in what order event handlers are present, this flexibility arguably also makes it more difficult to design the specifications of events such that they are sufficiently restrictive for the event announcer, but sufficiently permissive for any event handlers that might register to the event. An @advisedBy clause is more restrictive, as it announces which advice are expected, in what order, but it leaves open which (sub)types should implement the listed advice. Another difference between translucid contracts and our approach is that translucid contracts are grey-box specifications, as they also expose how event handlers should alter control flow, i.e. when a proceed call is made or not. Our contracts in ContractAJ are black-box, yet the use of the proc keyword often gives away on what conditions a proceed call is made. Nonetheless, the proc keyword is nothing but a placeholder for another module's pre- or postcondition, and is not a guarantee that an advice body will (or will not) make a proceed call on certain conditions.

Pipa and CONA - In Zhao et al. [43], the design of Pipa is presented, a language to specify contracts for AspectJ programs, as an extension to the JML specification language. The interaction of an advice with the base system is viewed from a weaving perspective, at a syntactical level: the contracts of an advice are woven into the contracts of the corresponding advised methods. There is no notion of an advice substitution principle however, as no constraints are placed on how an advice's contracts should relate to those of advised methods. In Lorenz et al. [28], aspects are classified as agnostic, obedient or rebellious. Each of the three types correspond to aspects with only ASP-compliant advice. To enforce that an aspect is of a particular type, blame assignment tables are presented for each type. Developers can indicate which of the three types an aspect belongs to, and a prototype implementation called CONA will then perform contract enforcement using these blame assignment tables. The CONA tool uses aspects to enforce contracts on objects, but uses objects to enforce contracts on aspects. The work of Agostinho et al. [1] as well is based on the advice substitution principle in Wampler [41] and informally discusses its application to various concrete aspect-oriented languages (AspectJ, CaesarJ and FuseJ).

Modular reasoning in AOP-like languages - Related work can also be found for other types of languages similar to AOP: the work of Thüm [40] discusses design by contract for feature-oriented programming. Several different approaches to integrate design by contract are discussed and compared in a number of use cases. The "explicit contract refinement" approach is closest to the ASP, as it is based on method refinement and has the original keyword, which is similar to proc. The different approaches are compared on a number of case studies, and some cases were identified where none of the approaches were sufficiently expressive, which could indicate the need for a construct similar to the @advisedBy clause.

In Hähnle et. al [36], design by contract is discussed for delta-oriented programming, which is as well closely related to AOP. Liskov substitution [27] is adapted to this type of languages. It also demonstrates that making a language's constructs more dynamic also makes it more difficult to reason about: a dynamic element is present, in the sense that the feature configuration of delta-oriented programs can take on various different forms. As a consequence, method contracts will need to take into account more than just the superclass. This is similar to the fact that our `proc` keyword depends on the advised join point.

Finally, there are also several related papers that focus on restoring modular reasoning by establishing new kinds of interfaces between aspects and the modules they advise, such as open modules [2], crosscutting program interfaces (XPIs) [35,39], join point types [38] or join point interfaces [7]. While some of these interfaces restrict what each aspect is allowed to advise, this work is mostly complementary to ours, in the sense that such intermediate interfaces can alleviate the fragile pointcut problem and reduce the number of reasoning tasks for developers of aspects.

9   Conclusion

In this paper an approach has been presented to achieve modular reasoning in aspect-oriented languages, using the ContractAJ language. This approach is centred around an advice substitution principle and the `@advisedBy` clause. For those advice that satisfy the ASP, obliviousness can be preserved without affecting modular reasoning. For all other advice, the `@advisedBy` clause should be used to become aware of such advice. Apart from the fact that each advice should take into account the contracts of any (implicit) proceed calls, there are no restrictions on what an advice is allowed to do. The approach is shown to preserve modular reasoning when making method/proceed calls and an algorithm is provided to perform runtime contract enforcement.

In terms of future work, case studies can be performed to study our approach on existing AspectJ applications and to answer questions such as: What proportion of all advice is ASP-compliant versus non-ASP-compliant? If an advice advises a large amount of join point shadows, can there be a lot of coupling between the advice and its shadows? In other words, does the developer always need to pay close attention to the value of the `proc` keyword or is it unlikely to cause conflicts with our approach?

Another interesting path of future work is to provide support for static contract enforcement. That is, the ability to determine statically whether an advice satisfies the ASP or not. If not, we should examine whether the advice is mentioned in the relevant `@advisedBy` clauses. Finally, another path worth exploring is to study invariants and frame conditions in more detail, and to extend the approach with e.g. an ownership type system such that it can be used for formal verification.

References

1. Agostinho, S., Moreira, A., Guerreiro, P.: Contracts for aspect-oriented design. In: Proceedings of the 2008 AOSD workshop on Software Engineering Properties of Languages and Aspect Technologies (SPLAT), pp. 1:1–1:6. ACM, New York, NY, USA (2008)
2. Aldrich, J.: Open modules: modular reasoning about advice. In: Gao, X.-X. (ed.) ECOOP 2005. LNCS, vol. 3586, pp. 144–168. Springer, Heidelberg (2005)
3. America, P.: Designing an object-oriented programming language with behavioural subtyping. In: de Bakker, J.W., de Roever, W.P., Rozenberg, G. (eds.) Foundations of Object-Oriented Languages. LNCS, vol. 489, pp. 60–90. Springer, Heidelberg (1991)
4. Apel, S., Batory, D.: How AspectJ is used: an analysis of eleven AspectJ programs. J. Object Technol. (JOT) **9**(1), 117–142 (2010)
5. Aracic, I., Gasiunas, V., Mezini, M., Ostermann, K.: An overview of CaesarJ. In: Rashid, A., Akşit, M. (eds.) Transactions on Aspect-Oriented Software Development I. LNCS, vol. 3880, pp. 135–173. Springer, Heidelberg (2006)
6. Bagherzadeh, M., Rajan, H., Leavens, G.T., Mooney, S.: Translucid contracts: expressive specification and modular verification for aspect-oriented interfaces. In: Proceedings of the Tenth International Conference on Aspect-Oriented Software Development, AOSD 2011, pp. 141–152. ACM, New York, NY, USA (2011)
7. Bodden, E., Tanter, É., Inostroza, M.: Join point interfaces for safe and flexible decoupling of aspects. ACM Trans. Softw. Eng. Methodol. **23**(1), 7:1–7:41 (2014)
8. Borgida, A., Mylopoulos, J., Reiter, R.: On the frame problem in procedure specifications. IEEE Trans. Softw. Eng. **21**(10), 785–798 (1995)
9. Clarke, D.G., Potter, J.M., Noble, J.: Ownership types for flexible alias protection. SIGPLAN Not. **33**(10), 48–64 (1998)
10. Clement, A., Colyer, A., Kersten, M.: Aspect-oriented programming with AJDT. In: ECOOP Workshop on Analysis of Aspect-Oriented Software (2003)
11. Clifton, C., Leavens, G.T.: Observers and assistants: a proposal for modular aspect-oriented reasoning. In: Proceedings of the 1st Workshop on Foundations of Aspect-Oriented Languages, FOAL 2002, p. 33 (2002)
12. Clifton, C., Leavens, G.T.: Obliviousness, modular reasoning, and the behavioral subtyping analogy. In: Workshop on Software Engineering Properties of Languages for Aspect Technologies (SPLAT) (2003)
13. Clifton, C., Leavens, G.T.: A design discipline and language features for modular reasoning in aspect-oriented programs. Ph.D. thesis, Iowa State University (2005)
14. Clifton, C., Leavens, G.T., Boyland, J.: MAO: ownership and effects for more effective reasoning about aspects. In: Ernst, E. (ed.) ECOOP 2007. LNCS, vol. 4609, pp. 451–475. Springer, Heidelberg (2007)
15. Dantas, D.S., Walker, D.: Harmless advice. In: Conference Record of the 33rd ACM SIGPLAN-SIGACT Symposium on Principles of Programming Languages, POPL 2006, pp. 383–396. ACM, New York, NY, USA (2006)
16. Dhara, K.K., Leavens, G.T.: Forcing behavioral subtyping through specification inheritance. In: Proceedings of the 18th International Conference on Software Engineering, 1996, pp. 258–267 (1996)
17. Filman, R.E., Friedman, D.P.: Aspect-oriented programming is quantification and obliviousness. In: Workshop on Advanced separation of Concerns, OOPSLA (2000)

18. Findler, R.B., Felleisen, M.: Contract soundness for object-oriented languages. In: Proceedings of the 16th ACM SIGPLAN Conference on Object-Oriented Programming, Systems, Languages, and Applications (OOPSLA), pp. 1–15. ACM, New York, NY, USA (2001)
19. Flatt, M., Krishnamurthi, S., Felleisen, M.: Classes and mixins. In: Proceedings of the 25th ACM SIGPLAN-SIGACT Symposium on Principles of Programming Languages (POPL), pp. 171–183. ACM Press, New York, USA, January 1998
20. Hirschfeld, R., Costanza, P., Nierstrasz, O.: Context-oriented programming. J. Technol. **7**(3), 125–151 (2008)
21. Katz, S.: Aspect categories and classes of temporal properties. In: Rashid, A., Akşit, M. (eds.) Transactions on Aspect-Oriented Software Development I. LNCS, vol. 3880, pp. 106–134. Springer, Heidelberg (2006)
22. Koppen, C., Störzer, M.: PCDiff: attacking the fragile pointcut problem. In: European Interactive Workshop on Aspects in Software (2004)
23. Leavens, G.T., Baker, A.L., Ruby, C.: Preliminary design of JML: a behavioral interface specification language for java. SIGSOFT Softw. Eng. Notes **31**(3), 1–38 (2006)
24. Leavens, G.T., Naumann, D.A.: Behavioral subtyping, specification inheritance, and modular reasoning (2006)
25. Rustan, K., Leino, M.: Data groups: specifying the modification of extended state. SIGPLAN Not. **33**(10), 144–153 (1998)
26. Rustan, K., Leino, M., Müller, P.: Object invariants in dynamic contexts. In: Odersky, M. (ed.) ECOOP 2004. LNCS, vol. 3086, pp. 491–515. Springer, Heidelberg (2004)
27. Liskov, B.H., Wing, J.M.: A behavioral notion of subtyping. ACM Trans. Program. Lang. Syst. (TOPLAS) **16**(6), 1811–1841 (1994)
28. Lorenz, D.H., Skotiniotis, T.: Extending design by contract for aspect-oriented programming, January 2005. http://arxiv.org/abs/cs/0501070
29. Meyer, B.: Object-Oriented Software Construction, vol. 2. Prentice Hall, New York (1988)
30. Meyer, B.: Applying "Design by contract". Computer **25**(10), 40–51 (1992)
31. Müller, P., Poetzsch-Heffter, A., Leavens, G.T.: Modular invariants for layered object structures. Sci. Comput. Program. **62**(3), 253–286 (2006)
32. Naumann, D.A., Barnett, M.: Towards imperative modules: Reasoning. Theor. Comput. Sci. **365**(1–2), 143–168 (2006)
33. Rajan, H., Leavens, G.T.: Ptolemy: a language with quantified, typed events. In: Vitek, J. (ed.) ECOOP 2008. LNCS, vol. 5142, pp. 155–179. Springer, Heidelberg (2008)
34. Rajan, H., Sullivan, K.J.: Classpects: unifying aspect- and object-oriented language design. In: 27th International Conference on Software Engineering (ICSE), pp. 59–68 (2005)
35. Rebelo, H., Leavens, G.T., Lima, R.M.F., Borba, P. Ribeiro, M.: Modular aspect-oriented design rule enforcement with XPIDRs. In: Proceedings of the 12th workshop on Foundations of Aspect-Oriented Languages, FOAL 2013, pp. 13–18. ACM, New York, NY, USA (2013)
36. Hähnle, R., Schaefer, I.: A Liskov principle for delta-oriented programming. In: Margaria, T., Steffen, B. (eds.) Leveraging Applications of Formal Methods, Verification and Validation. Technologies for Mastering Change. LNCS, vol. 7609, pp. 32–46. Springer, Heidelberg (2012)

37. Rinard, M., Salcianu, A., Bugrara, S.: A classification system and analysis for aspect-oriented programs. In: Proceedings of the 12th ACM SIGSOFT Twelfth International Symposium on Foundations of Software Engineering, SIGSOFT 2004/FSE-12, pp. 147–158. ACM, New York, NY, USA (2004)
38. Steimann, F., Pawlitzki, T., Apel, S., Kästner, C.: Types and modularity for implicit invocation with implicit announcement. ACM Trans. Softw. Eng. Methodol. **20**(1), 1:1–1:43 (2010)
39. Sullivan, K., Griswold, W.G., Rajan, H., Song, Y., Cai, Y., Shonle, M., Tewari, N.: Modular aspect-oriented design with XPIs. ACM Trans. Softw. Eng. Methodol. **20**(2), 5:1–5:42 (2010)
40. Thüm, T., Schaefer, I., Kuhlemann, M., Apel, S., Saake, G.: Applying design by contract to feature-oriented programming. In: de Lara, J., Zisman, A. (eds.) Fundamental Approaches to Software Engineering. LNCS, vol. 7212, pp. 255–269. Springer, Heidelberg (2012)
41. Wampler, D.: Aspect-oriented design principles: Lessons from object-oriented design. In: Sixth International Conference on Aspect-Oriented Software Development (2007). http://aosd.net/2007/program/industry/I6-AspectDesignPrinciples. pdf
42. Wright, A.K., Felleisen, M.: A syntactic approach to type soundness. Inf. Comput. **115**(1), 38–94 (1994)
43. Zhao, J., Rinard, M.: Pipa: a behavioral interface specification language for AspectJ. In: Pezzè, M. (ed.) FASE 2003. LNCS, vol. 2621, pp. 150–165. Springer, Heidelberg (2003)

Selected Papers from Modularity 2014

Propagation of Behavioral Variations with Delegation Proxies

Camille Teruel[1]($\boxtimes$), Erwann Wernli[2], Stéphane Ducasse[1],
and Oscar Nierstrasz[2]

[1] RMOD, INRIA Lille Nord Europe, Villeneuve d'ascq, France
`camille.teruel@inria.fr`
[2] Software Composition Group, University of Bern, Bern, Switzerland

Abstract. Scoping behavioral variations to dynamic extents is useful to support non-functional concerns that otherwise result in cross-cutting code. Unfortunately, such forms of scoping are difficult to obtain with traditional reflection or aspects. We propose *delegation proxies*, a dynamic proxy model that supports behavioral intercession through the interception of various interpretation operations. Delegation proxies permit different behavioral variations to be easily composed together. We show how delegation proxies enable behavioral variations that can *propagate* to dynamic extents. We demonstrate our approach with examples of behavioral variations scoped to dynamic extents that help simplify code related to safety, reliability, and monitoring.

Keywords: Reflection · Proxy · Delegation · Propagation · Dynamic extent

1 Introduction

Non-functional concerns like monitoring or reliability typically result in code duplication in the code base. The use of aspects is the de-facto solution to factor out such boilerplate code into a single place. Aspects enable the scoping of behavioral variations in space (with a rich variety of static pointcuts), in time (with dynamic aspects), and in the control flow (with the corresponding pointcuts). Scoping a behavioral variation to the *dynamic extent* [TFD+09] of an expression is however challenging, since scoping between threads is not easily realized with aspects. Traditional reflection and meta-object protocols suffer from similar limitations.

This is unfortunate since scoping behavioral variations to dynamic extents increases the expressiveness of the language in useful ways [Tan08, TFD+09]. With such a form of scoping, it is possible to execute code in a read-only manner [ADD+10] (thus improving safety), or to track all state mutations to ease recovery in case of errors (thus improving reliability), or to trace and profile code at a fine-grained level (thus improving monitoring).

We show in this paper that with minor changes to the way dynamic proxies operate, it becomes possible to implement behavioral variations that are scoped

© Springer-Verlag Berlin Heidelberg 2015
S. Chiba et al. (Eds.): Transactions on AOSD XII, LNCS 8989, pp. 63–95, 2015.
DOI: 10.1007/978-3-662-46734-3_2

to dynamic extents. A dynamic proxy [VCM10, MPBD+11, Eug06][1] is a special object that mediates interactions between a client object and another target object. When the client sends a message to the proxy, the message is intercepted and reified to allow specific processing. To scope variations to dynamic extents using proxies, we must first slightly adapt the dynamic proxy mechanism. We refer to our approach as *delegation proxies*.

Delegation proxies have the following characteristics:

- They operate by delegation [Lie86], *i.e.*, by rebinding self-references as in prototype-based languages,
- they intercept state accesses, both for regular fields and variables captured in closures, and
- they intercept object creation.

With delegation proxies, a proxy can encode a behavioral variation that will be consistently *propagated* to all objects accessed during the evaluation of a message send (*i.e.*, its dynamic extent).

Delegation proxies have several positive properties. First, delegation proxies can avoid *infinite regressions*. In aspect-oriented programming, infinite regressions can arise when an advice triggers the associated pointcut.[2] In reflective architectures, infinite regression arises when reflecting on code that is used to implement the reflective behavior itself. The conventional solution to this problem is to explicitly model the different levels of execution [CKL96, DSD08, Tan10]. With delegation proxies, a proxy and its target are distinct objects and the propagation is enabled only for the proxy. No variation is active when executing the code that implements the behavioral variation as long as all messages are sent to base objects. Second, behavioral variations expressed with delegation proxies *compose*, similarly to aspects. For instance, tracing and profiling behavioral variations can be implemented by separate proxies that can be combined to apply both behavioral variations. Third, like other dynamic proxy implementations, delegation proxies naturally support *partial reflection* [TNCC03] at an object-level granularity. Behavioral intercession is enabled only for proxies. All other objects in the system — including the target — remain unaffected and pay no performance overhead.

In this paper, we explore and demonstrate the flexibility of delegation proxies in Smalltalk with the following contributions:

- A model of proxies based on delegation that intercepts object instantiations and state accesses (including variables in closures) (Sect. 2);
- A technique to use delegation proxies to scope variations to dynamic extents (Sect. 2);
- Several examples of useful applications of variations scoped to dynamic extents (Sect. 4);

---

[1] A similar mechanism is called encapsulator [Pas86].

[2] A typical workaround for this problem is to constrain pointcut definitions: *e.g.*, a pointcut p within an aspect A is rewritten: p && !cflow(adviceexecution()) && within(A).

- A formalization of delegation proxies and the propagation technique (Sect. 6);
- An implementation of delegation proxies in Smalltalk based on code generation (Sect. 7).

2 Delegation Proxies

Delegation proxies are dynamic proxies that operate by delegation in contrast to classical dynamic proxies that operate by forwarding. After presenting dynamic proxies, we show why delegation is a better choice than forwarding for proxy-based behavioral intercession.

To the best of our knowledge only EcmaScript 6 proxies use delegation. However, this is incidental since EcmaScript, as a prototype-based object language, uses delegation to implement object inheritance [Lie86].

We will see that delegation enables the interception of interpretation operations that occur during method execution — like object state accesses and object creation — and allows behavioral variations to be composed naturally. This is an important matter to consider in the context of class-based object-oriented languages.

2.1 Dynamic Proxies

A dynamic proxy is an object that acts as a surrogate for another object, called its *target*. A proxy mediates interactions between its target and its clients. The behavior of a proxy is typically defined by a separate object called its *handler*, whose methods are called *traps* [VCM10]. When an interpretation operation — like the reception of a message, an access to an object instance variable, *etc.*— is applied to a proxy, the proxy reifies the operation and instead invokes the trap that corresponds to that operation in its handler. The handler can take some actions before, after or even instead of performing the original operation on the target. Figure 1 shows the relationships between a proxy, its handler and its target with an example of message interception.

The dynamic proxy mechanism implements a kind of behavioral intercession that alters the interpretation of a program at the granularity of objects. We refer to the different alterations of the interpretation process as *behavioral variations*. Tracing, profiling, read-only, *etc.*, are examples of behavioral variations.

The distinction between proxies and handlers is the application of a principle called *stratification* [BU04, VCM10, MPBD+11]. Stratification stipulates that the meta-level must be separated from base-level. In the context of dynamic proxies, this principle avoids name conflicts between application methods and handler traps, *i.e.*, between the base-level and the meta-level. This means that a proxy can expose exactly the same interface as its target.

By using proxies as the targets of other proxies, we obtain chains of proxies as depicted in Fig. 2. In this case, when an interpretation operation is intercepted, the corresponding trap should be triggered in each of the handlers of the proxies in the order specified by the chain. This offers a natural and convenient way to compose multiple behavioral variations.

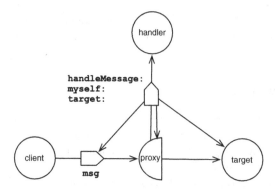

Fig. 1. Example of message interception. First, the client sends the message `msg` to a proxy. Then, the proxy intercepts the message and invokes the handler trap associated with message reception (`handleMessage:proxy:target:`) with three arguments: the reified message, the proxy itself and the target.

2.2   Forwarding *vs* Delegation

We explore the differences between forwarding and delegation semantics in the context of proxy-based intercession. The operational difference reduces to how self-references are bound in methods that match intercepted messages. Traditional dynamic proxy implementations found in class-based object-oriented languages operate by forwarding. Once a message has been intercepted by a proxy, the proxy may decide to *forward* the message to its target: the method corresponding to the message is executed with self-references bound to the target. This implies that the proxy loses control of the execution. With delegation, the proxy may decide to *delegate* the message: the method corresponding to the intercepted message is executed with self-references bound to the proxy itself. This implies that the proxy keeps the control of the execution.

With delegation, the proxy can intercept interpretation operations that occur during a method execution: object state reads, object state writes, object creation, literal resolution, *etc.* We refer to these interpretation operations as *sub-method operations*. Moreover, with delegation the identity of the proxy that originally intercepted the operation is maintained; this permits behavioral variations to be composed in the case of chains of proxies.

In Fig. 2, we have two proxies *p1* and *p2*, their respective handlers *h1* and *h2*, and an object *target*. The target of *p1* is *p2* and the target of *p2* is *target*. This forms a chain of two proxies. A client object sends a message *incr* that is supposed to change the state of the target object by modifying its instance variable *iv*.

With forwarding execution begins with the message by *p1* being intercepted and triggering the *message-reception* trap of its handler *h1*. The handler may at some point forward the intercepted message to the target of *p1* — namely the proxy *p2* — losing control of the execution at the same time. The same scenario applies to *p2*: it intercepts the message, invokes its handler's message-reception

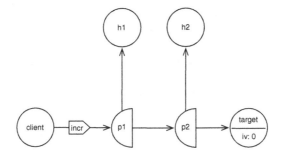

Fig. 2. A chain of two proxies. When an interpretation operation is intercepted, the corresponding trap is triggered in the handlers *h1* and *h2* in order.

trap, its handler forwards the message to *target* which then executes the method associated with the message normally and increments the value of its instance variable *iv*.

We can see that the behavioral variations of *p1* and *p2* are necessarily limited to interception of message reception since *p1* — the proxy that originally intercepted the message — loses the control of the execution. It thus cannot intercept sub-method operations. Even if the execution of the method of *target* associated with the message performs a self-send, this latter message send will not be intercepted.

With delegation the execution begins the same: *p1* intercepts the message and invokes the message-reception trap of its handler. But instead of forwarding the message to *p2*, *h1* instead delegates the message: it specify that the receiver should be rebound to *p1*. Then *p2* intercepts that message, passes it to *h2*, which applies its behavioral variation and delegates the message to *target*. At this point *p1* is still the receiver and has still control over the execution: it can intercept sub-method operations, in particular the modification of *iv*. In reaction to this interception, *p1* invokes the state-write trap of its handler *h1*. The state-write trap of *h2* is then invoked. This example shows that delegation permits behavioral variations to be composed in the context of sub-method operation interception.

To sum up, using delegation instead of forwarding for proxy-based intercession permits proxies to intercept sub-method operations and to compose behavioral variations by forming chains of proxies.

3   Propagation

In the previous section we saw how delegation proxies work. In this section we present the concept of *propagation* of behavioral variation and its reflective implementation in terms of delegation proxies. This technique permits a proxy to be created for a target object that will scope a behavioral variation to the dynamic extents of the messages it receives. These dynamic extents are the parts of the execution delimited by the processing of a message received by the proxy, from the reception of the message until the corresponding method returns. All objects accessed during this dynamic extent are consistently represented by proxies that are created on-demand. We refer to the first proxy that initiates the propagations as the *root proxy*. Other proxies created during the propagation are called *non-root proxies*. The root proxy can be seen as the entry point to a lazily-created parallel object graph as depicted in Fig. 3.

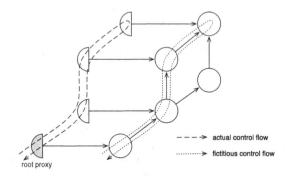

Fig. 3. A depiction of propagation (handlers are omitted for clarity). A root proxy (in grey) wraps a target object that is connected to some object graph. The dashed line depicts the actual control flow of the execution. Proxies are created on need and are eligible for garbage collection once the control flow leaves them. The actual control flow parallels a fictitious control flow (dotted line) *i.e.*, the control flow that would have resulted if execution had not been intercepted by the root proxy.

3.1 Tracing Example

We will illustrate propagation with a tracing example. Let us consider the Smalltalk method `Integer>>fib`[3] which computes the Fibonacci value of an integer using recursion:

```
Integer>>fib
    self < 2 ifTrue: [ ↑ self ].
    ↑ (self - 1) fib + (self - 2) fib
```
Listing 1. Fibonacci computation

The computation of the Fibonacci value of 2 corresponds to the following sequence of message sends (first the receiver of the message, then the message with its arguments):

---

[3] The notation `Integer>>fib` refers to the method `fib` of the class `Integer`. In Smalltalk, closures are expressed with square brackets ([...]) and booleans are objects. The method `ifTrue:` takes a closure as argument: if the receiver is the object `true`, the closure is evaluated by sending it the message `value`. The up-arrow (↑ ...) denotes a return expression.

```
2 fib
2 < 2
false ifTrue: [ ↑ self ]
2 - 1
1 fib
1 < 2
true ifTrue: [ ↑ self ]
[ ↑ self ] value
2 - 2
0 fib
0 < 2
true ifTrue: [ ↑ self ]
[ ↑ self ] value
1 + 0
```

Listing 2. Trace of 2 `fib`

To automatically trace message sends, we can use a proxy to intercept message sends and print them. A tracing proxy can be obtained by instantiating a proxy with a tracing handler. For convenience, we define the method `Object>>tracing`, which returns a tracing proxy for any object. For instance, the expression 2 `tracing` returns a tracing proxy for the number 2.

```
Object>>tracing
    ↑ Proxy handler: TracingHandler new target: self.
```

Listing 3. Creation of a tracing proxy

To trace messages, the tracing handler must define a *message reception* trap that prints the name of the reified message. Listing 4 shows the code of such a *message* trap:

```
TracingHandler>>handleMessage: m myself: p target: t
    Transcript
            print: t asString;
            space;
            print: m asString;
            cr.
    ↑ t perform: m myself: p.
```

Listing 4. A simple tracing handler

The reflective invocation with **perform:** takes one additional parameter **myself**, which specifies how **self** is rebound in the reflective invocation. This permits us to encode delegation. The handler can thus either rebind **self** to the proxy (delegation) or rebind **self** to the target (forwarding). Delegation proxies thus trivially subsume traditional forwarding proxies.

Delegation ensures that messages received by the proxy are traced, including self-sends in the method executed with delegation. However, it would fail to trace messages sent to other objects. The evaluation of 2 `tracing` `fib` would print 2 `fib`, 2 < 2, 2 - 1, 2 - 2, but all the messages sent to 1, 0, true, false and [↑ self] would not be traced.

To consistently apply a behavioral variation during the execution of a message send, all objects accessed during the execution must be represented with proxies.

3.2 Wrapping Rules

To scope a behavioral variation to a dynamic extent, we can implement a handler that replaces all object references accessed by proxies. This way, the behavioral variation will *propagate* during the execution.

In a given method activation, a reference to an object can be obtained from:

- an argument,
- a field read,
- the return value of message sends,
- the instantiation of new objects
- the resolution of literals[4]

The following rules suffice to make sure that all objects are represented by proxies:

- *Wrap the initial arguments.* When the root proxy receives a message, the arguments are wrapped with proxies. We don't need to wrap the arguments of messages sent to non-root proxies because the other rules ensure that the arguments are already wrapped in the context of the caller.
- *Wrap field reads.* References to fields are represented by proxies.
- *Wrap object instantiation.* The return value of primitive message sends that "create" new objects must be wrapped. Such primitive messages include explicit instantiations with **new** and arithmetic computations that are typically implemented natively.
- *Wrap literals.* Similarly, literals occurring in the method must be wrapped.

We don't need to wrap the return value of other message sends. Indeed, if the receiver and the arguments of a message send are already wrapped, and if the results of state reads and object instantiations are also wrapped in the execution of the method triggered by this message send, this message send will necessarily return a proxy.

Additionally, we need two rules to control how objects must be unwrapped:

- *Unwrap field writes.* When a field is written, we unwrap the value of the assignment before performing it. This way, the proxies created during the propagation are only referred to from within the call stack and don't corrupt the object graph connected to the target.
- *Unwrap the initial return value.* The root proxy unwraps the objects returned to the clients. This rule may be omitted to implement other forms of propagation as discussed in Subsect. 5.2.

Applying this technique to the code in Listing 1, the subtractions `self-2` and `self-1` return proxies as well. Figure 4 depicts the situation. This way, tracing is consistently applied during the computation of Fibonacci numbers.

---

[4] We consider closures to be special kinds of literals.

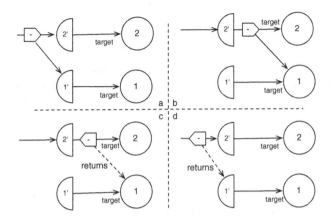

Fig. 4. Illustration of propagation during the subtraction 2 - 1. A proxy to 2 receives the subtraction message "-" with a proxy to 1 as argument (a). The message is forwarded to 2 to perform the actual subtraction (b) that returns 1 (c). Finally the result is wrapped (d).

3.3 Propagation Handler

To implement a handler that applies the wrapping rules presented previously, we need to have specific traps. In Smalltalk, an object is instantiated by sending the message **new** to a class, which is an object as well. The interception of object instantiations does thus not require a specific trap and is realized indirectly. The following set of traps is thus sufficient to intercept all method invocations, state accesses, and object instantiations:

- handleMessage:myself:target:
  The trap for message sends takes as parameters the reified message, the original proxy[5] and the target.
- handleReadField:myself:target:
  The trap for field reads takes as parameters the field name, the original proxy and the target.
- handleWriteField:value:myself:target:
  The trap for field writes takes as parameters the field name, the value to write, the original proxy and the target.
- handleLiteral:myself:target:
  The trap for the resolution of literals (symbols, string, numbers, class names, and closures) takes as parameters the resolved literal, the original proxy and the target.

   This set of traps is sufficient to implement propagation in Smalltalk. However, the set of necessary traps depends on the host language. In Java, additional traps

---

[5] In case of chain proxies, the original proxy is not necessarily the one that intercepted the operation but the root of the chain.

would be needed to intercept constructor invocations, accesses to static fields and invocation of static methods.

Similarly to `perform:`, reflective methods used to read fields, to write fields and to resolve literals need to be extended with an additional parameter `myself`. They become `instVarNamed:myself:`, `instVarNamed:put:myself` and `literal: myself:`. In the case of a chain of proxies, the parameter `myself` is passed to the traps along the chain to preserve the identity of the proxy that originally intercepted the operation.

Listing 5 shows the traps for state writes and state reads traps. Other traps are similar. This handler just applies the previous wrapping rules.

It is impossible to deconstruct a proxy to obtain its handler or its target without using reflective capabilities. For simplicity, we assume the existence of a class `Reflect` that exposes the following methods globally:

– `Reflect class>>isProxy: aProxy`
 Returns whether the argument is a proxy or not.
– `Reflect class>>handlerOf: aProxy`
 If the argument is a proxy, returns its handler. Fails otherwise.
– `Reflect class>>targetOf: aProxy`
 If the argument is a proxy, returns its target. Fails otherwise.

For increased security, these methods could be stratified with *mirrors* (*i.e.*, dedicated objects that provide access to reflective features for a given object [BU04]), in which case handlers would need to have access to a mirror when they are instantiated.

```
PropagationHandler>>handleReadField: f myself: p target: t
  ↑ self wrap: (super handleReadField: f myself: p target: t)

PropagationHandler>>handleWriteField: f value: v proxy: p target: t
  ↑ super handleWriteField: f value: (self unwrap: v) proxy: p target: t
```

Listing 5. State reads and state writes traps of a propagating handler.

3.4 Closures

Closures deserve special treatment. A closure should be evaluated with the variations that are active in the current dynamic extent, and not the variations that were active when it was created. Consider, for instance, if the closure `[ self printString ]` is created when tracing is enabled, its evaluation during a regular execution should not trace the message `printString`. Conversely, if the closure `[ self printString ]` is created during a regular execution, its evaluation when tracing is enabled should trace the message `printString`. For this to work correctly, closures are always created in an *unproxied* form, and are transformed on demand when wrapped.

Variables captured in a closure are stored in indexed fields. Let us see first how creation works and illustrate it with the closure `[ self printString ]` and tracing:

1. The closure is created by the runtime and captures variables as-is. *Tracing example:* the closure captures `self`, which refers to a proxy.
2. The closure creation is intercepted by the *literal* trap of the creator. *Tracing example:* the closure is treated like other literals and thus proxied.
3. If the closure was proxied, the runtime invokes the *write* trap of the closure's proxy for all captured variables. *Tracing example:* the runtime invokes the *write* trap of the closure's proxy passing 0 as field index and the `self` proxy as value. The trap unproxies the value and reflectively invokes `instVarNamed: put:myself:` for field 0. This overwrites the previous value in the closure with a reference to the base object.

Evaluation of closures follows the inverse scheme:

1. If the closure is evaluated via a proxy, the runtime invokes the *read* trap each time a captured variable is accessed. *Tracing example:* the runtime invokes the *read* trap of the closure's proxy passing 0 as field index. The trap reflectively invokes `instVarNamed:` for field 0 and wraps the result with a proxy. The message `printString` is sent to the proxy.

Note that this scheme is quite natural if we consider that closures could be encoded with regular objects, similarly to anonymous classes in Java. In that case, captured variables are effectively stored in synthetic fields initialized in the constructor. The instantiation of the anonymous class would trigger *write* traps, and evaluation would trigger *read* traps.

Adding method `valueWithHandler:` in `BlockClosure`, tracing `2 fib` can also be achieved with `[ 2 fib ] valueWithHandler: TracingHandler new` instead of `2 tracing fib`. Closures provide a convenient way to activate a behavioral variation in the dynamic extent of expression.

```
BlockClosure>>valueWithHandler: aHandler
   ↑ (Proxy handler: aHandler target: self) value.
```

Listing 6. Convenience method to wrap and evaluate a closure

4   Examples

Delegation proxies subsume dynamic proxies and can be used to implement all classical examples of dynamic proxies such as lazy values, membranes, *etc.* We omit examples that can be found in the literature [VCM13, Eug06, MPBD+11].

We focus in this section on new examples enabled by delegation proxies. They all rely on the propagation technique presented earlier. We assume that the exemple handlers subclass a `PropagationHandler` that implements the propagation technique (see Listing 5). There are advantages to using delegation proxies to scope these behavioral variations to a dynamic extent. Behavioral variations can be composed: different parties can add their own variations without being aware of others already active for the same target. A behavioral variation is enabled only for the proxy: a variation is enabled for clients who possess a reference to the proxy while other clients may have a reference to the target or to another proxy implementing another behavioral variation. It is up to the creator of the proxy to decide whether to pass the proxy or the target.

4.1   Read-Only Execution

Read-only execution [ADD+10] prevents mutation of state during evaluation. Read-only execution can dynamically guarantee that the evaluation of a given piece of code is either free of side effects or raises an error.

Classical proxies could restrict the interface of a given object to the subset of read-only methods. However, they would fail to enable read-only execution of arbitrary methods, or to guarantee that methods are deeply read-only. Read-only execution can be implemented trivially with a propagating handler that fails upon state writes.

```
ReadOnlyHandler>>handleWriteField: f value: v myself: p target: t
  ReadOnlyError signal
```
Listing 7. Read-only handler

Thanks to proxy-based intercession, the target object is still available to trusted clients that can modify it. Only clients holding a reference to the proxy are affected by the read-only policy.

4.2   Object Versioning

To tolerate errors, developers implement recovery blocks that undo mutations and leave the objects in a consistent state [PLW09]. Typically, this entails cloning objects to obtain snapshots. Our propagation technique enables the implementation of object versioning concisely. Before any field is mutated, the handler shown below records the old value into a log using a reflective field read. The log can be used in recovery block, for instance to implement rollback.

```
RecordingHandler>>handleWriteField: f value: v myself: p target: t
  | oldValue |
  oldValue := t instVarNamed: f myself: t.
  log add: { t. f. oldValue deepCopy }.
  ↑ super handleWriteField: f value: v myself: p target: t
```
Listing 8. Recording handler

A convenience method can be added to closures to enable recording with [...] recordInLog: aLog.

```
BlockClosure>>recordInLog: aLog
  ↑ self valueWithHandler: (RecordingHandler log: aLog)
```
Listing 9. Enabling recording

The log can then be used to reflectively undo changes if needed.

```
aLog reverseDo: [ :change |
  change first instVarNamed: change second put: change third ]
```
Listing 10. Undoing changes

4.3 Dynamic Scoping

In most modern programming languages, variables are lexically scoped and can't be dynamically scoped. Dynamic scoping is sometimes desirable, for instance in web frameworks to access easily the ongoing request. Developers must in this case use alternatives like thread locals. It is for instance the strategy taken by Java Server Faces in the static method `getCurrentInstance()` of class `FacesContext`[6]).

Dynamic scoping can be realized in Smalltalk using call stack manipulation [Deu81] or by accessing the active process. Delegation proxies offer an additional approach to implement dynamic bindings by simply sharing a common (key,value) pair between handlers. If multiple dynamic bindings are defined, objects will be wrapped multiple times, once per binding. When a binding value must be retrieved, a utility method locates the handler corresponding to the request key, and returns the corresponding value:

```
ScopeUtils>>valueOf: aKey for: aProxy
  | h p |
  p := aProxy.
  [ Reflect isProxy: p ] whileTrue: [
    h := Reflect handlerOf: p.
    ( h bindingKey == aKey ) ifTrue: [ ↑ h bindingValue ].
    p := Reflect targetOf: p ].
  ↑ nil. "Not found"
```
Listing 11. Inspection of a chain of proxies

During the evaluation of a block, a dynamic variable can be bound with `[...] valueWith: #currentRequest value: aRequest` and accessed pervasively with `ScopeUtils valueOf: #currentRequest for: self`.

4.4 Profiling

Previous sections already illustrated delegation proxies using tracing. The same approach could be used to implement other interceptors like profiling or code contracts. The following handler implements profiling. It stores records of the different execution durations in an instance variable `tallies` for later analysis.

```
ProfilingHandler>>initialize
    tallies := OrderedCollection new
```

```
ProfilingHandler>>handleMessage: m myself: p target: t
```

---

[6] http://www.webcitation.org/6FOF4DFab.

```
| start |
start := Time now.
[ ↑ super handleMessage: m myself: p target: t ]
  ensure: [
      | duration |
      duration := Time now - start.
      tallies add: {t. m. duration} ]
```

Listing 12. A simple profiling handler

5   Other Forms of Propagation

Since propagation is implemented reflectively, it can be customized in many ways. Delegation proxies provide flexible building blocks to implement various forms of scopes, possibly blurring the line between static and dynamic scoping, similarly to Tanter's *scoping strategies* [TFD+09].

5.1   Filtering on Package

Propagation can for instance be adapted to enable a behavioral variation only for instances of classes belonging to specific packages. This can be used to select which parts of an execution are subject to a behavioral variation such as tracing. It is especially useful for excluding kernel classes (string, dictionaries, arrays, *etc.*) and focusing instead on the classes of the analysed application.

To implement this form of scoping, it is possible to implement a filtering handler with a set of packages. This handler apply its behavioral variation only when the class of the target is declared in one of the packages of interest. Listing 13 shows the message trap of such a filtering handler.

```
FilteringHandler>>handleMessage: m myself: p target: t
  ↑ (packages includes: t class package)
    ifTrue: [ super handleMessage: m myself: p target: t ]
    ifFalse: [ t perform: m myself: t ]
```

Listing 13. Message trap of the filtering handler

5.2   Defensive Proxies

Behavioral variations that are concerned with security can be used in two cases. The first case is when we want to apply the behavioral variation to protect the target from its clients. The second case is when we want to apply the behavioral variation to protect the clients from the target.

Protecting the target from the clients. With full propagation a read-only behavioral variation ensures that no state is modified from within the dynamic extent of messages received by the root proxy. We can customize propagation to relax the constraint imposed on clients. We can ensure that no state *of the object graph connected to the target* is modified from within the dynamic extent of messages received by the root proxy. To achieve that we can have an alternative propagation handler that does not wrap initial arguments, *i.e.*, the arguments of messages sent to the root proxy. The rationale is that the client necessarily has a reference to each of the objects it passes as arguments in the message to the root proxy. The client can therefore access these objects with the behavioral variation disabled in any case. In such scenarios, we also typically want initial returns to be wrapped so that objects returned by the target are still protected by the behavioral variation. Consequently, this alternative propagation does not apply this unwrapping rule.

Protecting the clients from the target. Other security-related behavioral variations can be used to protect the clients from the target. This means that propagation should be enabled only for the arguments that are passed to the proxy. In that case, the proxy created to wrap the initial target (initial proxy) does not propagate by itself but it wraps the arguments of messages it receives with proxies that propagate. The return values of messages sent to that initial proxy are also proxies (with the same wrapping rules) to ensure that clients are also protected from returned objects. This scenario is in fact a combination of a membrane [VCM10, TCD13] with our propagation technique. The initial proxy's handler implements the wrapping rules of membranes. The membrane handler is parameterized with two handlers: one that defines the inside-out policy and another that defines the outside-in policy [TCD13]. The inside-out handler is typically an identity handler and the outside-in handler is a propagating handler that implements the behavioral variations used to protect the clients from the target.

6   Semantics

We formalize delegation proxies by extending SMALLTALKLITE [BDNW08], a lightweight calculus in the spirit of CLASSICJAVA [FKF98] that captures the core execution semantics of a Smalltalk-like language and omits static types. We assume no prior knowledge of it. Our formalization simplifies three aspects of the semantics presented in the previous sections: it doesn't model first-class classes, literals or closures. Consequently, *literal* traps are not considered. Instead, we introduce a *new* trap that intercepts object instantiations.

The syntax of our extended calculus, SMALLTALKPROXY, is shown in Fig. 5. The only addition to the original syntax is the new expression **proxy** *e e*.

During evaluation, the expressions of the program are annotated with the object and class context of the ongoing evaluation, since this information is missing from the static syntax. An annotated expression is called a *redex*. For

$$P = \mathbf{defn}^* e$$
$$\mathbf{defn} = \mathbf{class}\ c\ \mathbf{extends}\ c\ \{\ f^* meth^*\ \}$$
$$meth = m(x^*)\ \{\ e\ \}$$
$$e = \mathbf{new}\ c\ \mid\ x\ \mid\ \mathbf{self}\ \mid\ \mathsf{nil}\ \mid\ f\ \mid\ f = e$$
$$\mid\ e.m(e^*)\ \mid\ \mathbf{super}.m(e^*)\ \mid\ \mathbf{let}\ x = e\ \mathbf{in}\ e$$
$$\mid\ \mathbf{proxy}\ e\ e$$

Fig. 5. Syntax of SMALLTALKPROXY

instance, the super call $\mathbf{super}.m(v^*)$ is decorated with its object and class into $\mathbf{super}\langle c\rangle.m\langle o\rangle(v^*)$ before being interpreted; $\mathbf{self}$ is translated into the value of the corresponding object; message sends $o.m(v^*)$ are decorated with the current object context to keep track of the sender of the message. The rules for translating expressions into redexes are shown in Fig. 7.

$$o[\![\mathbf{new}\ c']\!]_c = \mathbf{new}\langle o\rangle\ c'\ \textit{(where o is fresh)}$$
$$o[\![x]\!]_c = x$$
$$o[\![\mathbf{self}]\!]_c = o$$
$$o[\![\mathsf{nil}]\!]_c = \mathsf{nil}$$
$$o[\![f]\!]_c = f\langle o\rangle$$
$$o[\![f = e]\!]_c = f\langle o\rangle = o[\![e]\!]_c$$
$$o[\![e.m(e_i^*)]\!]_c = o[\![e]\!]_c.m\langle o\rangle(o[\![e_i]\!]_c^*)$$
$$o[\![\mathbf{super}.m(e_i^*)]\!]_c = \mathbf{super}\langle c\rangle.m\langle o\rangle(o[\![e_i]\!]_c^*)$$
$$o[\![\mathbf{let}\ x = e\ \mathbf{in}\ e']\!]_c = \mathbf{let}\ x = o[\![e]\!]_c\ \mathbf{in}\ o[\![e']\!]_c$$
$$o[\![\mathbf{proxy}\ e\ e']\!]_c = \mathbf{proxy}\ o[\![e]\!]_c\ o[\![e']\!]_c$$

Fig. 6. Translating expressions to redexes

Redexes and their subredexes reduce to a value, which is either an address a, nil, or a proxy. A proxy has a handler h and a target t. A proxy is itself a value. Both h and t can be proxies as well. Redexes may be evaluated within an expression context E. An expression context corresponds to an redex with a hole that can be filled with another redex. For example, $E[expr]$ denotes an expression that contains the sub-expression $expr$.

Translation from the main expression to an initial redex is carried out by the function $o[\![e]\!]_c$ (see Fig. 6). This binds fields to their enclosing object context and binds $\mathbf{self}$ to the value o of the receiver. The initial object context for a program is nil. (*i.e.*, there are no global fields accessible to the main expression). So if e is the main expression associated to a program P, then $\mathsf{nil}[\![e]\!]_{\mathsf{Object}}$ is the initial redex.

$P \vdash \langle \epsilon, \mathcal{H}\rangle \hookrightarrow \langle \epsilon', \mathcal{H}'\rangle$ means that we reduce an expression (redex) ϵ in the context of a (static) program P and an object heap $\mathcal{H}$ to a new expression ϵ' and (possibly) updated heap $\mathcal{H}'$. The heap consists of a set of mappings from

$$\epsilon = o \mid \mathbf{new}\langle o \rangle \ c \mid x \mid \mathbf{self} \mid \mathsf{nil} \mid f\langle o \rangle \mid f\langle o \rangle = \epsilon$$
$$\mid \epsilon.m\langle o \rangle(\epsilon^*) \mid \mathbf{super}\langle c \rangle.m\langle o \rangle(\epsilon^*) \mid \mathbf{let} \ x = \epsilon \ \mathbf{in} \ \epsilon$$
$$\mid \mathbf{proxy} \ \epsilon \ \epsilon$$
$$E = [\ ] \mid f\langle o \rangle = E \mid E.m\langle o \rangle(\epsilon^*) \mid o.m\langle o \rangle(o^* \ E \ \epsilon^*)$$
$$\mid \mathbf{super}\langle c \rangle.m\langle o \rangle(o^* \ E \ \epsilon^*) \mid \mathbf{let} \ x = E \ \mathbf{in} \ \epsilon$$
$$\mid \mathbf{proxy} \ E \ \epsilon \mid \mathbf{proxy} \ o \ E$$
$$o = a \mid \mathsf{nil} \mid \mathbf{proxy} \ o \ o$$

Fig. 7. Redex syntax

addresses $a \in \mathrm{dom}(\mathcal{H})$ to tuples $\langle c, \{f \mapsto v\} \rangle$ representing the class c of an object and the set of its field values. The initial value of the heap is $\mathcal{H} = \{\}$.

The reductions are summarized in Fig. 8. Predicate $\in_P^*$ is used for field lookup in a class ($f \in_P^* c$) and method lookup ($\langle c, m, x^*, e \rangle \in_P^* c'$, where c' is the class where the method was found in the hierarchy). Predicates $\leq_P$ and $\prec_P$ are used respectively for subclass and direct subclass relationships.

If the object context $\langle o \rangle$ of an instantiation with $\mathbf{new}\langle o \rangle$ c is a regular object (*i.e.*, not a proxy), the expression reduces to a fresh address a, bound in the heap to an object whose class is c and whose fields are all nil(reduction [*new*]). If the object context of the instantiation is a proxy, the **newTrap** is invoked on the handler instead (reduction [*new-proxy*]). The trap takes the result of the instantiation $\mathbf{new}\langle t \rangle$ c as parameter; it can take further action or return it as-is.

The object context $\langle o \rangle$ of field reads and field writes can be an object or a proxy. A local field read in the context of an object address reduces to the value of the field (reduction [*get*]). A local field read in the context of a proxy invokes the trap **readTrap** on the handler h (reduction [*get-proxy*]). A local field write in the context of an object simply updates the corresponding binding of the field in the heap (reduction [*set*]). A local field read in the context of a proxy invokes the trap **writeTrap** on the handler h (reduction [*set-proxy*]).

Messages can be sent to an object or to a proxy. When we send a message to an object, the corresponding method body e is looked up, starting from the class c of the receiver a. The method body is then evaluated in the context of the receiver, binding **self** to the address a. Formal parameters to the method are substituted by the actual arguments. We also pass in the actual class in which the method is found, so that **super** sends have the right context to start their method lookup (reduction [*message*]). When a message is sent to a proxy, the trap **messageTrap** is invoked on the handler. The object context $\langle s \rangle$ that decorates the message corresponds to the sender of the message. The trap takes as parameters the message and its arguments, and the initial receiver of the message **proxy** h t.

Super-sends are similar to regular message sends, except that the method lookup must start in the superclass of the class of the method in which the **super** send was declared. In the case of a super-send, the object context $\langle s \rangle$ corresponds to the sender of the message as well as the receiver. The object context is used to rebind **self** (reduction [*super*]). When we reduce the super-send,

$$P \vdash \langle E[\mathbf{new}\langle r \rangle\ c], \mathcal{H} \rangle$$
$$\hookrightarrow \langle E[a], \mathcal{H}[a \mapsto \langle c, \{f \mapsto \mathsf{nil} \mid \forall f, f \in_P^* c\}\rangle]\rangle \qquad \qquad [new]$$
$$\text{where } a \notin \mathrm{dom}(\mathcal{H})$$

$$P \vdash \langle E[\mathbf{new}\langle \mathbf{proxy}\ h\ t \rangle\ c], \mathcal{H} \rangle$$
$$\hookrightarrow \langle E[h.\mathbf{newTrap}(\mathbf{new}\langle t \rangle c, \mathbf{proxy}\ h\ t)], \mathcal{H} \rangle \qquad \qquad [new\text{-}proxy]$$

$$P \vdash \langle E[f\langle a \rangle], \mathcal{H} \rangle$$
$$\hookrightarrow \langle E[o], \mathcal{H} \rangle \qquad \qquad [get]$$
$$\text{where } \mathcal{H}(a) = \langle c, \mathcal{F} \rangle \text{ and } \mathcal{F}(f) = o$$

$$P \vdash \langle E[f\langle \mathbf{proxy}\ h\ t \rangle], \mathcal{H} \rangle$$
$$\hookrightarrow \langle E[h.\mathbf{readTrap}(t, f, \mathbf{proxy}\ h\ t)], \mathcal{H} \rangle \qquad \qquad [get\text{-}proxy]$$

$$P \vdash \langle E[f\langle a \rangle = o], \mathcal{H} \rangle$$
$$\hookrightarrow \langle E[o], \mathcal{H}[a \mapsto \langle c, \mathcal{F}[f \mapsto o]\rangle]\rangle \qquad \qquad [set]$$
$$\text{where } \mathcal{H}(a) = \langle c, \mathcal{F} \rangle$$

$$P \vdash \langle E[f\langle \mathbf{proxy}\ h\ t \rangle = o], \mathcal{H} \rangle$$
$$\hookrightarrow \langle E[h.\mathbf{writeTrap}(t, f, o, \mathbf{proxy}\ h\ t)], \mathcal{H} \rangle \qquad \qquad [set\text{-}proxy]$$

$$P \vdash \langle E[a.m\langle s \rangle(o^*)], \mathcal{H} \rangle$$
$$\hookrightarrow \langle E[a[e[o^*/x^*]]_{c'}], \mathcal{H} \rangle \qquad \qquad [message]$$
$$\text{where } \mathcal{H}[a] = \langle c, \mathcal{F} \rangle \text{ and } \langle c, m, x^*, e \rangle \in_P^* c'$$

$$P \vdash \langle E[(\mathbf{proxy}\ h\ t).m\langle s \rangle(o^*)], \mathcal{H} \rangle$$
$$\hookrightarrow \langle E[h.\mathbf{messageTrap}(t, m, o^*, \mathbf{proxy}\ h\ t)], \mathcal{H} \rangle \qquad [message\text{-}proxy]$$

$$P \vdash \langle E[\mathbf{super}\langle c \rangle.m\langle s \rangle(o^*)], \mathcal{H} \rangle$$
$$\hookrightarrow \langle E[s[e[o^*/x^*]]_{c''}], \mathcal{H} \rangle \qquad \qquad [super]$$
$$\text{where } c \prec_P c' \text{ and } \langle c', m, x^*, e \rangle \in_P^* c'' \text{ and } c' \leq_P c''$$

$$P \vdash \langle E[\mathbf{let}\ x = o\ \mathbf{in}\ \epsilon], \mathcal{H} \rangle$$
$$\hookrightarrow \langle E[\epsilon[o/x]], \mathcal{H} \rangle \qquad \qquad [let]$$

Fig. 8. Reductions for SMALLTALKPROXY

we must take care to pass on the class c'' of the method in which the super reference was found, since that method may make further super-sends. Finally, **let in** expressions simply represent local variable bindings (reduction [let]).

Errors occur if an expression does not reduce to an a or to nil. This may occur if a non-existent variable, field or method is referenced (for example, when sending any message to nil, or applying traps on a handler h that isn't suitable). For the purpose of this paper we are not concerned with errors, so we do not introduce any special rules to generate an error value in these cases.

6.1 Identity Proxy

The language requires the ability to reflectively apply operations for proxies to be useful. For simplicity, we extend the language with three additional non-stratified reflective primitives: **send**, **read**, and **write**. The semantics of these primitives is given in Fig. 9.

$$P \vdash \langle E[a.\mathbf{send}(m, o^*, my)], \mathcal{H} \rangle$$
$$\hookrightarrow \langle E[my[\![e[o^*/x^*]]\!]_{c'}], \mathcal{H} \rangle \qquad [\textit{reflect-message}]$$
where $\mathcal{H}[a] = \langle c, \mathcal{F} \rangle$ and $\langle c, m, x^*, e \rangle \in_P^* c'$

$$P \vdash \langle E[(\mathbf{proxy}\ h\ t).\mathbf{send}(m, o^*, my)], \mathcal{H} \rangle$$
$$\hookrightarrow \langle E[h.\mathbf{messageTrap}(t, m, o^*, my)], \mathcal{H} \rangle \quad [\textit{reflect-message-proxy}]$$

$$P \vdash \langle E[a.\mathbf{read}(f, my)], \mathcal{H} \rangle$$
$$\hookrightarrow \langle E[o], \mathcal{H} \rangle \qquad [\textit{reflect-get}]$$
where $\mathcal{H}(a) = \langle c, \mathcal{F} \rangle$ and $\mathcal{F}(f) = o$

$$P \vdash \langle E[(\mathbf{proxy}\ h\ t).\mathbf{read}(f, my)], \mathcal{H} \rangle$$
$$\hookrightarrow \langle E[h.\mathbf{readTrap}(t, f, my)], \mathcal{H} \rangle \qquad [\textit{reflect-get-proxy}]$$

$$P \vdash \langle E[a.\mathbf{write}(f, o, my)], \mathcal{H} \rangle$$
$$\hookrightarrow \langle E[o], \mathcal{H}[a \mapsto \langle c, \mathcal{F}[f \mapsto o] \rangle] \rangle \qquad [\textit{reflect-set}]$$
where $\mathcal{H}(a) = \langle c, \mathcal{F} \rangle$

$$P \vdash \langle E[(\mathbf{proxy}\ h\ t).\mathbf{write}(f, o, my)], \mathcal{H} \rangle$$
$$\hookrightarrow \langle E[h.\mathbf{writeTrap}(t, f, o, my)], \mathcal{H} \rangle \qquad [\textit{reflect-set-proxy}]$$

$$P \vdash \langle E[\mathbf{unproxy}\ (\mathbf{proxy}\ h\ t)], \mathcal{H} \rangle$$
$$\hookrightarrow \langle E[t], \mathcal{H} \rangle \qquad [\textit{unproxy}]$$

$$P \vdash \langle E[\mathbf{unproxy}\ a], \mathcal{H} \rangle$$
$$\hookrightarrow \langle E[a], \mathcal{H} \rangle \qquad [\textit{unproxy-object}]$$

Fig. 9. Reflective facilities added to SMALLTALKPROXY

All three primitives take a final argument my (shortcut for "myself") representing the object context that will be rebound. When applied to a proxy, the operations invoke the corresponding trap in a straightforward manner, passing my as is. When **read** or **write** are applied to an object address, the argument my is ignored. When **send** is applied to an object address, my defines how **self** will be rebound during the reflective invocation.

With these primitives, we can trivially define the identity handler idHandler that defines the following methods:

```
class idHandler extends Object {
    newTrap(t, my){ t }
    readTrap(t, f, my){ t.read(f, my) }
    writeTrap(t, f, o, my){ t.write(f, o, my) }
    messageTrap(t, m, o*, my){ t.send(m, o*, my) }}
```

6.2 Proof of Compositionality

Here we prove that proxy composition works as expected. That is, when the first proxy in a chain of proxies intercepts a message send, the message traps of the corresponding handlers are evaluated in order (given that these traps delegate the message to the corresponding targets). In addition, the operations applied during the execution of the matching method are also intercepted and consequently, the corresponding traps are also evaluated in order.

Theorem 1. *Let $p_1, p_2, \ldots, p_n$ be a proxy chain (i.e., $p_n = \textbf{proxy } h_n\, t$ and $\forall i \in [1, n[\,.\, p_i = \textbf{proxy } h_i\, p_{i+1})$ such that each handler h_i unconditionally delegates the intercepted operations on their respective target. Then, the behavioral variations implemented by each h_i compose, i.e., (1) a message m intercepted by p_1 triggers the message trap of each handler h_i in order for $i \in [1, n]$ and (2) each consequent operations performed in the method that t associates with the message m, will be intercepted and will trigger the corresponding trap of each handler h_i in order for $i \in [1, n]$.*

Proof:

Lemma 1. *For all $i \in [1, n[$, invoking the message trap of a handler h_i with p bound to the my parameter triggers the message trap of each subsequent handler h_j in order for $j \in]i, n]$ with p still bound to the my parameter.*

Proof of Lemma 1 by reverse induction:
Basis: The proposition holds for $n - 1$.

$$\langle h_{n-1}.\textbf{messageTrap}(p_n, m, o^*, p), \mathcal{H}\rangle$$
$$\hookrightarrow^* \langle E[p_n.\textbf{send}(m, o^*, p)], \mathcal{H}\rangle \qquad \text{by hypothesis}$$
$$\hookrightarrow \langle E[h_n.\textbf{messageTrap}(t, m, o^*, p)], \mathcal{H}\rangle \quad \text{by } [message\text{-}proxy]$$

Inductive step: If the proposition holds for $i + 1 > 1$ then it holds for i.

$$\langle h_i.\textbf{messageTrap}(p_{i+1}, m, o^*, p), \mathcal{H}\rangle$$
$$\hookrightarrow^* \langle E[p_{i+1}.\textbf{send}(m, o^*, p)], \mathcal{H}\rangle \qquad \text{by hypothesis}$$
$$\hookrightarrow \langle E[h_{i+1}.\textbf{messageTrap}(target_{i+1}, m, o^*, p)], \mathcal{H}\rangle \qquad \text{by } [message\text{-}proxy]$$
$$\text{where } target_{i+1} = t \text{ when } i = n - 1 \text{ and } p_{i+2} \text{ otherwise}$$

Hence the proposition holds for all $i \in [1, n[$.   □

We know from the reduction rule [*message-proxy*] that a message sent to a proxy triggers the message trap of that proxy's handler, that is $\langle E[p_1.m(o^*)], \mathcal{H}\rangle$ reduces to $\langle E[h_1.\textbf{messageTrap}(p_2, m, o^*, p_1)], \mathcal{H}\rangle$. Together with Lemma 1, we know that the proposition *(1)* of Theorem 1 holds.

Now, we need to prove the proposition *(2)* also holds in these conditions. First we know by hypothesis that $\langle E[h_n.\textbf{messageTrap}(t, m, o^*, p_1)], \mathcal{H}\rangle$ will eventually reduce to $\langle E[t.\textbf{send}(m, o^*, p_1)], \mathcal{H}\rangle$. Then, we know from the reduction rule [*reflect-message*] that this reduces to $\langle E[p_1 [\![meth[o^*/x^*]]\!]_{c'}, \mathcal{H}\rangle$ where $\mathcal{H}[t] = \langle c, \mathcal{F}\rangle$ and $\langle c, m, x^*, meth\rangle \in_P^* c'$. In other words, the code *meth* of the method that t associates with the message m is executed with p_1 as receiver.

This method can perform different operations: self or super sends, writes, reads. In case of self-sends, similarly to the proposition (1) we know from Lemma 1 and from the reduction rule [*message-proxy*] that the proposition (2) holds.

Lets now consider the case of writes.

Lemma 2. *For all $i \in [1, n[$, invoking the write trap of a handler h_i with p_1 bound to the my parameter triggers the write trap of each subsequent handler h_j in order for $j \in]i, n]$ with p_1 still bound to the my parameter.*

The proof of Lemma 2 is similar to that of Lemma 1. From [*set-proxy*] we see that $\langle E[f\langle p_1 \rangle = o], \mathcal{H} \rangle$ gives $\langle E[h_1.\mathbf{writeTrap}(p_2, f, o, p_1)], \mathcal{H} \rangle$. Together with Lemma 2 and the fact that p_1 is the receiver during the evaluation of *meth*, we know that proposition *(2)* holds for writes. The situation is similar for reads, super-send and instantiation. We omit these cases for the sake of conciseness as the proof can easily be expended to take them into account. Hence the proposition *(2)* holds and so does the Theorem 1.   □

6.3 Propagating Identity Proxy

Following the technique of propagation presented in Sect. 3, we propose a propagating identity handler, PropHandler. This handler defines the behavior of the root proxy and uses another handler PropHandler* to create the other proxies during the propagation. This technique requires the ability to unwrap a proxy. The expression **unproxy** is added to the language as defined in Fig. 9. We also assume the existence of the traditional sequencing operation $(;)$. We allow ourselves to use a notation for the multiple arguments of **messageTrap** that deviates from the given syntax and semantics.

The handler PropHandler is defined as follows:

```
class PropHandler extends Object {
    newTrap(t, my){ proxy PropHandler* t }
    readTrap(t, f, my){ t.read(f, my) }
    writeTrap(t, f, o, my){ t.write(f, o, my) }
    messageTrap(t, m, (o₁, ..., oₙ), my){
        unproxy(t.send(m,
            (proxy PropHandler* o₁, ..., proxy PropHandler* oₙ), my)) }}
```

The handler PropHandler* is defined as follows:

```
class PropHandler* extends PropHandler {
    messageTrap(t, m, (o₁, ..., oₙ), my){ t.send(m, (o₁, ..., oₙ), my) }}
```

6.4 Proof of Soundness of Propagation

We can formally express the intuitive explanation of Sect. 3 about soundness of the propagation.

Theorem 2. *Lets t, o_1, ..., o_n be objects. Then, during the evaluation of the expression $Expr := (\mathbf{proxy}\ \mathsf{PropHandler}\ t).m(o_1, \ldots, o_n)$ everything reduces to a proxy or to nil except Expr itself.*

Proof:

Let $pr = \mathbf{proxy}\ \mathsf{PropHandler}\ t$. We begin by reducing the expression $pr.m(o^*)$ in the context of a program P where $o^* = (o_1, \ldots, o_n)$.

$$\langle pr.m(o_1, \ldots, o_n), \mathcal{H} \rangle$$
$\hookrightarrow\ \langle \mathsf{PropHandler}.\mathbf{messageTrap}(t, m, (o_1, \ldots, o_n), p), \mathcal{H} \rangle \quad$ by $[message\text{-}proxy]$
$\hookrightarrow^*\ \langle \mathbf{unproxy}(t.\mathbf{send}(m, po^*, p)), \mathcal{H} \rangle$
  where $po^* = ((\mathbf{proxy}\ \mathsf{PropHandler}^* o_1), \ldots, (\mathbf{proxy}\ \mathsf{PropHandler}^* o_n))$
  by definition
$\hookrightarrow\ \langle \mathbf{unproxy}(pr\ [\![e[po^*/x^*]]\!]_{c'}, \mathcal{H} \rangle$
  where $\mathcal{H}[t] = \langle c, \mathcal{F} \rangle$ and $\langle c', m, x^*, e \rangle \in_P^* c$ by $[reflect\text{-}message]$

Now we prove by structural induction on e that during the evaluation of $\langle pr\ [\![e[po^*/x^*]]\!]_{c'}, \mathcal{H} \rangle$ everything reduces to a proxy or to nil. Then, the remaining **unproxy** operation ensures that the value of the initial expression is unwrapped and thus that Theorem 2 holds.

We call *(H)* the inductive hypothesis: *during the evaluation of e everything reduces to a proxy or to nil.*

Case $e := x$: Here x can refer to an argument or to a local variable (see $[let]$). In the first case we have $\langle pr\ [\![x[po^*/x^*]]\!]_{c'}, \mathcal{H} \rangle = \langle p_{o_i}, \mathcal{H} \rangle$ where i is the index of the argument in question. In the second case we know by *(H)* that it reduce to a proxy or nil.

Case $e := \mathbf{self}$: $\langle pr\ [\![\mathbf{self}[po^*/x^*]]\!]_{c'}, \mathcal{H} \rangle = \langle pr, \mathcal{H} \rangle$

Case $e := \mathsf{nil}$: $\langle pr\ [\![\mathsf{nil}[po^*/x^*]]\!]_{c'}, \mathcal{H} \rangle = \langle \mathsf{nil}, \mathcal{H} \rangle$

Case $e := \mathbf{new}\ c$:

$$\langle pr\ [\![\mathbf{new}\ c[po^*/x^*]]\!]_{c'}, \mathcal{H} \rangle = \langle \mathbf{new}\langle pr \rangle\ c, \mathcal{H} \rangle$$
$\hookrightarrow\ \langle \mathsf{PropHandler}.\mathbf{newTrap}(\mathbf{new}\langle t \rangle c, pr), \mathcal{H} \rangle \quad$ by $[new\text{-}proxy]$
$\hookrightarrow\ \langle \mathsf{PropHandler}.\mathbf{newTrap}(a, pr), \mathcal{H}' \rangle$
  where $\mathcal{H}' = \mathcal{H}[a \mapsto \langle c, \{f \mapsto \mathsf{nil} \mid \forall f, f \in_P^* c\} \rangle]$ by $[new]$
$\hookrightarrow^*\ \langle \mathbf{proxy}\ \mathsf{PropHandler}^*\ a, \mathcal{H}'] \rangle$ by definition

Case $e := f$:

$$\langle pr\ [\![f[po^*/x^*]]\!]_{c'}, \mathcal{H} \rangle = \langle f\langle pr \rangle, \mathcal{H} \rangle$$
$\hookrightarrow\ \langle \mathsf{PropHandler}.\mathbf{readTrap}(t, f, pr), \mathcal{H} \rangle \quad$ by $[get\text{-}proxy]$
$\hookrightarrow^*\ \langle \mathbf{proxy}\ \mathsf{PropHandler}^*\ (t.\mathbf{read}(f, p)), \mathcal{H} \rangle$ by definition
$\hookrightarrow\ \langle \mathbf{proxy}\ \mathsf{PropHandler}^*\ o, \mathcal{H} \rangle$ by $[reflect\text{-}get]$

Case $e := f = e'$:

We know by inductive hypothesis that e' reduces to a value which is a proxy or nil. Let v be that value.

$$\langle pr \, [\![f = e'[po^*/x^*]]\!]_{c'} , \mathcal{H} \rangle = \langle f \langle pr \rangle = e', \mathcal{H} \rangle$$
$\hookrightarrow^* \langle f \langle pr \rangle = v, \mathcal{H}' \rangle$ by *(H)*
$\hookrightarrow \langle \mathsf{PropHandler.writeTrap}(t, f, v, p), \mathcal{H}' \rangle$ by *[set-proxy]*
$\hookrightarrow^* \langle t.\mathbf{write}(f, \mathbf{unproxy} \; v, p); v, \mathcal{H}' \rangle$ by definition
$\hookrightarrow \langle t.\mathbf{write}(f, v', p); v, \mathcal{H}' \rangle$ by *[unproxy(-object)]*
     where $v' = t'$ if $v = \mathbf{proxy} \; h \; t'$ or nil if $v = $ nil
$\hookrightarrow \langle v'; p', \mathcal{H}'' \rangle$
     where $\mathcal{H}'' = \mathcal{H}'[t \mapsto \langle c, \mathcal{F}[f \mapsto o] \rangle]$
     and $\mathcal{H}'(t) = \langle c, \mathcal{F} \rangle$ by *[reflect-set]*
$= \langle v, \mathcal{H}'' \rangle$

Case $e := e'.m(e_1'', \dots, e_n'')$:
We know by *(H)* that e', e_1'', ..., e_n'' all reduce to a proxy or nil. We need to prove that *(H)* holds in case e' is a proxy p whose handler is a $\mathsf{PropHandler}^*$. Since only **messageTrap** differs from PropHandler in PropHandler*, we thus just need to prove that the expression $p.m(p_1, \dots, p_n)$ reduces to a proxy or nil when each p_i are already proxies or nil.

$\langle p.m(p_1, \dots, p_n), \mathcal{H} \rangle$
$\hookrightarrow \langle \mathsf{PropHandler}^*.\mathbf{messageTrap}(t', m, (p_1, \dots, p_n), p), \mathcal{H} \rangle$ by *[message-proxy]*
$\hookrightarrow \langle t'.\mathbf{send}(m, (p_1, \dots, p_n), p), \mathcal{H} \rangle$ by definition
$\hookrightarrow \langle p \, [\![meth[(p_1, \dots, p_n)/x^*]]\!]_{c_m} , \mathcal{H} \rangle$
     where $\mathcal{H}[t'] = \langle c_{t'}, \mathcal{F} \rangle$ and $\langle c_m, m, x^*, meth \rangle \in_P^* c_m$ by *[reflect-message]*

That last expression is known to reduce to a proxy or nil by *(H)*.
Case $e := \mathbf{super}.m(e_1', \dots, e_n')$: Similar to the previous case.
Case $e := \mathbf{let} \; x = e' \; \mathbf{in} \; e''$: We know by *(H)* that e' reduces to a proxy or nil. In case x is referred in e'', it will be replaced by e' (see case $e := x$).
Case $e := \mathbf{proxy} \; e' \; e''$: This case already satisfies the proposition. $\square$

7 Implementation

We have implemented a prototype of delegation proxies[7] in Pharo[8], a Smalltalk dialect. This implementation generates code using the compiler infrastructure of Pharo. For each existing method in a base class, a hidden method with an additional parameter `myself` and a transformed body is generated and installed in a *proxy class*. Instead of `self`, `myself` is used in the generated method body (this is similar to Python's explicit `self` argument). Following the same approach as Uniform Proxies for Java [Eug06], proxy classes are auto-generated.

7.1 Example

Let us consider the class `Suitcase`:

---

[7] http://scg.unibe.ch/research/DelegationProxies.
[8] http://pharo.org/.

```
Object>>subclass: #Suitcase
  instanceVariableNames: 'content'
```

```
Suitcase>>printString
  ↑ 'Content:' concat: content
```

Listing 14. Original code of class `Suitcase`

Applying our transformation, the class `Suitcase` is augmented with synthetic methods to read and write the field `content` and to resolve literals.

```
Suitcase>>literal: aLiteral myself: myself
  ↑ aLiteral
```

```
Suitcase>>readContentMyself: myself
  ↑ content
```

```
Suitcase>>writeContent: value myself: myself
  ↑ content := value
```

Listing 15. Synthetic methods to read and write instance variable `content` and literal resolution

In Smalltalk, fields are encapsulated and can be accessed only by their respective object. The sender of a state access is always `myself`, and can thus be omitted from the traps. For each existing method in class `Suitcase`, a hidden method with a transformed body and one additional parameter `myself` is generated.

```
Suitcase>>printStringMyself: myself
  ↑ (myself literal:'Content:' myself: myself)
    concat: (self readContentMyself: myself)
```

Listing 16. A transformed version of method `printString`

A proxy class for `Suitcase` is then generated. It inherits from a class `Proxy`, which defines the `handler` field common to all proxies. The generated class implements the same methods as the `Suitcase` class, *i.e.*, , `printStringMyself:`, `readContentMyself:`, and `writeContent:myself:`. The methods invoke respectively *message*, *read* and *write* traps on the handler. In addition, a method `printString` forwards to `printStringMyself:` with `self` as argument.

```
SuitcaseProxy>>printString
  ↑ self printStringMyself: self
```

```
SuitcaseProxy>>printStringMyself: myself
  | msg |
  msg := Message selector: #printString arguments: {}.
  ↑ handler message: msg myself: myself target: target
```

Listing 17. Sample generated method in proxy class of `Suitcase`

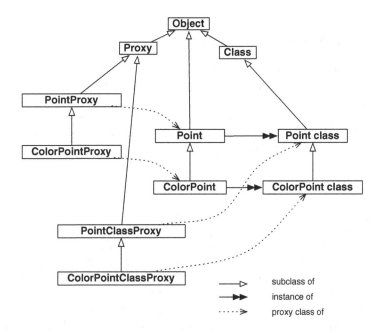

Fig. 10. Inheritance of classes, meta-classes, and auto-generated proxy classes.

Proxy class generation. Smalltalk has first-class classes whose behaviors are defined in meta-classes. The meta-class hierarchy parallels the class hierarchy. Classes can be proxied like any object. Consequently, meta-classes are rewritten and extended with synthetic methods similarly to classes. However, the generated proxy classes do not inherit from `Class`, but `Proxy`, as shown in Fig. 10.

Handling closures. Closures are regular objects that are adapted upon creation and evaluation as described in Subsect. 3.4. If a closure defined in an original uninstrumented method is wrapped with a proxy, the code of the closure is transformed lazily when the closure is evaluated.

Weaving. Sending a message to a proxy entails reification of the message, invocation of the handler's trap, and then reflective invocation of the message on the target. In addition, the handler might take additional actions that entail costs. The handler and the proxy can be woven into specialized classes for fewer levels of indirection. For instance, a `SuitcaseProxy` with a `Tracing` handler can be woven into a `SuitcaseTracingProxy`:

```
SuitcaseTracingProxy>>printStringMyself: myself
  | msg |
  msg := Message selector: #printString arguments: {}.
  Transcript
    print: target asString;
```

```
  space;
  print: msg asString;
  cr.
↑ target printStringMyself: myself
```

Listing 18. Sample woven method

We have implemented a simple weaver that works for basic cases. We plan to mature it in the future and leverage techniques for partial evaluation [Fut99] developed for aspect compilers [MKD03].

7.2 Performance

Delegation proxies have no impact on performance when they are not used: the transformation adds new code but does not alter existing code. Only the proxies pay a performance overhead. We need to distinguish between the performance of delegation proxies themselves and the performance of the propagation technique.

Used sparingly, delegation proxies do not entail serious performance issues because the cost of an interception is reasonably low. To measure the cost of a message interception, we use a proxy with an identity handler (*i.e.*, a handler that performs the intercepted operations reflectively) and send a message that dispatches to an empty method. The result is compared with sending the same message to the target object. The average performance degradation is 20.49 over 1 million iterations. With weaving, this number drops to 1.45 because there is less indirections and no reflective call is needed anymore (see the last line of Listing 18 for example).

However, with propagation, all the operations that happen in the dynamic extent of a message send are intercepted. Consequently, the cost of delegation proxies with propagation becomes prohibitive unless weaving is used. With weaving, computing the 20th Fibonacci number 10 thousands times reveals an average performance degradation of 8.72.

We believe these are encouraging results given that delegation proxies enable unanticipated behavioral reflection, which is known to be costly. Also the performance could be improved if delegation proxies were implemented directly by a runtime that supports delegation at its core [HS07].

8 Discussion

Myself parameter. To encode the fact that delegation proxies operate by delegation, we add an explicit parameter `myself` to all the available reflective operations. While this exposes the rebinding of self references for the sake of understandability, this extra parameter can be hidden from the users. The reifications of the operations can handle the delegation themselves. Otherwise, delegation can be implemented natively in which case delegation becomes mandatory. It is thus not absolutely required to modify the reflective API of a language to be able to implement delegation proxies.

Usability. From the developer's point of view, proxies operating by delegation or by forwarding are not very different. If the `myself` parameter is exposed, the developer has to take care to provide the right receiver. Similarly, if a handler sends additional messages in its traps, it may have to unwrap the receivers if they are proxies. Another consequence for a developer is that delegation proxies permit behavioral variations to be composed together dynamically by forming a chain of proxies.

Static Typing. There is no major obstacle to port our implementation to a statically-typed language. Delegation proxies preserve the interface of their target, like traditional forwarding proxies. For type compatibility, the generated proxy class must inherit from the original class. Reflective operations and traps can fail with run-time type errors. Forwarding and delegation proxies suffer from the same lack of type safety from this perspective.

If closures cannot be adapted at run time with the same flexibility as in Smalltalk, the implementation might require a global rewrite of the sources to adapt the code of the closures at compile-time.

Our implementation of delegation proxies requires that reflective operations have an additional parameter `myself` that specifies how to rebind `self`. Naturally, this parameter must be of a valid type: in practice it will be either the target of the invocation or a proxy of the target. Both implement the same interface.

9   Related Work

Proxy-based intercession. Many languages provide support for dynamic proxies. When a message is sent to a dynamic proxy, the message is intercepted and reified. Dynamic proxies have found many usefully applications that can be categorized as *interceptors* or *virtual objects* [VCM10]. An important question for proxies is whether to support them at the language level or natively at the runtime level. The performance gain brought by native support of proxies is appreciable for serious use in production but native implementations generally lack the flexibility needed for experimentation.

Most dynamic languages support proxies via traps that are invoked when a message cannot be delivered [MPBD+11]. Modern proxy mechanisms stratify the base and meta levels with a handler [MPBD+11,Eug06,VCM10,STHFF12]. These solutions are generally limited to message intercession. However, many interpretation operations — such access to instance variables and literal resolution — are not typically realized via message-sending. It is important to be able to intercept these operations to implement useful behavioral variations. The inability to intercept these operations make the implementation of dynamically-scoped behavioral variations difficult.

A notable exception is that of EcmaScript 6 direct proxies. EcmaScript direct proxies operate by delegation [VCM10] and can intercept additional operations. However, they do not enable the interception of object instantiations. Also, the variables captured in a closure cannot be intercepted upon reads and writes. This makes the form of propagation presented here is not easily implementable with EcmaScript 6 direct proxies as captured variables cannot easily be unwrapped upon capture and wrapped upon evaluation.

Pointcut-advice model. Proxy-based intercession differs from the traditional poincut-advice model of aspect oriented programming. In the pointcut-advice model, an aspect groups definition of pointcuts with corresponding advices, *i.e.*, a behavioral variation and its deployment. With proxy-based intercession, a handler specifies the actions taken upon interception of certain operations. This looks similar to the pointcut-advice model: the body of a trap is akin to an advice and the trap itself matches certain points of execution, just like a pointcut does. However, a trap does not specify which objects it will affect. A trap defines points of interception relatively to a proxy: only operations applied on a proxy are intercepted and trigger the actions defined by the corresponding traps. This allows developpers to deploy a behavioral variation on specific object references.

Composition Filters. In the *Composition Filters* model [AWB+94], objects filter and transform incoming and outgoing messages. This model could be used to implement dynamic scoping similar to the presented propagation technique. With composition filters, an object can rewrite outgoing messages to change their receiver to an object with that same behavior. Delegation could be implemented with a *dispatch* filter. However, as far as we are aware of, the composition filters model does not offer a mechanism to intercept instance variable accesses. Intercepting instance variables accesses is what permits delegation proxies to implement clean propagation (leaving the target objects unaffected by unwrapping proxies on writes). Adding this facility to the model would allow composition filters to realize the kind of dynamic scoping enabled by the propagation technique presented here.

Infinite regression. AOP and MOP inherently suffer from infinite regression issues unless the meta-levels are explicitly modeled [CKL96, DSD08, Tan10]. In contrast to AOP and MOPs, delegation proxies limit infinite regression issues since the adapted object and the base object are distinct. For instance, the tracing handler in Listing 4 does not lead to an infinite regression since it sends the message `asString` to the target, which is distinct from the proxy (in parameter `myself`). Handlers that send messages only to non-proxy objects do not lead to meta-regressions, but failure to do so can lead to meta-regressions, possibly infinite. Consequently, handlers may have to unwrap proxies before sending messages in traps. Also, delegation proxies naturally enable partial reflection [TNCC03] since objects are selectively wrapped and proxies can be selectively passed around to client code.

Composing Behavior. Inheritance leads to an explosion in the number of classes when multiple variations of a given set of classes must be designed. Static traits

[SDNB03] or mixins enable the definition of units of reuse that can be composed into classes, but they do not solve the issue of class explosion.

One solution to this problem is the use of decorators that refine a specific set of known methods, *e.g.*, the method `paint` of a window. Static and dynamic approaches have been proposed to decoration. Unlike decorators, proxies find their use when the refinement applies to unknown methods, *e.g.*, to trace all invocations. Büchi and Weck proposed a mechanism [BW00] to statically parameterize classes with a decorator (called wrapper in their terminology). Bettini *et al.* [BCG07] proposed a similar construct but composition happens at creation time. Ressia *et al.* proposed *talents* [RGN+12] which enable adaptations of the behavior of individual objects by composing trait-like units of behavior dynamically. Other works enable dynamic replacement of behavior in a trait-like fashion [BCD13].

The code snippet below illustrates how to achieve the decoration of a `Window` with a `Border` and shows the conceptual differences between these approaches. The two first approaches can work with forwarding or delegation (but no implementations with delegation are available). The third approach replaces the behavior or the object so the distinction does not apply.

```
Window w = new Window<Border>(); // Buchi and Weck
Window w = new BorderWrap( new Window() ); // Bettini
Window w = new WindowEmptyPaint(); // Ressia
w.acquire( new BorderedPaint() );
```

Listing 19. Differences between approaches to decoration

Several languages that combine class-based inheritance and object inheritance (*i.e.*, delegation) have been proposed [Kni99, VTB98]. Delegation enables the behavior of an object to be composed dynamically from other objects with partial behaviors. Essentially, delegation achieves trait-like dynamic composition of behavior.

Ostermann proposed delegation layers [Ost02], which extend the notion of delegation from objects to collaborations of nested objects, *e.g.*, a graph with edges and nodes. An outer object wrapped with a delegation layer will affects its nested objects as well. Similary to decorators, the mechanism refines specific sets of methods of the objects in the collaboration.

Dynamic Scoping. The dynamic extent of an expression corresponds to all operations that happen during the evaluation of the expression by a given thread of execution. Control-flow pointcuts are thus not sufficient to scope to dynamic extents, since they lack control over the thread scope. Control-flow pointcuts are popular and supported by mainstream AOP implementations, *e.g.*, AspectJ's `cflow` and `cflowbelow`. Aware of the limitations of control-flow pointcuts, some AOP implementations provide specific constructs to scope to the dynamic extent of a block of code, *e.g.*, CaesarJ's `deploy` [AGMO06]. Implemented naively, control-flow pointcuts are expensive since they entail a traversal of the stack at run time, but they can be implemented efficiently using partial evaluation [MKD03].

In context-oriented programming (COP) [HCN08,vLDN07], variations can be encapsulated into layers that are dynamically activated in the dynamic extent of an expression. Unlike the propagation technique presented in this paper that work better with *homogenous* variations, COP has a better support for *heterogenous* variations [ALS08]. COP can be seen as a form of multi-dimensional dispatch, where the context is an additional dimension.

Other mechanisms to vary the behavior of objects in a contextual manner are roles [Kri96], perspectives [SU96], and subjects [HO93]. Delegation proxies can realize dynamic scoping via reference flow, by wrapping and unwrapping objects accessed during an execution. Delegation proxies may provide a foundation to design contextual variations.

Similarly to our approach, Arnaud *et al.*'s *Handle* model [ADD+10, Arn13] enables the adaptation of references with behavioral variations that propagate. The propagation belongs to the semantics of the handles, whereas in our approach, the propagation is encoded reflectively in a specific handler. Our approach is more flexible since it decouples the notion of propagation from the notion of proxy but the handle approach is more efficient since it is implemented at the runtime level.

10   Conclusions

We can draw the following conclusions about the applicability of delegation proxies:

- *Expressiveness.* Delegation proxies subsume forwarding proxies and enable variations to be propagated to dynamic extents. This suits well non-functional concerns like monitoring (tracing, profiling), safety (read-only references), or reliability (rollback with object versioning). Since the propagation is written reflectively, it can be customized to achieve other forms of scopes.
- *Metaness.* Delegation proxies naturally compose, support partial behavioral reflection, and help developers avoid meta-regression. We can for instance trace and profile an execution by using tracing proxies and profiling proxies that form chains of delegation (composition). Objects are wrapped selectively. Adapting objects during an execution will not affect other objects in the system (partial reflection). Proxies and targets represent the same object at two different levels but have distinct identities (no meta-regression).
- *Encoding.* Delegation proxies can be implemented with code generation. In our Smalltalk implementation, only new code needs to be added; existing code remains unchanged. Delegation proxies have thus no overhead if not used. Delegation proxies do not entail performance issues when used sporadically (same situation as with classical dynamic proxies). The overhead of our propagation technique is of factor 8 when the code of handlers are woven into dedicated proxies classes. For optimal performance, the language could provide native support of delegation proxies.

Acknowledgments. We thank Jorge Ressia, Mircea Lungu, Niko Schwarz and Jan Kurš for support and feedback about ideas in the paper. We gratefully acknowledge the financial support of the Swiss National Science Foundation for the project "Agile Software Assessment" (SNSF project Np. 200020-144126/1, Jan 1, 2013 - Dec. 30, 2015) and of the French General Directorate for Armament (DGA).

References

[ADD+10] Arnaud, J.-B., Denker, M., Ducasse, S., Pollet, D., Bergel, A., Suen, M.: Read-only execution for dynamic languages. In: Vitek, J. (ed.) TOOLS 2010. LNCS, vol. 6141, pp. 117–136. Springer, Heidelberg (2010)

[AGMO06] Aracic, I., Gasiunas, V., Mezini, M., Ostermann, K.: An overview of CaesarJ. In: Rashid, A., Akşit, M. (eds.) Transactions on Aspect-Oriented Software Development I. LNCS, vol. 3880, pp. 135–173. Springer, Heidelberg (2006)

[ALS08] Apel, S., Leich, T., Saake, G.: Aspectual feature modules. IEEE Trans. Software Eng. **34**(2), 162–180 (2008)

[Arn13] Arnaud, J.-B.: Towards First Class References as a Security Infrastructure in Dynamically-Typed Languages. Ph.D. thesis, Université de Lille (2013)

[AWB+94] Aksit, M., Wakita, K., Bosch, J., Bergmans, L., Yonezawa, A.: Abstracting object interactions using composition filter. In: Guerraoui, R., Nierstrasz, O., Riveill, M. (eds.) Object-Based Distributed Programming. LNCS, vol. 791, pp. 152–184. Springer, Heidelberg (1994)

[BCD13] Bettini, L., Capecchi, S., Damiani, F.: On flexible dynamic trait replacement for Java-like languages. Sci. Comput. Program. **78**(7), 907–932 (2013)

[BCG07] Bettini, L., Capecchi, S., Giachino, E.: Featherweight wrap Java. In: Proceedings of the ACM symposium on Applied computing (2007)

[BDNW08] Bergel, A., Ducasse, S., Nierstrasz, O., Wuyts, R.: Stateful traits and their formalization. J. Comput. Lang. Syst. Struct. **34**(2–3), 83–108 (2008)

[BU04] Bracha, G., Ungar, D.: Mirrors: design principles for meta-level facilities of object-oriented programming languages. In: Proceedings of the International Conference on Object-Oriented Programming, Systems, Languages, and Applications (2004)

[BW00] Büchi, M., Weck, W.: Generic wrappers. In: Bertino, E. (ed.) ECOOP 2000 — Object-Oriented Programming. LNCS, vol. 1850, pp. 201–225. Springer, Heidelberg (2000)

[CKL96] Chiba, S., Kiczales, G., Lamping, J.: Avoiding confusion in metacircularity: The meta-helix. In: Futatsugi, K., Matsuoka, S. (eds.) Object Technologies for Advanced Software. LNCS, vol. 1049, pp. 157–172. Springer, Heidelberg (1996)

[Deu81] Deutsch, P.L.: Building control structures in the Smalltalk-80 system. BYTE Magazine Special Issue on Smalltalk **6**(8), 322–346 (1981)

[DSD08] Denker, M., Suen, M., Ducasse, S.: The meta in meta-object architectures. In: Paige, R.F., Meyer, B. (eds.) TOOLS EUROPE 2008. LNBIP, vol. 11, pp. 218–237. Springer, Heidelberg (2008)

[Eug06] Eugster, P.: Uniform proxies for Java. In: Proceedings of Object-oriented programming systems, languages, and applications (2006)

[FKF98]   Flatt, M., Krishnamurthi, S., Felleisen, M.: Classes and mixins. In: Proceedings of Principles of Programming Languages (1998)

[Fut99]   Futamura, Y.: Partial evaluation of computation process–an approach to a compiler-compiler. Higher-Order and Symbolic Comput. **12**(4), 381–391 (1999)

[HCN08]   Hirschfeld, R., Costanza, P., Nierstrasz, O.: Context-oriented programming. J. Object Technol. **7**(3), 125–151 (2008)

[HO93]   Harrison, W., Ossher, H.: Subject-oriented programming (a critique of pure objects). In: Proceedings of Object-Oriented Programming, Systems, Languages, and Applications (1993)

[HS07]   Haupt, M., Schippers, H.: A machine model for aspect-oriented programming. In: Ernst, E. (ed.) ECOOP 2007. LNCS, vol. 4609, pp. 501–524. Springer, Heidelberg (2007)

[Kni99]   Kniesel, G.: Type-safe delegation for run-time component adaptation. In: Guerraoui, R. (ed.) ECOOP 1999. LNCS, vol. 1628, pp. 351–366. Springer, Heidelberg (1999)

[Kri96]   Kristensen, B.B.: Object-oriented modeling with roles. Springer, London (1996)

[Lie86]   Lieberman, H.: Using prototypical objects to implement shared behavior in object oriented systems. In: Proceedings of Object-Oriented Programming, Systems, Languages, and Applications (1986)

[MKD03]   Masuhara, H., Kiczales, G., Dutchyn, C.: A compilation and optimization model for aspect-oriented programs. In: Hedin, G. (ed.) CC 2003. LNCS, vol. 2662, pp. 46–60. Springer, Heidelberg (2003)

[MPBD+11]   Peck, M.M., Bouraqadi, N., Denker, M., Ducasse, S., Fabresse, L.: Efficient proxies in smalltalk. In: Proceedings of ESUG International Workshop on Smalltalk Technologies (2011)

[Ost02]   Ostermann, K.: Dynamically composable collaborations with delegation layers. In: Proceedings of European Conference on Object-Oriented Programming (2002)

[Pas86]   Pascoe, G.A.: Encapsulators: a new software paradigm in smalltalk-80. In: Proceedings of Object-Oriented Programming, Systems, Languages, and Applications (1986)

[PLW09]   Pluquet, F., Langerman, S., Wuyts, R.: Executing code in the past: efficient in-memory object graph versioning. In: Proceedings of Object-Oriented Programming, Systems, Languages, and Applications (2009)

[RGN+12]   Ressia, J., Gîrba, T., Nierstrasz, O., Perin, F., Renggli, L.: Talents: an environment for dynamically composing units of reuse. Softw. Pract. Experience **44**(4), 413–432 (2014)

[SDNB03]   Schärli, N., Ducasse, S., Nierstrasz, O., Black, A.P.: Traits: composable units of behaviour. In: Cardelli, L. (ed.) ECOOP 2003. LNCS, vol. 2743, pp. 248–274. Springer, Heidelberg (2003)

[STHFF12]   Stephen Strickland, T., Tobin-Hochstadt, Sam., Findler, R.B., Flatt, M.: Chaperones and impersonators: run-time support for reasonable interposition. In: Proceedings of Object-Oriented Programming, Systems, Languages, and Applications (2012)

[SU96]   Smith, R.B., Ungar, D.: A simple and unifying approach to subjective objects. Theory and Practice of Object Systems (TAPOS) **2**, 161–178 (1996). Special issue on Subjectivity in Object-Oriented Systems

[Tan08]   Tanter, É.: Expressive scoping of dynamically-deployed aspects. In: Proceedings of Aspect-Oriented Software Development (2008)

[Tan10] Tanter, É.: Execution levels for aspect-oriented programming. In: Proceedings of Aspect-Oriented Software Development (2010)

[TCD13] Teruel, C., Cassou, D., Ducasse, S.: Object Graph Isolation with Proxies. In: Workshop on Dynamic Languages and Applications - European Conference on Object-Oriented Programming (2013)

[TFD+09] Tanter, É., Fabry, J., Douence, R., Noyé, J., Südholt, M.: Expressive scoping of distributed aspects. In: Proceedings Aspect-Oriented Software Development (2009)

[TNCC03] Tanter, É., Noyé, J., Caromel, D., Cointe, P.: Partial behavioral reflection: Spatial and temporal selection of reification. Languages, and Applications. In: Proceedings of Object-Oriented Programming, Systems (2003)

[VCM10] Van Cutsem, T., Miller, M.S.: Proxies: design principles for robust object-oriented intercession APIs. In: DLS '10 Proceedings of the 6th symposium on Dynamic languages (2010)

[VCM13] Van Cutsem, T., Miller, M.S.: Trustworthy proxies. In: Castagna, G. (ed.) ECOOP 2013. LNCS, vol. 7920, pp. 154–178. Springer, Heidelberg (2013)

[vLDN07] von Löwis, M., Denker, M., Nierstrasz, O.: Context-oriented programming: Beyond layers. In: Proceedings of International Conference on Dynamic Languages (2007)

[VTB98] Viega, J., Tutt, B., Behrends, R.: Automated elegation is a viable alternative to multiple inheritance in class based languages. University of Virginia, Charlottesville (1998)

Co-change Clusters: Extraction and Application on Assessing Software Modularity

Luciana Lourdes Silva[1,3]([✉]), Marco Tulio Valente[1],
and Marcelo de A. Maia[2]

[1] Department of Computer Science, Federal University of Minas Gerais,
Belo Horizonte, Brazil
{luciana.lourdes,mtov}@dcc.ufmg.br
[2] Faculty of Computing, Federal University of Uberlândia, Uberlândia, Brazil
marcmaia@facom.ufu.br
[3] Federal Institute of the Triângulo Mineiro, Uberaba, Brazil

Abstract. The traditional modular structure defined by the package hierarchy suffers from the dominant decomposition problem and it is widely accepted that alternative forms of modularization are necessary to increase developer's productivity. In this paper, we propose an alternative form to understand and assess package modularity based on co-change clusters, which are highly inter-related classes considering co-change relations. We evaluate how co-change clusters relate to the package decomposition of four real-world systems. The results show that the projection of co-change clusters to packages follows different patterns in each system. Therefore, we claim that modular views based on co-change clusters can improve developers' understanding on how well-modularized are their systems, considering that modularity is the ability to confine changes and evolve components in parallel.

Keywords: Modularity · Software changes · Version control systems · Co-change graphs · Co-change clusters · Agglomerative hierarchical clustering algorithm

1 Introduction

Modularity is the key concept to embrace when designing complex software systems [3]. The central idea is that modules should hide important design decisions or decisions that are likely to change [33]. In this way, modularity contributes to improve productivity during initial development and maintenance phases. Particularly, well-modularized systems are easier to maintain and evolve, because their modules can be understood and changed independently from each other.

For this reason, it is fundamental to consider modularity when assessing the internal quality of software systems [23,28]. Typically, the standard approach to assess modularity is based on coupling and cohesion, calculated using the structural dependencies established between the modules of a system (coupling) and

© Springer-Verlag Berlin Heidelberg 2015
S. Chiba et al. (Eds.): Transactions on AOSD XII, LNCS 8989, pp. 96–131, 2015.
DOI: 10.1007/978-3-662-46734-3_3

between the internal elements from each module (cohesion) [9,45]. However, typical cohesion and coupling metrics measure a single dimension of the software implementation (the static-structural dimension). For this reason, it is widely accepted that traditional modular structures and metrics suffer from the dominant decomposition problem and tend to hinder different facets that developers may be interested in [22,38,39]. Therefore, to improve current modularity views, it is important to investigate the impact of design decisions concerning modularity in other dimensions of a software system, as the evolutionary dimension.

Specifically, we propose a novel approach for assessing modularity, based on co-change graphs [5]. The approach is directly inspired by the common criteria used to decompose systems in modules, i.e., modules should confine implementation decisions that are likely to change together [33]. We first extract co-change graphs from the history of changes in software systems. In such graphs, the nodes are classes and the edges link classes that were modified together in the same commits. After that, co-change graphs are automatically processed to produce a new modular facet: co-change clusters, which abstract out common changes made to a system, as stored in version control platforms. Basically, co-change clusters are sets of classes that frequently changed together in the past.

Our approach relies on distribution maps [14]—a well-known visualization technique—to reason about the projection of the extracted clusters in the traditional decomposition of a system in packages. We then rely on a set of metrics defined for distribution maps to characterize the extracted co-change clusters. Particularly, we describe recurrent distribution patterns of co-change clusters, including patterns denoting well-modularized and crosscutting clusters. Moreover, we also evaluate the meaning of the obtained clusters using information retrieval techniques. The goal in this particular case is to understand how similar are the issues whose commits were clustered together. We used our approach to assess the modularity of four real-world systems (Geronimo, Lucene, Eclipse JDT Core, and Camel).

Our main contributions are threefold. First, we propose a methodology for extracting co-change graphs and co-change clusters, including several pre and post-processing filters to avoid noise in the generated clusters. This methodology relies on a graph clustering algorithm designed for sparse graphs, as is usually the case of co-change graphs. Second, we propose a methodology to contrast the co-change modularity with the standard package decomposition. This methodology includes metrics to detect both well-modularized and crosscutting co-change clusters. Third, we found that the generated clusters are not only dense in terms of co-changes, but they also have high similarity from the point of view of the meaning of the maintenance issues that originated the respective commits.

This paper is a revised and extended version of our work that appeared in [43]. The key additions in this new version are as follows. First, Sect. 2 describes several concepts needed to comprehend our methodology and analysis. Second, we improved Sect. 3 by adding examples and new information concerning the extraction of co-change clusters. Third, this paper contains new experimental results in Sects. 5 and 6, including the extraction of co-change clusters for a new system (Camel). Finally, we improved the discussion on using association rules to retrieve co-change relations in Sect. 7.2.

The paper is organized as follows. Section 2 presents background on clustering techniques and Latent Semantic Analysis. Section 3 presents the methodology to extract co-change graphs and co-change clusters from version control systems. Section 4 presents the results of co-change clustering, when applied to four systems. Section 5 analyzes the modularity of such systems under the light of co-change clusters. Section 6 analyzes the semantic similarity regarding the set of issues related to the extracted clusters. Section 7 discusses our results and presents threats to validity. Section 8 describes related work and finally Sect. 9 concludes the paper.

2   Background

This section provides background on clustering and information retrieval techniques. We use clustering techniques to retrieve clusters of software artifacts that changed together in the past, which are called co-change clusters. We also use linguistic preprocessing, Latent Semantic Analysis (LSA), and cosine similarity techniques to evaluate the meaning of issue reports related to software maintenance activities.

2.1   Clustering Techniques

Clustering techniques are broadly classified in partitioning and hierarchical. On one hand, a partitioning approach divides the set of data objects into K clusters such that each data object is in exactly one cluster. On the other hand, hierarchical clustering yields a tree of clusters, known as a dendrogram. It is further subdivided into agglomerative (bottom-up) and divisive (top-down). An agglomerative clustering starts with each data object being a single cluster and repeatedly merges two, or more, most appropriate clusters. A divisive clustering starts with a single cluster containing all data objects and repeatedly splits the most appropriate cluster. The process continues until a stop criterion is achieved, usually the requested number of K clusters.

2.2   Chameleon Clustering Algorithm

Chameleon [20] is an agglomerative hierarchical clustering algorithm designed to handle sparse graphs in which nodes represent data objects, and weighted edges represent similarities among these objects.

Input. Chameleon requires as input a matrix whose entries represent the similarity between data objects. A sparse graph representation is created following a k-nearest-neighbor graph algorithm. Each vertex represents a data object and there is an edge between two vertices u and v if v is among the k most similar points to u or vice-versa.

Constructing a Sparse Graph. In this step, data objects that are far away are disconnected in order to reduce noise. As Chameleon operates on a sparse graph, each cluster is a subgraph of the sparse graph. The sparse graph allows Chameleon to deal with large data sets and to successfully use data sets in similarity space.

First Phase (Partitioning the Graph): A min-cut graph partitioning algorithm is used to partition the k-nearest-neighbor graph into a pre-defined number of subclusters M. If the graph contains a single connected component, then the algorithm returns k subclusters. Otherwise, the number of subclusters after this phase is M plus C, where C is the number of connected components. Since each edge represents similarity among objects, a min-cut partitioning is able to minimize the connection among data objects through the partitions.

Second Phase (Merging Partitions): This phase uses an agglomerative hierarchical algorithm to merge the small clusters, created by the first phase, repeatedly. Clusters are combined to maximize the number of links within a cluster (internal similarity) and to minimize the number of links between clusters (external similarity). Chameleon models similarity based on the Relative Interconnectivity (RI) and Relative Closeness (RC) of the clusters. A pair of clusters C_i and C_j is selected to be merge when both RI and RC are high, suggesting that they are highly interconnected as well as close together. Chameleon's authors provide a software package, named Cluto[1], which supports different agglomerative merging schemes in this second phase. As our goal is to find co-change clusters in a sparse graph, we are interested in functions that do not cluster all data objects (in our case, classes). The artifacts discarded by Chameleon are considered noisy data because they do not share any edges with the rest of the artifacts.

2.3 Latent Semantic Analysis

The discussion on Latent Semantic Analysis (LSA) [13] is relevant to our approach, since we evaluate the semantic similarity of issue reports that are related to a specific cluster in order to improve our understanding of the clusters' meaning. LSA is a statistical approach for extracting and representing the meaning of words. The semantic information is retrieved from a word-document co-occurrence matrix, where words and documents are considered as points in an Euclidean space. LSA is based on the Vector Space Model (VSM), an algebraic representation of documents frequently used in information retrieval [41]. The vector space of a text collection is constructed by representing each document as a vector with the frequencies of its words. The document vectors add to a term-by-document matrix representing the full text collection. First, the vocabulary of terms is determined using feature selection techniques such as tokenization, stop words removal, domain vocabulary, case-folding, stemming, and weighting schemes (TF-IDF, binary weight) before representing the textual data in a

---

[1] http://glaros.dtc.umn.edu/gkhome/views/cluto.

numerical form. Moreover, LSA applies singular value decomposition (SVD) to the term-by-document matrix as a way of factor analysis. In SVD, a rectangular matrix is decomposed into the product of three other matrices — an orthogonal matrix U, a diagonal matrix Σ, and the transpose of an orthogonal matrix V. Suppose an original term-document matrix $C_{M \times N}$, where M is the number of terms and N is the number of documents. The matrix C is then decomposed via SVD into the term vector matrix U, the document vector matrix V, and the diagonal matrix Σ (consisting of eigenvalues) as follows:

$$C_{m \times n} = U_{m \times m} \Sigma_{m \times n} V_{n \times n}^T$$

where $U^T U = I$ and $V^T V = I$. The columns of U are the orthogonal eigenvectors of CC^T and I is the identity matrix. The columns of V are the orthogonal eigenvectors of $C^T C$, and Σ is a diagonal matrix containing the square roots of eigenvalues from U or V in descending order.

Text Pre-processing Tasks. When analyzing text documents, an adequate pre-processing step is crucial to achieve good results [27]. After collecting the documents to be analyzed, some steps are usually performed as follows:

Tokenization. The tokenization process is applied on the text chopping character streams into tokens, discarding special characters, such as punctuation and numbers. Furthermore, when dealing with software artifacts, CamelCase identifiers are also split into tokens.

Stop Words Removal. In this step, common words that are irrelevant when selecting documents matching an end-user needs are removed from the vocabulary. For example, words such as *a, an, and, was,* and *were.*

Case-Folding. It is a common strategy by reducing all letters to lower case.

Stemming. Due to grammatical reasons, documents usually contain different forms of a word, such as *run, runs,* and *running.* The goal of stemming is to reduce the possible inflectional forms of a word to a common base form.

Cosine Similarity. Since we consider the semantic similarity between two issue reports, i and j, cosine similarity measures the cosine of the angle between the vectors $\vec{v_i}$ and $\vec{v_j}$ corresponding to the issue reports d_i and d_j in the semantic space constructed by LSA:

$$sim(\vec{v_i}, \vec{v_j}) = \frac{\vec{v_i} \bullet \vec{v_j}}{|\vec{v_i}| \times |\vec{v_j}|}$$

where $\vec{v}$ is the vector norm and $\bullet$ is the vector internal product operator and $sim(\vec{v_i}, \vec{v_j}) \in [-1, 1]$.

3   Methodology

This section presents the methodology we followed for retrieving co-change graphs and then for extracting the co-change clusters.

3.1   Extracting Co-change Graphs

As proposed by Beyer et al. [5], a co-change graph is an abstraction for a version control system (VCS). Suppose a set of change transactions (commits) in a VCS, defined as $T = \{T_1, T_2, \ldots, T_n\}$, where each transaction T_i changes a set of classes. Conceptually, a co-change graph is an undirected graph $G = \{V, E\}$, where V is a set of classes and E is a set of edges. An edge (C_i, C_j) is defined between classes (vertices) C_i and C_j whenever there is a transaction T_k, such that $C_i, C_j \in T_k$, for $i \neq j$. Finally, each edge has a weight that represents the number of transactions changing the connected classes.

Our approach relies on two inputs: issue reports available in issue trackers, e.g., Jira, Bugzilla, and Tigris; and commit transactions retrieved from version control repositories (SVN or GIT). In a further step, several processing tasks are applied and then a co-change graph is build. Finally, sets of classes that frequently change together are retrieved, called co-change clusters.

Pre-processing Tasks. When extracting co-change graphs, it is fundamental to preprocess the considered commits to filter out commits that may pollute the graph with noise. We propose the following preprocessing tasks:

Removing commits not associated to maintenance issues: In early implementation stages, commits can denote partial implementations of programming tasks, since the system is under construction [29]. When such commits are performed multiple times, they generate noise in the edges' weights. For this reason, we consider just commits associated to maintenance issues. More specifically, we consider as maintenance issues those that are registered in an issue tracking system. Moreover, we only consider issues labeled as *bug correction, new feature*, or *improvement*. We followed the usual procedure to associate commits to maintenance issues: a commit is related to an issue when its textual description includes a substring that represents a valid Issue-ID in the system's bug tracking system [12, 44, 51].

Removing commits not changing classes: The co-changes considered by our approach are defined for classes. However, there are commits that only change artifacts like configuration files, documentation, script files, etc. Therefore, we discard such commits in order to only consider commits that change at least one class. Finally, we eliminate unit testing classes from commits because co-changes between functional classes and their respective testing classes are usually common and therefore may dominate the relations expressed in co-change graphs.

Merging commits related to the same maintenance issue: When there are multiple commits referring to the same Issue-ID, we merge all of them—including the

changed classes—in a single commit. Figure 1 presents an example for the Geronimo system.[2] The figure shows the short description of four commits related to
the issue GERONIMO-3003. In this case, a single change set is generated for the
four commits, including 13 classes. In the co-change graph, an edge is created
for each pair of classes in this merged change set. In this way, it is possible to
have edges connecting classes modified in different commits, but referring to the
same maintenance issue.

```
------------------------------------
Revision: 918360
Date: Wed Mar 03 05:07:00 BRT 2010
Short Description: GERONIMO-3003 create karaf command wrpaper
for encryptCommand
Changed Classes: [1 class]
------------------------------------
Revision: 798794
Date: Wed Jul 29 03:54:50 BRT 2009
Short Description: GERONIMO-3003 Encrypt poassoreds and morked
attributes in serialized gbeans and config.xml. Modified from
patch by [developer name], many thanks.
Changed Classes: [9 new classes]
------------------------------------
Revision: 799023
Date: Wed Jul 29 16:13:02 BRT 2009
Short Description: GERONIMO-3003 Encrypt poassoreds and morked
attributes in serialized gbeans and config.xml. Modified from
patch by [developer name], many thanks. 2nd half of patch.missed
adding one file and several geronimo-system changes earlier.
Changed Classes: [3 new classes]
------------------------------------
Revision: 799037
Date: Wed Jul 29 16:49:52 BRT 2009
Short Description: GERONIMO-3003 Use idea from [developer name]
to encrypt config.xml attributes that are encryptable but reset
to plaintext by users
Changed Classes: [1 class, also modified in revision 799023]
```

Fig. 1. Multiple commits for the issue GERONIMO-3003

Removing commits associated to multiple maintenance issues: We remove commits that report changes related to more than one maintenance issue, which are
usually called tangled code changes [17]. Basically, such commits are discarded
because otherwise they would result on edges connecting classes modified to
implement semantically unrelated maintenance tasks (which are included in the
same commit just by convenience, for example). Figure 2 presents a tangled code
change for the Geronimo system.

Removing highly scattered commits: We remove commits representing highly
scattered code changes, i.e., commits that modify a massive number of classes.
Typically, such commits are associated to refactorings (like rename method) and
other software quality improving tasks (like dead code removal), implementation
of new features, or minor syntactical fixes (like changes to comment styles) [50].

---

[2] Geronimo is an application server, http://geronimo.apache.org.

```
Revision: 565397
Date: Mon Aug 13 13:21:44 BRT 2007
Short Description: GERONIMO-3254 Admin Console Wizard to auto
generate geronimo-web.xml and dependencies GERONIMO-3394,
GERONIMO-3395, GERONIMO-3396, GERONIMO-3397,
GERONIMO-3398
- First commit of "Create Plan" portlet code. ....
Changed Classes: [25 classes]
```

Fig. 2. Single commit handling multiple issues (3254, 3394 to 3398)

Figure 3 illustrates a highly scattered commit in Lucene. This commit changes 251 classes, located in 80 packages. Basically, in this commit redundant throws clauses are refactored.

```
Revision: 1355069
Date: Thu Jun 28 13:39:25 BRT 2012
Short Description: LUCENE-4172: clean up redundant throws clauses
Changed Classes: [251 classes]
```

Fig. 3. Highly scattered commit (251 changed classes)

Recent research shows that scattering in commits tends to follow heavy-tailed distributions [50]. Therefore, the existence of massively scattering commits cannot be neglected. Particularly, such commits may have a major impact when considered in co-change graphs, due to the very large deviation between the number of classes changed by them and by the remaining commits in the system. Figure 4 illustrates this fact by showing a histogram with the number of packages changed by commits made to the Lucene system.[3] As we can observe, 1,310 commits (62 %) change classes in a single package. Despite this fact, the mean value of this distribution is 51.2, due to the existence of commits changing for example, more than 10 packages.

Considering that our goal is to model recurrent maintenance tasks and considering that highly scattered commits typically do not present this characteristic, we decided to remove them during the co-change graph creation. For this purpose, we define that a package pkg is changed by a commit cmt if at least one of the classes modified by cmt are located in pkg. Using this definition, we ignore commits that change more than $MAX\_SCATTERING$ packages. In Sect. 4, we define and explain the values for thresholds in our method.

Post-processing Task. In co-change graphs, the edges' weights represent the number of commits changing the connected classes. However, co-change graphs typically have many edges with small weights, i.e., edges representing co-changes that occurred very few times. Such co-changes are not relevant considering that our goal is to model recurrent maintenance tasks. For this reason, there is a post-processing phase after extracting a first co-change graph. In this phase, edges with weights less than a MIN_WEIGHT threshold are removed. In fact,

---

[3] An information retrieval library, http://lucene.apache.org.

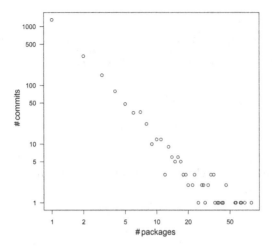

Fig. 4. Packages changed by commits in the Lucene system

this threshold is analogous to the *support* threshold used by co-change mining approaches based on association rules [52].

3.2 Extracting Co-change Clusters

After extracting the co-change graph, our goal is to retrieve sets of classes that frequently change together, which we call co-change clusters. We propose to extract co-change clusters automatically, using a graph clustering algorithm designed to handle sparse graphs, as is typically the case of co-change graphs [5]. More specifically, we decided to use the Chameleon clustering algorithm, which is an agglomerative and hierarchical clustering algorithm recommended to sparse graphs.

As reported in Sect. 2.2, there are several clustering criterion functions that can be applied in the agglomerative phase available in Cluto package. We conducted pre-experiments with those functions to find which one produces clusters with higher internal similarity, lower external similarity and higher density. The function i2 (Cohesion based on graphs) is the one that best fitted to our goal. We observed that other functions retrieved several clusters with low density. The i2 function searches for subclusters to combine, maximizing the similarity by evaluating how close are the objects in a cluster, as follows:

$$maximize \sum_{i=1}^{k} \sqrt{\sum_{v,u \in S_i} sim(v,u)}$$

Defining the Number of Clusters. A critical decision when applying Chameleon—and many other clustering algorithms—is to define the number of partitions M that should be created in the first phase of the algorithm. To define the "best value" for M we execute Chameleon multiple times, with different values of M, starting with a *M_INITIAL* value. Furthermore, in the subsequent executions, the previous tested value is decremented by a *M_DECREMENT* constant.

After each execution, we discard small clusters, as defined by a *MIN_CLUSTER_SZ* threshold. Considering that our goal is to extract groups of classes that may be used as alternative modular views, it is not reasonable to consider clusters with only two or three classes. If we accept such small clusters, we may eventually generate a decomposition of the system with hundreds of clusters.

For each execution, the algorithm provides two important statistics to evaluate the quality of each cluster:

- *ESim* - The average similarity of the classes of each cluster and the remaining classes (average *external similarity*). This value must tend to zero because minimizing inter-cluster connections is important to support modular reasoning.
- *ISim* - The average similarity between the classes of each cluster (average *internal similarity*).

After pruning small clusters, the following clustering quality function is applied to the remaining clusters:

$$coefficient(M) = \frac{1}{k} * \sum_{i=1}^{k} \frac{ISim_{C_i} - ESim_{C_i}}{max(ISim_{C_i}, ESim_{C_i})}$$

where k is the number of clusters after pruning the small ones.

The proposed *coefficient(M)* combines the concepts of cluster cohesion (tight co-change clusters) and cluster separation (highly separated co-change clusters). The *coefficients* ranges from $[-1; 1]$, where -1 indicates a very poor round and 1 an excellent round. The selected M value is the one with the highest *coefficient(M)*. If the highest *coefficient(M)* is the same for more than one value of M, then the highest *mean(ISim)* is used as a tiebreaker. Clearly, internal similarity is relevant because it represents how often the classes changed together in a cluster.

4 Co-change Clustering Results

In this section, we report the results we achieved after following the methodology described in Sect. 3 to extract co-change clusters for four systems.

4.1 Target Systems and Thresholds Selection

Table 1 describes the systems considered in our study, including information on their function, number of lines of code (LOC), number of packages (NOP), and number of classes (NOC). Table 2 shows the number of commits extracted for each system and the time frame used in this extraction.

In order to run the approach, we define the following thresholds:

Table 1. Target systems (size metrics)

System	Description	Release	LOC	NOP	NOC
Geronimo	Web application server	3.0	234,086	424	2,740
Lucene	Text search library	4.3	572,051	263	4,323
JDT Core	Eclipse Java infrastructure	3.7	249,471	74	1,829
Camel	Integration framework	2.13.1	964,938	828	11,395

Table 2. Initial commits sample

System	Commits	Period
Geronimo	9,829	08/20/2003 – 06/04/2013 (9.75 years)
Lucene	8,991	01/01/2003 – 07/06/2013 (10.5 years)
JDT Core	24,315	08/15/2002 – 08/21/2013 (10 years)
Camel	13,769	04/18/2007 – 06/14/2014 (7 years)

- $MAX\_SCATTERING = 10$ packages, i.e., we discard commits changing classes located in more than ten packages. We based on the hypothesis that large transactions typically correspond to noisy data, such as changes in comments formatting and rename method [1,52]. However, excessive pruning is also undesirable, so we adopted a conservative approach working at package level.
- $MIN\_WEIGHT = 2$ co-changes, i.e., we discard edges connecting classes with less than two co-changes because an unitary weight does not reflect how often two classes usually change together [5].
- $M\_INITIAL = NOC_G * 0.20$, i.e., the first phase of the clustering algorithm creates a number of partitions that is one-fifth of the number of classes in the co-change graph (NOC_G). The higher the M, the higher the final clusters' size because the second phase of the algorithm works by aggregating the partitions. In this case, the $ISim$ tends to be low because subgraphs that are not well connected are grouped in the same cluster. We performed several experiments varying $M's$ value, and observed that whenever M is high, the clustering tends to have clusters of unbalanced size.
- $M\_DECREMENT = 1$ class, i.e., after each clustering execution, we decrement the value of M by 1.
- $MIN\_CLUSTER\_SZ = 4$ classes, i.e., after each clustering execution, we remove clusters with less than 4 classes.

We defined the thresholds after some preliminary experiments with the target systems. We also based this selection on previous empirical studies reported in the literature. For example, Walker showed that only 5.93 % of the patches in the Mozilla system change more than 11 files [50]. Therefore, we claim that commits changing more than 10 packages are in the last quantiles of the heavy-tailed distributions that normally characterize the degree of scattering in commits. As another example, in the systems included in the Qualitas Corpus—a well-known dataset of Java programs—the packages on average have 12.24 classes [46,47]. In our four target systems, the packages have on average 15.87 classes. Therefore, we claim that clusters with less than four classes can be characterized as small clusters.

4.2 Co-change Graph Extraction

We start by characterizing the extracted co-change graphs. Table 3 shows the percentage of commits in our sample, after applying the preprocessing filters described in Sect. 3.1: removal of commits not associated to maintenance issues (Pre #1), removal of commits not changing classes and also referring to testing classes (Pre #2), merging commits associated to the same maintenance issue (Pre #3), removal of commits denoting tangled code changes (Pre #4), and removal of highly scattering commits (Pre #5).

Table 3. Percentage of unitary commits (i.e., changing a single class) discarded in the first phase and commits discarded after each preprocessing filters

System	Pre #1	Unitary Commits	Pre #2	Pre #3	Pre #4	Pre #5
Geronimo	32.6	39.6	25.2	17.3	16.1	14.3
Lucene	39.2	35.3	34.6	23.6	23.3	22.4
JDT Core	38.4	58.1	32.8	21.7	20.3	20.1
Camel	45.0	44.5	39.7	25.7	21.7	21.3

As can be observed in Table 3, our initial sample for the Geronimo, Lucene, JDT Core, and Camel systems was reduced to 14.3 %, 22.4 %, 20.1 % and 21.3 % of its original size, respectively. The most significant reduction was due to the first preprocessing task. Basically, only 32.6 %, 39.2 %, 38.4 %, and 45.0 % of the commits in Geronimo, Lucene, JDT Core, and Camel are associated to mainte-nance issues (as stored in the systems issue tracking platforms). Moreover, we analyzed the commits discarded in first preprocessing task. We observed a sub-stantial number of commits changing a single class, 39.6 % of Geronimo's, 35.3 % of Lucene's, 58.1 % of JDT's, and 44.5 % of Camel's commits. These unitary com-mits may contain configuration or/and script files, for instance. In addition, as some of these commits are not linked to issue reports, we cannot assume they represent a complete maintenance task. We also had not analyzed if these unitary commits are partial implementations of maintenance tasks. This could be done by inspecting their time frame, for instance. However, these unitary commits are not useful anyway to evaluate a system in terms of co-changes. There are also significant reductions after filtering out commits that do not change classes or that only change testing classes (preprocessing task #2) and after merging com-mits related to the same maintenance issue (preprocessing task #3). Finally, a reduction affecting 3 % of the Geronimo's commits, 4 % of the Camel's commits, and nearly 1 % of the commits of the other systems is observed after the last two preprocessing tasks.

After applying the preprocessing filters, we extracted a first co-change graph for each system. We then applied the post-processing filter defined in Sect. 3.1, to remove edges with unitary weights. Table 4 shows the number of vertices ($|V|$) and the number of edges ($|E|$) in the co-change graphs, before and after this post-processing task. The table also presents the graph's density (column D).

Table 4. Number of vertices ($|V|$), edges ($|E|$) and co-change graphs' density (D) before and after the post-processing filter

System	Post-Processing					
	Before			After		
	$|V|$	$|E|$	D	$|V|$	$|E|$	D
Geronimo	2,099	24,815	0.01	695	4,608	0.02
Lucene	2,679	63,075	0.02	1,353	18,784	0.02
JDT Core	1,201	75,006	0.01	823	25,144	0.04
Camel	3,033	42,336	0.01	1,498	15,404	0.01

By observing the results in Table 4, two conclusions can be drawn. First, co-change graphs are clearly sparse graphs, having density close to zero in the evaluated systems. This fact reinforces our choice to use Chameleon as the clustering algorithm, since this algorithm is particularly well-suited to handle sparse graphs [20]. Second, most edges in the initial co-change graphs have weight equal to one (more precisely, around 81 %, 70 %, 66 %, and 64 % of the edges for Geronimo, Lucene, JTD Core, and Camel graphs, respectively). Therefore, these edges connect classes that changed together in just one commit and for this reason they were removed after the post-processing task. As result, the number of vertices after post-processing is reduced to 33.1 % (Geronimo), 50.5 % (Lucene), 68.5 % (JDT Core), and 49.4 % (Camel) of their initial value.

4.3   Co-change Clustering

We executed the Chameleon algorithm having as input the co-change graphs created for each system (after applying the pre-processing and post-processing filters).[4] Table 5 shows the value of M that generated the best clusters, according to the clustering selection criteria defined in Sect. 3.2. The table also reports the initial number of co-change clusters generated by Chameleon and the number of clusters after eliminating the small clusters, i.e., clusters with less than four classes, as defined by the *MIN_CLUSTER_SZ* threshold. Finally, the table shows the ratio between the final number of clusters and the number of packages in each system (column %NOP).

---

[4] To execute Chameleon, we relied on the CLUTO clustering package, http://glaros. dtc.umn.edu/gkhome/cluto/cluto/overview.

Table 5. Number of co-change clusters

System	M	# clusters		%NOP
		All	$|V| \geq 4$	
Geronimo	108	46	21	0.05
Lucene	68	98	49	0.19
JDT Core	100	35	24	0.32
Camel	251	130	47	0.06

Table 6. Co-change clusters size (in number of classes)

System	Cluster size			
	Min	Max	Avg	Std
Geronimo	4	20	8.8	4.7
Lucene	4	27	11.7	7.0
JDT Core	4	43	14.0	10.4
Camel	4	74	10.2	11.5

For example, for Geronimo, we achieved the "best clusters" for $M = 108$, i.e., the co-change graph was initially partitioned into 108 clusters, in the first phase of the algorithm. In the second phase (agglomerative clustering), the initial clusters were successively merged, stopping with a configuration of 46 clusters. However, only 21 clusters have four or more classes ($|V| \geq 4$) and the others were discarded, since they represent "small modules", as defined in Sect. 4.1. We can also observe that the number of clusters is considerably smaller than the number of packages. Basically, this fact is an indication that the maintenance activity in the systems is concentrated in few classes.

Table 6 shows standard descriptive statistics measurements regarding the size of the extracted co-change clusters, in terms of number of classes. The extracted clusters have 8.8 ± 4.7 classes, 11.7 ± 7.0 classes, 14 ± 10.4 classes, and 10.2 ± 11.48 (average $\pm$ standard deviation) in the Geronimo, Lucene, JDT Core, and Camel systems, respectively. Moreover, the biggest cluster has a considerable number of classes: 20 classes (Geronimo), 27 classes (Lucene), 43 classes (JDT Core), and 74 classes (Camel).

Table 7 presents standard descriptive statistics measurements regarding the density of the extracted co-change clusters. The clusters have density of 0.80 ± 0.24 (Geronimo), 0.68 ± 0.25 (Lucene), 0.54 ± 0.29 (JDT Core), and 0.77 ± 0.25 (Camel). The median density is 0.90 (Geronimo), 0.71 (Lucene), 0.49 (JDT Core), and 0.83 (Camel). Therefore, although co-change graphs are sparse graphs, the results in Table 7 show they have dense subgraphs with a considerable size (at least four classes). Density is a central property in co-change clusters, because it assures that there is a high probability of co-changes between each pair of classes in the cluster.

Table 7. Co-change clusters density

System	Cluster density				
	Min	Max	Avg	Std	Median
Geronimo	0.31	1.0	0.80	0.24	0.90
Lucene	0.17	1.0	0.68	0.25	0.71
JDT Core	0.18	1.0	0.54	0.29	0.49
Camel	0.16	1.0	0.77	0.25	0.83

Table 8. Cluster average edges' weight

System	Average edges' weight				
	Min	Max	Avg	Std	Median
Geronimo	2	5.5	2.4	0.8	2.1
Lucene	2	7.1	2.7	1.0	2.4
JDT Core	2	7.6	4.3	1.5	3.8
Camel	2	5	2.6	0.8	2.3

Table 8 presents standard descriptive statistics measurements regarding the average weight of the edges in the extracted co-change clusters. For a given co-change cluster, we define this average as the sum of the weights of all edges divided by the number of edges in the cluster. We can observe that the median edges' weight is not high, being slightly greater than two in Geronimo, Lucene, and Camel. Whereas, in the JDT Core it is about four.

5   Modularity Analysis

In this section, we investigate the application of co-change clusters to assess the quality of a system's package decomposition. Particularly, we investigate the distribution of the co-change clusters over the package structure. For this purpose, we rely on distribution maps [14], which are typically used to compare two partitions P and Q of the entities of a system S. In our case, the entities are classes, the partition P is the package structure, and Q is composed by the co-change clusters. Moreover, entities (classes) are represented as small squares and the partition P (package structure) groups such squares into large rectangles (packages). In the package structure, we only consider classes that are members of co-change clusters, in order to improve the maps visualization. Finally, partition Q (co-change clusters) is used to color the classes (all classes in a cluster have the same color).

In addition to visualization, distribution maps can be used to quantify the *focus* of a given cluster q in relation to the partition P (package structure), as follows:

Table 9. Focus

System	Focus				
	Min	Max	Avg	Std	Median
Geronimo	0.50	1.00	0.93	0.12	1.00
Lucene	0.06	1.00	0.57	0.30	0.55
JDT Core	0.07	1.00	0.36	0.26	0.30
Camel	0.23	1.00	0.87	0.20	1.00

$$focus(q, P) = \sum_{p_i \in P} touch(q, p_i) * touch(p_i, q)$$

where

$$touch(p, q) = \frac{|p \cap q|}{|q|}$$

In this definition, $touch(q, p_i)$ is the number of classes of cluster q located in the package p_i divided by the number of classes in p_i that are included in at least a co-change cluster. Similarly, $touch(p_i, q)$ is the number of classes in p_i included in the cluster q divided by the number of classes in q. Focus ranges between 0 and 1, where the 1 means that the cluster q dominates the packages that it touches, i.e., it is well-encapsulated in such packages. In contrast, when co-change clusters crosscut many packages, but touching few classes in each of them, their focus is low.

There is also a second metric that measures how *spread* is a cluster q in P, i.e., the number of packages touched by q.

$$spread(q, P) = \sum_{p_i \in P} \begin{cases} 1, touch(q, p_i) > 0 \\ 0, touch(q, p_i) = 0 \end{cases}$$

Tables 9 and 10 show the standard descriptive statistics measurements regarding respectively the focus and spread of the co-change clusters. We can observe that the co-change clusters in Geronimo and Camel have a higher focus than in Lucene and JDT Core. For example, the median focus in Geronimo and Camel is 1.00, against 0.55 and 0.30 in Lucene and JDT Core, respectively. Regarding spread, Camel has a lower value than the others, on average the spread is 2.96 against 3.50 (Geronimo), 3.35 (Lucene), and 3.83 (JDT Core). Figure 5 shows a scatterplot with the values of focus (horizontal axis) and spread (vertical axis) for each co-change cluster. In Geronimo and Camel, we can see that there is a concentration of clusters with high focus. On the other hand, for Lucene, the clusters are much more dispersed along the two axis. Eclipse JDT tends to have lower focus, but also lower spread.

In the following sections, we analyze examples of well-encapsulated and crosscutting clusters, using distribution maps.[5] Section 5.1 emphasizes

---

[5] To extract and visualize distribution maps, we used the Topic Viewer tool [42], available at https://code.google.com/p/topic-viewer).

Table 10. Spread

System	Spread					
	Min	Max	Avg	Std	Median	Mode
Geronimo	1	8	3.50	2.10	3	1
Lucene	1	8	3.35	1.90	3	3
JDT Core	1	10	3.83	2.60	3	1
Camel	1	13	2.96	2.52	2	1

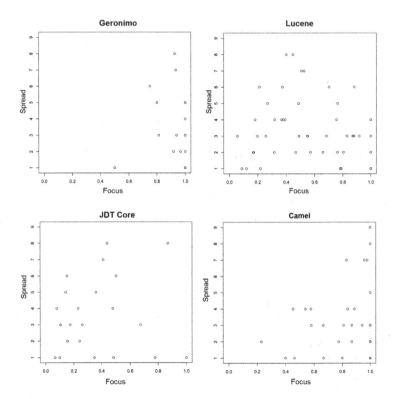

Fig. 5. Focus versus Spread

well-encapsulated clusters, since they are common in Geronimo. On the other hand, Sect. 5.2 emphasizes crosscutting concerns, which are most common in Lucene. Section 5.3 reports on both types of clusters in Eclipse JDT. Finally, Sect. 5.4 emphasizes well-encapsulated and partially encapsulated clusters, since they are common in Camel.

5.1   Distribution Map for Geronimo

Figure 6 shows the distribution map for Geronimo. To improve the visualization, besides background colors, we use a number in each class (small squares) to

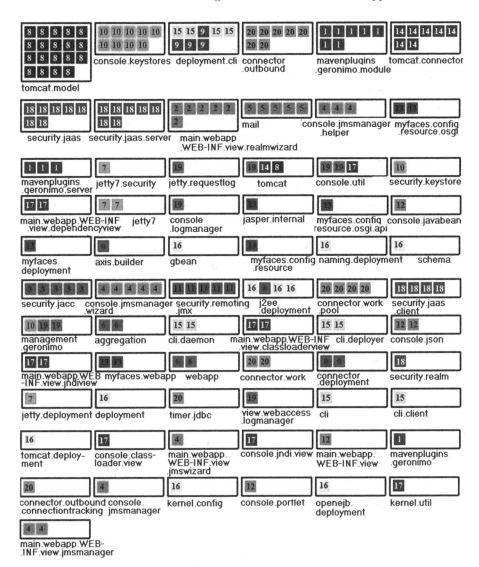

Fig. 6. Distribution map for Geronimo

indicate their respective clusters. The large boxes are the packages and the text
below is the package name.

Considering the clusters that are *well-encapsulated* (high focus) in Geronimo,
we found three package distribution patterns:

– *Clusters encapsulated (focus = 1.0) in a single package (spread = 1).* Four clusters have this behavior. As an example, we have Cluster 2, which dominates
the co-change classes in the package `main.webapp.WEBINF.view.realmwizard`

(line 2 in the map, column 3). This package implements a wizard to configure or create security domains. Therefore, since it implements a specific functional concern, maintenance is confined in the package. As another example, we have Cluster 5 (package `mail`, line 2 in the map, column 4) and Cluster 11 (package `security.remoting.jmx`, line 6, column 3).

- *Clusters encapsulated (focus = 1.0) in more than one package (spread > 1).* We counted eight clusters with this behavior. As an example, we have Cluster 18 (*spread = 4*), which touches all co-change classes in the following packages: `security.jaas.server`, `security.jaas.client`, `security.jaas`, and `security.realm` (displayed respectively in line 2, columns 1 and 2; line 6, column 6; and line 8, column 6). As suggested by their names, these packages are related to security concerns, implemented using the Java Authentication and Authorization Service (JAAS) framework. Therefore, the packages are conceptually related and their spread should not be regarded as a design problem. In fact, the spread in this case is probably due to a decision to organize the source code in sub-packages. As another example, we have Cluster 20 (*spread = 5*), which touches all classes in `connector.outbound`, `connector.work.pool`, `connector.work`, `connector.outbound.connectiontracking`, and `timer.jdbc` (displayed respectively in line 1, column 4; line 6, column 5; line 8, column 4; line 9, column 3; line 11 and column 1). These packages implement EJB connectors for message exchange.

- *Clusters partially encapsulated (focus ≈ 1.0) and touching classes in other packages (spread > 1).*[6] As an example, we have Cluster 8 (*focus = 0.97, spread = 2*), which dominates the co-change classes in the package `tomcat.model` (line 1 and column 1 in the map), but also touches the class `TomcatServerGBean` from package `tomcat` (line 3, column 4). This class is responsible for configuring the web server used by Geronimo (Tomcat). Therefore, this particular co-change instance suggests an instability in the interface provided by the web server. In theory, Geronimo should only call this interface to configure the web server, but the co-change cluster shows that maintenance in the `model` package sometimes has a ripple effect on this class, or vice-versa. As another example, we have Cluster 14 (*focus = 0.92* and *spread = 2*), which dominates the package `tomcat.connector` (line 1 and column 6 in the map) but also touches the class `TomcatServerConfigManager` from package `tomcat` (line 3, column 4). This "tentacle" in a single class from another package suggests again an instability in the configuration interface provided by the underlying web server.

---

[6] These clusters are called octopus, because they have a body centered on a single package and tentacles in other packages [14].

5.2   Distribution Map for Lucene

We selected for analysis clusters that are *crosscutting* (focus ≈ 0.0), since they are much more common in Lucene. More specifically, we selected the three clusters in Lucene with the lowest focus and a spread greater than two. Figure 7 shows a fragment of the distribution map for Lucene, containing the following clusters:

– *Cluster 12 (focus = 0.06 and spread = 3)* with co-change classes in the following packages: `index`, `analysis`, and `store`. Since the cluster crosscuts packages that provide different services (indexing, analysis, and storing), we claim that it reveals a modularization flaw in the package decomposition followed by Lucene. For example, a package like `store` that supports binary I/O services should hide its implementation from other packages. However, the existence of recurring maintenance tasks crosscutting `store` shows that the package fails to hide its main design decisions from other packages in the system.

– *Cluster 13 (focus = 0.2 and spread = 3)*, with co-change classes in the following packages: `search`, `search.spans`, and `search.function`. In this case, we claim that crosscutting is less harmful to modularity, because the packages are related to a single service (searching).

– *Cluster 28 (focus = 0.21 and spread = 6)*, with co-change classes in the following packages: `index`, `search`, `search.function`, `index.memory`, `search-.highlight`, and `store. instantiated`. These packages are responsible for important services in Lucene, like indexing, searching, and storing. Therefore,

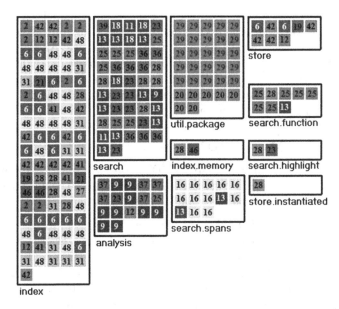

Fig. 7. Part of the Distribution map for Lucene

Table 11. Maintenance issues in Cluster 28

Maintenance Type	# issues	% issues
Functional concerns	22	59.50
Non-functional concerns	3	8.00
Refactoring	12	32.50

as in the case of Cluster 12, this crosscutting behavior suggests a modularization flaw in the system.

We also analyzed the maintenance issues associated to the commits responsible for the co-changes in Cluster 28. Particularly, we retrieved 37 maintenance issues related to this cluster. We then manually read and analyzed the short description of each issue, and classified them in three groups: (a) maintenance related to functional concerns in Lucene's domain (like searching, indexing, etc.); (b) maintenance related to non-functional concerns (like logging, persistence, exception handling, etc.); (c) maintenance related to refactorings. Table 11 shows the number of issues in each category. As can be observed, the crosscutting behavior of Cluster 28 is more due to issues related to functional concerns (59.5 %) than to non-functional concerns (8 %). Moreover, changes motivated by refactorings (32.5 %) are more common than changes in non-functional concerns.

Finally, we detected a distribution pattern in Lucene that represents neither well-encapsulated nor crosscutting clusters, but that might be relevant for analysis:

– *Clusters confined in a single package (spread = 1).* Although restricted to a single package, these clusters do not dominate the colors in this package. But if merged in a single cluster, they dominate their package. As an example, we have Cluster 20 (*focus = 0.22*) and Cluster 29 (*focus = 0.78*) that are both confined in package `util.packed` (line 1, column 3). Therefore, a refactoring that splits this package in sub-packages can be considered, in order to improve the focus of the respective clusters.

5.3   Distribution Map for JDT Core

Figure 8 shows the distribution map for JDT Core. We selected three distinct types of clusters for analysis: a *crosscutting* cluster (focus ≈ 0.0 and spread >= 3), clusters confined in a single package, and a cluster with high spread.

– *Clusters with crosscutting behavior.* We have Cluster 4 (focus = 0.08 and spread = 4) with co-change classes in the following packages: `internal.-compiler.lookup`, `internal.core`, `core.dom`, and `internal.core.util`. The `core.util` package provides a set of tools and utilities for manipulating `.class` files and Java model elements. Since the cluster crosscuts packages providing different services (document structure, files and elements manipulation, population of the model, compiler infrastructure), we claim that it reveals a modularization flaw in the system.

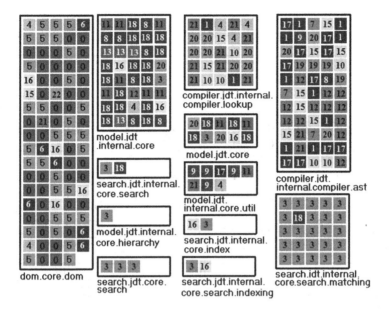

Fig. 8. Part of the Distribution map for JDT Core

– *Clusters confined in a single package (spread = 1).* We have Cluster 0 (*focus = 0.48*), Cluster 5 (*focus = 0.35*), and Cluster 6 (*focus = 0.07*) in the `core.dom` package (line 1, column 1).

– *Clusters partially encapsulated (focus ≈ 1.0) and touching classes in other packages (spread > 1).* We have Cluster 3 (focus = 0.87 and spread = 8), which dominates the co-change classes in the packages `search.jdt.inter-nal.core.search.matching` and `search.jdt.core.search`. These packages provide support for searching the workspace for Java elements matching a particular description. Therefore, a maintenance in this of the cluster usually has a ripple effect in classes like that.

5.4 Distribution Map for Camel

Figure 9 shows the distribution map for Camel. We selected two types of cluster patterns for analysis: a well-encapsulated cluster (focus = 1.0) and a partially encapsulated cluster (focus ≈ 1.0).

– *Clusters encapsulated (focus = 1.0) in a single package (spread = 1).* Twelve clusters have this behavior. As an example, we have Cluster 0, which domi-nates the co-change classes in the package `component.smpp` (line 3 in the map, column 5). This package provides access to a short message service. There-fore, since it implements a particular functional concern, the maintenance is confined in the package.

– *Clusters encapsulated (focus = 1.0) in more than one package (spread > 1).* We counted 13 clusters with this behavior. As an example, we have Cluster 17 (*spread = 9*), which touches all co-change classes in the following packages:

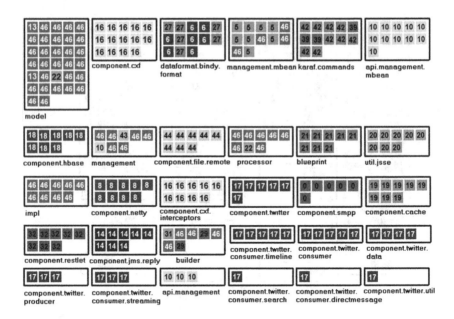

Fig. 9. Distribution map for Camel

component.twitter, component.twitter.data, component.twitter.
producer, component.twitter.consumer.streaming, component.twitter.
consumer.directmessage, component.twitter.consumer.search, compo-
nent.twitter.util, component.twitter.consumer, and component.twit-
ter.consumer.timeline. As revealed by their names, these packages are
related to the Twitter API. Therefore, these packages are conceptually related
and their spread should not be regarded as a design problem. In fact, the
spread in this case is probably due to a decision to organize the code in sub-
packages.

- *Clusters partially encapsulated (focus ≈ 1.0) and touching classes in other
  packages (spread > 1).* We counted 11 clusters with this behavior. As an
  example, we have Cluster 10 (*focus* = 0.94, *spread* = 3), which dominates
  the co-change classes in the packages api.management and api.management-
  .mbean (line 5, column 3; line 1, column 6 in the map), but also touches
  the class MBeanInfoAssembler from package management (line 2, columns 2).
  This class is responsible for reading details from different annotations, such
  as ManagedResource and ManagedAttribute. This co-change cluster shows
  that maintenance in api.management and api.management.mbean packages
  sometimes have a ripple effect on this class, or vice-versa.

6   Semantic Similarity Analysis

The previous section showed that the package structure of Geronimo and Camel
has more adherence to co-change clusters than Lucene's and JDT Core's. We also

observed that patterns followed by the relation clusters vs. packages can help to assess the modularity of systems. This section aims at evaluating the semantic similarity of the issues associated to a specific cluster in order to improve our understanding of the clusters' meaning. We hypothesize that if the issues related to a cluster have high semantic similarity, then the classes within that cluster are also semantically related and the cluster is semantically cohesive. We assume that an issue is related to a cluster if the change set of the issue contains at least a pair of classes from that cluster, not necessarily linked with an edge. In our strategy to evaluate the similarity of the issues related to a cluster, we consider each short description of an issue as a document and the collection of documents is obtained from the collection of issues related to a cluster. We use Latent Semantic Analysis - LSA [13] to evaluate the similarity among the collection of documents related to a cluster because it is a well-known method used in other studies concerning similarity among issues and other software artifacts [35,36].

6.1   Pre-processing Issue Description

When analyzing text documents with Information Retrieval techniques, an adequate pre-processing of the text is important to achieve good results. We define a domain vocabulary of terms based on words found in commits of the target system. The first step is stemming the terms. Next, the stop-words are removed. The final step produces a term-document matrix, where the cells have value 1 if the term occurs in the document and 0 otherwise. This decision was taken after some qualitative experimentation, in which we observed that different weighting mechanisms based on the frequency of terms, such as td-idf [27], did not improved the quality of the similarity matrix.

6.2   Latent Semantic Analysis

The LSA algorithm is applied to the binary term-document matrix and produces another similarity matrix among the documents (issues) with values ranging from -1 (no similarity) to 1 (maximum similarity). The LSA matrix should have high values to denote a collection of issues that are all related among them. However, not all pairs of issues have the same similarity level, so it is necessary to analyze the degree of similarity between the issues to evaluate the overall similarity within a cluster. We used heat maps to visualize the similarity between issues related to a cluster. Figure 10 shows examples of similarity within specific clusters. We show for each system the two best clusters in terms of similarity in the left, and the two clusters with several pairs of issues with low similarity in the right. The white cells represent issues that do not have any word in common, blue cells represent very low similarity, and yellow cells denote the maximum similarity between the issues.

We can observe that even for the cluster with more blue cells, there is still a dominance of higher similarity cells. The white cells in JDT's clusters suggest that there are issues with no similarity between the others in their respective cluster.

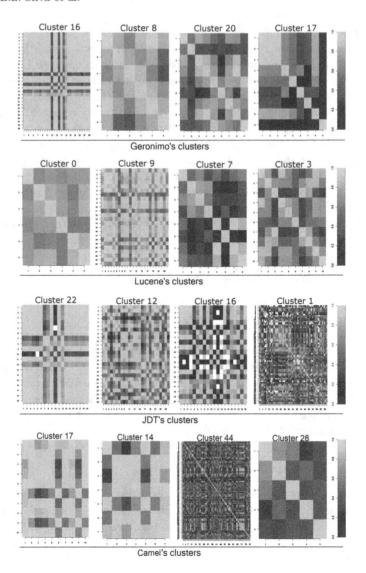

Fig. 10. Examples of heat maps for similarity of issues

6.3 Scoring Clusters

We propose the following metric to evaluate the overall similarity of a cluster c:

$$similarity\ score(c) = \frac{\displaystyle\sum_{\substack{0 < i,j < n-1 \\ j < i}} similar(i,j)}{\left(\frac{n^2}{2} - n\right)}$$

where
$$similar(i,j) = \begin{cases} 0, \text{ if } LSA\_Cosine(i,j) < SIM\_THRS \\ 1, \text{ Otherwise} \end{cases}$$
n = number of issues related to cluster c
$SIM\_THRS = 0.4$

The meaning of the *similarity score* of a cluster is defined upon the percentage of similar pair of issues. Therefore, a cluster with score = 0.5, means that 50 % of pairs of issues related to that cluster are similar to each other.

In this work, we defined a threshold to evaluate if two issues are similar or not. We consider the semantic similarity between two issue reports, i and j, as the cosine between the vectors corresponding to i and j in the semantic space created by LSA. After experimental testing, we observed that pairs of issues (i,j) that had $LSA\_Cosine(i,j) \geq 0.4$ had a meaningful degree of similarity. Nonetheless, we agree that this fixed threshold is not free of imprecision. Similar to our study, Poshyvanyk and Marcus [36] used LSA to analyze the coherence of the user comments in bug reports. The system's developers classified as high/very high similar the comments with average similarity greater than 0.33. For this reason, our more conservative approach seems to be adequate. Moreover, because our goal is to provide an overall evaluation of the whole collection of co-change clusters, some imprecision in the characterization of similarity between two issues would not affect significantly our analysis.

Figure 11 shows the distribution of score values for Geronimo's, Lucene's, JDT's, and Camel's clusters. We can observe that the systems' clusters follow a similar pattern of scoring, with 100 % (for Lucene, JDT, and Camel) and more than 90 % (for Geronimo) of clusters having more than half pairs of issues similar to each other. Only two Camel's clusters have score less than 50 % of similarity. Interestingly, one of these two clusters have 226 issue reports and their similarity is very low.

6.4   Correlating Similarity, Focus, and Spread

Another analysis that we carried out with clusters' scores was to evaluate the degree of correlation between the score, focus and spread. Table 12 shows the results obtained by applying the Spearman correlation test. For Geronimo, we observed a strong negative correlation between spread and score. In other words, the higher is the number of similar issues in a cluster, the higher is the capacity of the cluster to encompass a whole package in Geronimo. Interestingly, Lucene does not present the same behavior as Geronimo. We observe a weak correlation between focus and score, but we encounter no significant correlation between spread and score. In the case of Lucene, the higher is the number of similar issues in a cluster, the lower is the number of packages touched by the cluster. In the case of Eclipse JDT Core, there is no significant correlation between focus and score. Although, there is a moderate negative correlation between spread and score, it is only significant at p-value 0.074. For Camel, we observed a moderate negative correlation between spread and score. Similar to Geronimo, the higher

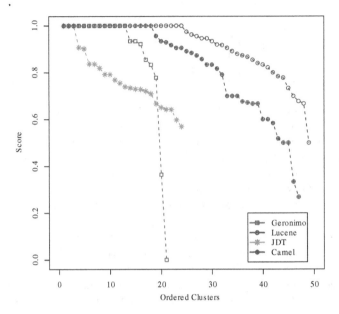

Fig. 11. Distribution of the clusters' score

Table 12. Correlation between score, focus and spread of clusters for Geronimo, Lucene, JDT Core, and Camel

Correlation Coefficient p-value	Score Geronimo	Score Lucene	Score JDT	Score Camel
Focus	0.264	0.308	−0.015	0.067
	0.131	0.016	0.473	0.327
Spread	−0.720	−0.178	−0.304	−0.337
	0.000	0.111	0.074	0.010

is the number of similar issues in a cluster, the higher is the capacity of the cluster to enfold a whole package in Camel. Considering that the clusters of the analyzed systems follow a similar pattern of similarity, this result suggests that the similarity between co-changes induces different properties in the clusters, either in spread or in focus.

7   Discussion

7.1   Practical Implications

Software architects can rely on the approach proposed in this paper to assess modularity under an evolutionary dimension. More specifically, we claim that our approach helps to reveal the following patterns of co-change behavior:

- When the package structure is adherent to the cluster structure, as in Geronimo's and Camel's clusters, localized co-changes are likely to occur.
- When there is not a clear adherence between co-change clusters and packages, a restructuring of the package decomposition may improve modularity. Particularly, there are two patterns of clusters that may suggest modularity flaws. The first pattern denotes clusters with crosscutting behavior (focus ≈ 0 and high spread). For example, in Lucene and JDT Core, we detected 12 and 10 clusters related to this pattern, respectively. The second pattern is the octopus cluster that suggest a possible ripple effect during maintenance tasks. In Geronimo, Lucene, and Camel, we detected four, five, and eleven clusters related to this pattern, respectively.

Nonetheless, we have no evidence that the proposed co-change clusters can fully replace traditional modular decompositions. Indeed, a first obstacle to this proposal is the fact that co-change clusters do not cover the whole population of classes in a system. However, we believe that they can be used as an alternative modular view during program comprehension tasks. For example, they may provide a better context during maintenance tasks (similar for example to the task context automatically inferred by tools like Mylyn [22]).

7.2 Clustering vs Association Rules Mining

Our approach is centered on the Chameleon hierarchical clustering algorithm, which is an algorithm designed to handle sparse graphs [20]. In our case studies, for example, the co-change graphs have densities ranging from 1 % (Camel) to 4 % (Eclipse JDT Core).

Particularly, in traditional clustering algorithms, like K-Means [26], the mapping of data items to clusters is a total function, i.e., each data item is allocated to a specific cluster. Likewise K-Means, Chameleon tries to cluster all data items. However, it is possible that some vertices are not allocated to any cluster. This may happen when some vertices do not share any edge with the rest of the vertices or when a vertice share edges to other vertices that belong to different clusters with no significant discrepancy among weights.

We also performed an algorithm to detect communities (clusters) [6], provided by the Gephi Tool[7], to compare with our co-change clusters. Similar to K-Means, this algorithm also allocates each vertice to a particular cluster. Thus, vertices with few or even one edge are assigned to a cluster leading these clusters to have lower density than Chameleon's. Nonetheless, we could define a pos-processing task to prune such vertices from clusters detected by the community algorithm to increase their densities. In spite of clusters with lower density, the result suggested the same pattern we presented in this paper, e.g., for Geronimo the package structure is adherent to the cluster structure and for Lucene, there is not a clear adherence between co-change clusters and packages.

An alternative to retrieve co-change relations is to rely on association rules mining [2]. In the context of evolutionary coupling, an association rule $C_{ant} \Rightarrow$

---

[7] http://gephi.github.io/.

C_{cons} expresses that commit transactions changing the classes C_{ant} (antecedent term) also change C_{cons} classes (consequent term), with a given probability.

However, hundreds of thousands of association rules can be easily retrieved from version histories. For example, we executed the Apriori algorithm [2] to retrieve association rules on Lucene's pre-processed dataset. By defining a minimum support threshold of four transactions, a minimum confidence of 50%, and limiting the size of the rules to 10 classes, we mined 976,572 association rules, with an average size of 8.14 classes. We repeated this experiment with the confidence threshold of 90%. In this case, we mined 831,795 association rules, with an average size of 8.23 classes. This explosion in the number of rules is an important limitation for using association rules to assess modularity, which ultimately is a task that requires careful judgment and analysis by software developers and maintainers. Another attempt to reduce the number of rules is to select the more interesting ones. There are several alternative measures available to complement the support and confidence measures [31,34]. One of the most well-known is the lift [8]. However, if the rules present high values of lift, it is very hard to make a precise selection. Another way to reduce the number of rules is to combine association rules and clustering [25].

7.3 Threats to Validity

In this section, we discuss possible threats to validity, following the usual classification in threats to internal, external, and construct validity:

Threats to External Validity: There are some threats that limit our ability to generalize our findings. The use of Geronimo, Lucene, JDT Core, and Camel may not be representative to capture co-change patterns present in other systems. However, it is important to note that we do not aim to propose general co-change patterns, but instead we just claim that the patterns founded in the target systems show the feasibility of using co-change clusters to evaluate modularity under a new dimension.

Threats to Construct Validity: A possible design threat to construct validity is that developers might not adequately link commit with issues, as pointed out by Herzing and Zeller [17]. Moreover, we also found a high number of commits not associated to maintenance issues. Thus, our results are subjected to missing and to incorrect links between commits and issues. However, we claim that we followed the approach commonly used in other studies that map issues to commits [10–12,51]. We also filtered out situations like commits associated to multiple maintenance issues and highly scattered commits. Another possible construction threat concerns the time frame used to collect the issues. We considered maintenance activity during a period of approximately ten years, which is certainly a large time frame. However, we did not evaluate how the co-change clusters evolved during this time frame or whether the systems' architecture has changed.

Finally, our approach only handles co-changes related to source code artifacts (.java files). However, the systems we evaluated have other types of artifacts, like

XML configuration files. Geronimo for example has 177 Javascript files, 1,004 XML configuration files, 19 configuration files, and 105 image files. Therefore, it is possible that we missed some co-change relations among non-Java based artifacts or between non-Java and Java-based artifacts. However, considering only source code artifacts makes possible the projection of co-change clusters to distribution maps, using the package structure as the main partition in the maps.

Threats to Internal Validity: Our approach relies on filters to select the commits used by the co-change graphs and clusters. Those filters are based on thresholds that can be defined differently, despite of our careful pre-experimentation. We also calibrated the semantic similarity analysis with parameters that define the dimensionality reduction in the case of LSA, and with a threshold in the case of the *LSA_Cosine* coefficient that defines when a pair of issues is similar. Although this calibration has some degree of uncertainty, it was not proposed to get better results favoring one system instead of the other. We defined the parameters and constants so that coherent results are achieved in all systems. Moreover, we observed that variations in the parameters' values would affect the results for all systems in a similar way.

8   Related Work

In this section, we discuss work related to our approach. The discussion is organized in three sections: concern mapping, co-change mining, and aspect mining.

8.1   Concern Mapping

Several approaches have been proposed to help developers and maintainers to manage concerns and features. For example, concern graphs model the subset of a software system associated with a specific concern [38,39]. The main purpose is to provide developers with an abstract view of the program fragments related to a concern. FEAT is a tool that supports the concern graph approach by enabling developers to build concern graphs interactively, as result of program investigation tasks. Aspect Browser [16] and JQuery [18] are other tools that rely on lexical or logic queries to find and document code fragments related to a certain concern. ConcernMapper [40] is an Eclipse Plug-in to organize and view concerns using an hierarchical structure similar to the package structure. However, in such approaches, the concern model is created manually or based on explicit input information provided by developers. Moreover, the relations between concerns are typically only syntactical and structural. By contrast, in the approach proposed in this paper, the elements and relationships are obtained by mining the version history.

8.2   Co-change Mining

Kouroshfar investigated the impact of co-change dispersion on software quality [24]. His results revealed that co-changes localized in the same subsystem involve fewer bugs than co-changes crosscutting distinct subsystems.

Zimmermann et al. propose an approach that uses association rule mining on version histories to suggest possible future changes [52]. Their approach differs from ours because they rely on association rules to recommend further changes (e.g., if class A usually co-changes with B, and a commit only changes A, a warning is given suggesting to check whether B should be changed too). Differently from their approach, we use co-change graphs to retrieve clusters semantically related to a target system's concern. Robillard and Barthélémy evaluated on seven open-source systems whether change clusters can support developers in their investigation of a software [37]. Similar to one of our pre-processing tasks, their approach discards commit transactions that contain too few or too many changed elements before clustering. Furthermore, in order to select clusters, like we do by using the *MIN_CLUSTER_SZ* threshold, they retrieved clusters that matched to a query. A quantitative analysis revealed that less than one in five tasks overlapped with a change cluster. The qualitative analysis of the recommended clusters showed that only 13 % of the recommendation for applicable change tasks are useful. However, our goal is not to recommend future changes, but to assess modularity, using distribution maps to compare and contrast co-change clusters with packages.

Beyer and Noack introduce the concept of co-change graphs and proposed a visualization of such graphs to reveal clusters of frequently co-changed artifacts [5]. Their approach clusters all co-change artifacts (code, configuration scripts, documentation, etc.), representing files as co-change graphs' vertices. These vertices are displayed as circles and their area is proportional to the frequency that the file was changed. Vanya et al. used co-change clusters to support the partitioning of system, reducing the coupling between its parts [49]. Their approach detects co-change clusters in which a group of files from one part of the system often changes with a group from another part. After the clustering step, they prune clusters containing files from the same part of the system. However, our central goal is not directly related with improving the visualization of co-change clusters as proposed by Beyer and Noack, but on using them to assess modularity. Finally, we do not prune clusters, such as Vanya et al., but we use them to visualize and to understand the system' package decomposition.

Oliva et al. mine version histories to extract logical dependencies between software artifacts to identify their origins [30]. They conducted a manual investigation of the origins of logical dependencies by reading revision comments and analyzing code diffs. Beck and Diehl combined evolutionary dependencies with syntactic dependencies to retrieve the modular structure of a system [4]. However, they cluster all classes in a system, since their original goal is to compare both approaches to software clustering. On the other hand, since our goal is to assess modularity, we consider only high-density co-change clusters.

Huzefa et al. present an approach that combines conceptual and evolutionary couplings for impact analysis in source code [19], using information retrieval and version history mining techniques. Gethers et al. propose an impact analysis that adapts to the specific maintenance scenario using information retrieval, historical data mining, and dynamic analysis techniques [15]. However, they do not use maintenance issues reports to discard noisy commits.

Palomba et al. propose HIST, an approach that uses association rule mining on version histories to detect code smells [32]. For each smell, they define a heuristics that relies on association rules for detecting bad smells. However, our goal is not to detect code smells but to assess modularity using co-change clusters.

A recent study by Negara et al. reveals that the use of data from version history presents many threats when investigating source code properties [29]. In this work, we proposed five pre-processing tasks and one post-processing task to tackle some of such threats.

8.3 Aspect Mining

Breu and Zimmermann proposed an approach (HAM) based on version history to detect crosscutting concerns in an object-oriented program to guide its migration to an aspect-oriented program [7]. They define the notion of transaction, which is the set of methods inserted by the developer to complete a single development task. They also consider that method calls inserted in eight or more locations (method bodies) define aspect candidates.

One important difference from their work and ours is that they consider not only methods that were changed together, but also those changes that are the same. Moreover, they rely on a fine-grained notion of change that is interested in finding methods calls to define aspect candidates.

Adams et al. propose a mining technique (COMMIT) to identify concerns from functions, variables, types, and macros that were changed together [1]. Similarly to HAM, COMMIT is based on the idea that similar calls and references that are added or removed into different parts of the program are candidates to concerns. This information produces several seed graphs which are concern candidates because nodes in the graph represent program entities to which calls or references have been co-added or co-removed. Their approach differs from ours because they generate independent seed graphs, while we are centered on a unique graph.

9 Conclusion

In this work, we proposed a method to extract an alternative view to the package decomposition based on co-change clusters. We applied our method to four real software systems, Geronimo, Lucene, JDT Core, and Camel. Our results show that meaningful co-change clusters can be extracted using the information available in version control systems. Although co-change graphs extracted from repositories are sparse, the co-change clusters are dense and have high internal similarity concerning co-changes and semantic similarity concerning their originating issues. We have shown that co-change clusters and their associated metrics are useful to assess the hierarchical modular decomposition of the target systems. Even if in some cases co-change clusters may be used to restructure the original package decomposition, we suggest that they are specially useful as an alternative view during maintenance tasks to improve the developer's understanding of the change impact.

We still need to investigate the reasons that induce co-change clusters and to identify the eventual patterns that produce those clusters, which would contribute in early modularization decisions. We plan to investigate and to compare our approach with other clustering algorithms for sparse graphs, like the approach proposed by Beyer et al. [5] and clustering algorithms based on density property. We also plan to consider co-changes at a finer-granularity level, more specifically among methods, and also including non-source code artifacts, like XML configuration files. Finally, we plan to investigate whether co-change clusters can be used as an alternative to the Package Explorer, supporting a mechanism for the virtual separation of concerns, inspired on the CIDE [21] and CIDE+ tools [48].

Acknowledgments. This work is supported by FAPEMIG, CAPES, and CNPq.

References

1. Adams, B., Jiang, Z.M., Hassan, A.E.: Identifying crosscutting concerns using historical code changes. In: 32nd International Conference on Software Engineering (ICSE), pp. 305–314 (2010)
2. Agrawal, R., Srikant, R.: Fast algorithms for mining association rules in large databases. In: 20th International Conference on Very Large Data Bases (VLDB), pp. 487–499 (1994)
3. Baldwin, C.Y., Clark, K.B.: Design Rules: The Power of Modularity. MIT Press, Cambridge (2003)
4. Beck, F., Diehl, S.: Evaluating the impact of software evolution on software clustering. In: 17th Working Conference on Reverse Engineering (WCRE), pp. 99–108 (2010)
5. Beyer, D., Noack, A.: Clustering software artifacts based on frequent common changes. In: 13th International Workshop on Program Comprehension (IWPC), pp. 259–268 (2005)
6. Blondel, V.D., Guillaume, J.L., Lambiotte, R., Lefebvre, E.: Fast unfolding of communities in large networks. J. Stat. Mech. Theory Exp. **2008**(10), P10008 (2008)
7. Breu, S., Zimmermann, T.: Mining aspects from version history. In: 21st Automated Software Engineering Conference (ASE), pp. 221–230 (2006)
8. Brin, S., Motwani, R., Ullman, J.D., Tsur, S.: Dynamic itemset counting and implication rules for market basket data. In: International Conference on Management of Data (SIGMOD), pp. 255–264 (1997)
9. Chidamber, S., Kemerer, C.: Towards a metrics suite for object oriented design. In: 6th Object-oriented Programming Systems, Languages, and Applications Conference (OOPSLA), pp. 197–211 (1991)
10. Couto, C., Pires, P., Valente, M.T., Bigonha, R., Anquetil, N.: Predicting software defects with causality tests. J. Syst. Softw. **93**, 24–41 (2014)

11. Couto, C., Silva, C., Valente, M.T., Bigonha, R., Anquetil, N.: Uncovering causal relationships between software metrics and bugs. In: 16th European Conference on Software Maintenance and Reengineering (CSMR), pp. 223–232 (2012)
12. D'Ambros, M., Lanza, M., Robbes, R.: An extensive comparison of bug prediction approaches. In: 7th Working Conference on Mining Software Repositories (MSR), pp. 31–41 (2010)
13. Deerwester, S., Dumais, S.T., Furnas, G.W., Landauer, T.K., Harshman, R.: Indexing by latent semantic analysis. J. Am. Soc. Inf. Sci. **41**, 391–407 (1990)
14. Ducasse, S., Gîrba, T., Kuhn, A.: Distribution map. In: 22nd IEEE International Conference on Software Maintenance (ICSM), pp. 203–212 (2006)
15. Gethers, M., Kagdi, H., Dit, B., Poshyvanyk, D.: An adaptive approach to impact analysis from change requests to source code. In: 26th Automated Software Engineering Conference (ASE), pp. 540–543 (2011)
16. Griswold, W.G., Yuan, J.J., Kato, Y.: Exploiting the map metaphor in a tool for software evolution. In: 23rd International Conference on Software Engineering (ICSE), pp. 265–274 (2001)
17. Herzing, K., Zeller, A.: The impact of tangled code changes. In: 10th Working Conference on Mining Software Repositories (MSR), pp. 121–130 (2013)
18. Janzen, D., Volder, K.D.: Navigating and querying code without getting lost. In: 2nd International Conference on Aspect-oriented Software Development (AOSD), pp. 178–187 (2003)
19. Kagdi, H., Gethers, M., Poshyvanyk, D.: Integrating conceptual and logical couplings for change impact analysis in software. Empirical Softw. Eng. (EMSE) **18**(5), 933–969 (2013)
20. Karypis, G., Han, E.H.S., Kumar, V.: Chameleon: hierarchical clustering using dynamic modeling. Computer **32**(8), 68–75 (1999)
21. Kästner, C., Apel, S., Kuhlemann, M.: Granularity in software product lines. In: 30th International Conference on Software Engineering (ICSE), pp. 311–320 (2008)
22. Kersten, M., Murphy, G.C.: Using task context to improve programmer productivity. In: 14th International Symposium on Foundations of Software Engineering (FSE), pp. 1–11 (2006)
23. Kiczales, G., Lamping, J., Mendhekar, A., Maeda, C., Lopes, C., Loingtier, J.M., Irwin, J.: Aspect-oriented programming. In: Akşit, M., Matsuoka, S. (eds.) ECOOP 1997. LNCS, vol. 1241. Springer, Heidelberg (1997)
24. Kouroshfar, E.: Studying the effect of co-change dispersion on software quality. In: 35th International Conference on Software Engineering (ICSE), pp. 1450–1452 (2013)
25. Lent, B., Swami, A.N., Widom, J.: Clustering association rules. In: 13th International Conference on Data Engineering (ICDE), pp. 220–231 (1997)
26. MacQueen, J.B.: Some methods for classification and analysis of multivariate observations. In: 5th Berkeley Symposium on Mathematical Statistics and Probability, pp. 281–297 (1967)
27. Manning, C.D., Raghavan, P., Schtze, H.: Introduction to Information Retrieval. Cambridge University Press, Cambridge (2008)
28. Meyer, B.: Object-Oriented Software Construction. Prentice-Hall, Upper Saddle River (2000)
29. Negara, S., Vakilian, M., Chen, N., Johnson, R.E., Dig, D.: Is it dangerous to use version control histories to study source code evolution? In: Noble, J. (ed.) ECOOP 2012. LNCS, vol. 7313, pp. 79–103. Springer, Heidelberg (2012)

30. Oliva, G.A., Santana, F.W., Gerosa, M.A., de Souza, C.R.B.: Towards a classification of logical dependencies origins: a case study. In: 12th International Workshop on Principles of Software Evolution and the 7th Annual ERCIM Workshop on Software Evolution (EVOL/IWPSE), pp. 31–40 (2011)

31. Omiecinski, E.: Alternative interest measures for mining associations in databases. IEEE Trans. Knowl. Data Eng. **15**(1), 57–69 (2003)

32. Palomba, F., Bavota, G., Penta, M.D., Oliveto, R., de Lucia, A., Poshyvanyk, D.: Detecting bad smells in source code using change history information. In: 28th IEEE/ACM International Conference on Automated Software Engineering (ASE), pp. 268–278 (2013)

33. Parnas, D.L.: On the criteria to be used in decomposing systems into modules. Commun. ACM **15**(12), 1053–1058 (1972)

34. Piatetsky-Shapiro, G.: Discovery, analysis and presentation of strong rules. In: Knowledge Discovery in Databases, pp. 229–248 (1991)

35. Poshyvanyk, D., Marcus, A.: Using information retrieval to support design of incremental change of software. In: 22th IEEE/ACM International Conference on Automated Software Engineering (ASE), pp. 563–566 (2007)

36. Poshyvanyk, D., Marcus, A.: Measuring the semantic similarity of comments in bug reports. In: 1st International ICPC Workshop on Semantic Technologies in System Maintenance (STSM), pp. 265–280 (2008)

37. Robillard, M.P., Dagenais, B.: Recommending change clusters to support software investigation: an empirical study. J. Softw. Maintenance Evol. Res. Pract. **22**(3), 143–164 (2010)

38. Robillard, M.P., Murphy, G.C.: Concern graphs: finding and describing concerns using structural program dependencies. In: 24th International Conference on Software Engineering (ICSE), pp. 406–416 (2002)

39. Robillard, M.P., Murphy, G.C.: Representing concerns in source code. ACM Trans. Softw. Eng. Methodol. **16**(1), 1–38 (2007)

40. Robillard, M.P., Weigand-Warr, F.: ConcernMapper: simple view-based separation of scattered concerns. In: OOPSLA Workshop on Eclipse Technology eXchange, pp. 65–69 (2005)

41. Salton, G., Wong, A., Yang, C.S.: A vector space model for automatic indexing. Commun. ACM **18**(11), 613–620 (1975)

42. Santos, G., Valente, M.T., Anquetil, N.: Remodularization analysis using semantic clustering. In: 1st CSMR-WCRE Software Evolution Week, pp. 224–233 (2014)

43. Silva, L., Valente, M.T., Maia, M.: Assessing modularity using co-change clusters. In: 13th International Conference on Modularity, pp. 49–60 (2014)

44. Śliwerski, J., Zimmermann, T., Zeller, A.: When do changes induce fixes? In: 2nd Working Conference on Mining Software Repositories (MSR), pp. 1–5 (2005)

45. Stevens, W.P., Myers, G.J., Constantine, L.L.: Structured design. IBM Syst. J. **13**(2), 115–139 (1974)

46. Tempero, E., Anslow, C., Dietrich, J., Han, T., Li, J., Lumpe, M., Melton, H., Noble, J.: Qualitas corpus: a curated collection of Java code for empirical studies. In: Asia Pacific Software Engineering Conference (APSEC), pp. 336–345 (2010)

47. Terra, R., Miranda, L.F., Valente, M.T., Bigonha, R.S.: Qualitas.class corpus: a compiled version of the qualitas corpus. Softw. Eng. Notes **38**, 1–4 (2013)

48. Valente, M., Borges, V., Passos, L.: A semi-automatic approach for extracting software product lines. IEEE Trans. Softw. Eng. **38**(4), 737–754 (2012)

49. Vanya, A., Hofland, L., Klusener, S., van de Laar, P., van Vliet, H.: Assessing software archives with evolutionary clusters. In: 16th IEEE International Conference on Program Comprehension (ICPC), pp. 192–201 (2008)

50. Walker, R.J., Rawal, S., Sillito, J.: Do crosscutting concerns cause modularity problems? In: 20th International Symposium on the Foundations of Software Engineering (FSE), pp. 1–11 (2012)
51. Zimmermann, T., Premraj, R., Zeller, A.: Predicting defects for Eclipse. In: 3rd
International Workshop on Predictor Models in Software Engineering, pp. 9 (2007)
52. Zimmermann, T., Weissgerber, P., Diehl, S., Zeller, A.: Mining version histories to
guide software changes. IEEE Trans. Softw. Eng. **31**(6), 429–445 (2005)

Reusable Components of Semantic Specifications

Martin Churchill[1], Peter D. Mosses[2][✉], Neil Sculthorpe[2], and Paolo Torrini[2]

[1] Google, Inc., London, UK
[2] PLanCompS Project, Swansea University, Swansea, UK
p.d.mosses@swansea.ac.uk
http://www.plancomps.org

Abstract. Semantic specifications of programming languages typically have poor modularity. This hinders reuse of parts of the semantics of one language when specifying a different language – even when the two languages have many constructs in common – and evolution of a language may require major reformulation of its semantics. Such drawbacks have discouraged language developers from using formal semantics to document their designs.

In the PLanCompS project, we have developed a component-based approach to semantics. Here, we explain its modularity aspects, and present an illustrative case study: a component-based semantics for Caml Light. We have tested the correctness of the semantics by running programs on an interpreter generated from the semantics, comparing the output with that produced on the standard implementation of the language.

Our approach provides good modularity, facilitates reuse, and should support co-evolution of languages and their formal semantics. It could be particularly useful in connection with domain-specific languages and language-driven software development.

Keywords: Modularity · Reusability · Component-based semantics · Fundamental constructs · Funcons · Modular SOS

1 Introduction

Various programming constructs are common to many languages. For instance, assignment statements, sequencing, conditional branching, loops and procedure calls are almost ubiquitous among languages that support imperative programming; expressions usually include references to declared variables and constants, arithmetic and logical operations on values, and function calls; and blocks are provided to restrict the scope of local declarations. The details of such constructs often vary between languages, both regarding their syntax and their intended behaviour, but sometimes they are identical.

Many constructs are also 'independent', in that their contributions to program behaviour are unaffected by the presence of other constructs in the same language. For instance, consider conditional expressions '$E_1?E_2 : E_3$'. How they

© Springer-Verlag Berlin Heidelberg 2015
S. Chiba et al. (Eds.): Transactions on AOSD XII, LNCS 8989, pp. 132–179, 2015.
DOI: 10.1007/978-3-662-46734-3_4

are evaluated is unaffected by whether expressions involve variable references, side effects, function calls, process synchronisation, etc. In contrast, the behaviour of a loop may depend on whether the language includes break and continue statements.

1.1 Modularity and Reusability

We consider a semantic specification framework to have *good modularity* when independent constructs can be specified separately, once and for all. Such frameworks support verbatim reuse of the specifications of common independent constructs between different language specifications. They also reduce the amount of reformulation needed when languages evolve.

Poor Modularity. It is well known that various semantic frameworks do not have good modularity. A particularly familiar example of a framework with poor modularity is structural operational semantics (SOS) [56]. As a simple illustration of the lack of modularity, consider specifying the evaluation of conditional expressions in the small-step SOS style developed by Plotkin:

$$\frac{E_1 \to E_1'}{E_1 \: ? \: E_2 : E_3 \to E_1' \: ? \: E_2 : E_3} \tag{1}$$

$$\mathtt{true} \: ? \: E_2 : E_3 \to E_2 \tag{2}$$

$$\mathtt{false} \: ? \: E_2 : E_3 \to E_3 \tag{3}$$

The transition formula $E \to E'$ asserts the possibility of a step of the computation of the value of E such that, after making the step, E' remains to be evaluated. The inference rule (1) specifies that computing the value of '$E_1 \: ? \: E_2 : E_3$' may involve computing the value of E_1; the axioms (2), (3) specify how the computation proceeds after E_1 has computed the value $\mathtt{true}$ or $\mathtt{false}$. If the computation of the value of E_1 does not terminate, neither does that of '$E_1 \: ? \: E_2 : E_3$'; if it terminates with a value other than $\mathtt{true}$ or $\mathtt{false}$, the computation of '$E_1 \: ? \: E_2 : E_3$' is stuck: it cannot make any further steps.

However, suppose we are specifying the semantics of a simple imperative language that includes also expressions of the form '$I = E$', intended to assign the value of E to a simple variable named I and return the value. We might specify the evaluation of such assignment expressions as follows.

$$\frac{\rho \vdash (E, \sigma) \to (E', \sigma')}{\rho \vdash (I = E, \sigma) \to (I = E', \sigma')} \tag{4}$$

$$\rho \vdash (I = V, \sigma) \to (V, \sigma[\rho(I) \mapsto V]) \tag{5}$$

The environment ρ above represents the current bindings of identifiers (e.g., to declared imperative variables) and the store σ represents the values currently assigned to such variables. The formula $\rho \vdash (E, \sigma) \to (E', \sigma')$ asserts that, after making the step, E' remains to be evaluated (or has been fully evaluated) and σ' reflects any side-effects. Axiom (5) specifies that when the value V of E has been computed, it is also the value of the enclosing expression; the resulting store reflects the assignment of that value to the variable bound to I in ρ.

Conventional SOS requires the semantics of all constructs in the same syntactic category to be specified using the same form of transition formulae. This is intrinsically a non-modular requirement. In the above example, it means we have to reformulate rules (1)–(3) as follows – in effect, *weaving* the extra arguments (here ρ, σ and σ') of the required transition formulae into the original rules.

$$\frac{\rho \vdash (E_1, \sigma) \to (E_1', \sigma')}{\rho \vdash (E_1 \mathbin{?} E_2 : E_3, \sigma) \to (E_1' \mathbin{?} E_2 : E_3, \sigma')} \tag{6}$$

$$\rho \vdash (\mathtt{true} \mathbin{?} E_2 : E_3, \sigma) \to (E_2, \sigma) \tag{7}$$

$$\rho \vdash (\mathtt{false} \mathbin{?} E_2 : E_3, \sigma) \to (E_3, \sigma) \tag{8}$$

Different SOS rules would be needed for specifying conditional expressions in other languages. For example, in a pure functional language, the transition formulae could be simply $\rho \vdash E \to E'$; in a process language, they would involve labels on transitions, e.g., $E \xrightarrow{a} E'$. The notation used to specify a language construct depends not only on the features of that particular construct, but also on the features of all the *other* constructs in the language. This flagrant disregard for modularity in conventional SOS implies that it is simply not possible to specify *once and for all* the semantics of conditional expressions (or any other programming constructs).

A Hindrance to Reuse. Several semantic frameworks are just as non-modular as SOS, whereas others have a somewhat higher degree of modularity (as discussed in Sect. 5). However, a further and almost universal feature of semantic descriptions of programming languages affects potential *reuse* of their parts: the common practice of using notation from the *concrete* syntax of a language when defining its semantics. For instance, the SOS rules for conditional expressions above might be based on a grammar including the following productions:

$$E : exp ::= exp \mathbin{?} exp : exp \mid \mathtt{true} \mid \mathtt{false} \tag{9}$$

Such grammars provide a concise and suggestive specification of the abstract syntax (i.e., compositional structure) of programs, and are generally preferred to the original style of abstract syntax specification developed by McCarthy [36]. These grammars are typically highly ambiguous, but parsing and disambiguation are usually handled as a preliminary step before the semantics, so ambiguity is not a problem. However, the use of concrete terminal symbols to distinguish language constructs entails that our SOS rules for '$E_1 \mathbin{?} E_2 : E_3$' cannot be directly reused for a language using different concrete syntax for conditional expressions, e.g., 'if E_1 then E_2 else E_3'.

Without support for both modularity and reuse, the development and subsequent revision of a formal semantics for a major programming language is inherently a huge effort, often regarded as disproportionate to its benefits [23].

1.2   Fundamental Constructs (Funcons)

Our component-based approach to semantics addresses both modularity and reusability. Its crucial novel feature is the introduction of an *open-ended* collection of so-called *fundamental constructs*, or *funcons*. Many of the funcons correspond closely to simplified language constructs. But in contrast to language constructs, each funcon has a fixed interpretation, which we specify, *once and for all*,[1] using a modular variant of SOS called MSOS [42]. For example, the collection includes a funcon written '**if-true**(E_1, E_2, E_3)', whose interpretation corresponds directly to that of the language construct '$E_1 \mathrel{?} E_2 : E_3$' considered above.

Language Specification. To specify the semantics of a language, we translate all its constructs to funcons. Thanks to the closeness of funcons to language constructs, the translation is generally rather simple to specify. For instance, the translation of '$E_1 \mathrel{?} E_2 : E_3$' could be trivial, simply using '**if-true**' to combine the translations of E_1, E_2, E_3; translation of conditional expressions that have a different type of condition (e.g., test for zero) involves inserting operations to test the value of E_1.

Each funcon has both static and dynamic semantics. A *single* translation of a language to funcons therefore defines *both* the static and dynamic semantics of the language. Sometimes it is necessary to adjust the induced static semantics by inserting further funcons, e.g., our '**if-true**' funcon requires its second and third arguments to have a common type, but the intended static semantics of '$E_1 \mathrel{?} E_2 : E_3$' might require inclusion between the minimal types of E_2 and E_3. Funcons for making such static checks have vacuous dynamic semantics.

Defining the semantics of a language by translating it to funcons is somewhat analogous to defining the semantics of a full language by translation to a kernel sublanguage whose semantics is defined directly, as for Standard ML [38]. However, the direct definition of a kernel language is language-specific, and does not provide reusable components.

Funcon Specification. The funcon specifications are expected to be highly reusable components of language specifications. Their crucial feature is that when funcons are combined in a language specification, or when a new funcon is added to the open-ended collection, the specifications *never* require any changes. MSOS has particular advantages in that respect, but it should be possible to specify funcons also using other highly modular frameworks, e.g., the K framework [58], as illustrated in [50].

When the syntax or semantics of a language construct changes, however, the specification of its translation to funcons has to change accordingly (since we never change the semantics of funcons) so the translation specification itself is inherently not so reusable. We explain all this further, and provide some simple introductory examples, in Sect. 2.

---

[1] The specifications of the current collection of funcons will not be finalised until we have tested their use in two further major case studies, as discussed in Sect. 6.

Case Study. The main contribution of this paper is in Sect. 3, where we illustrate the modularity and practical applicability of our approach by presenting excerpts from a moderate-sized case study: a component-based semantics of CAML LIGHT [32]. This language is used for teaching functional programming, but also has imperative features. For selected language constructs, we give conceptual explanations of the funcons involved in their translations, and present the MSOS specifications of the semantics of the funcons. We have made the complete case study available online [12]. The PLANCOMPS project [55] is carrying out two further major case studies to demonstrate the extent to which funcons can be reused in specifications of different languages.

Tool Support. We have tested the correspondence between our component-based semantics of CAML LIGHT and the standard implementation of the language [32, version 0.75], by running programs using a (modular!) interpreter generated from the MSOS specifications of the funcons [2,3,44]. Although the focus of this paper is on the features of component-based language specifications, we describe and illustrate our current tool support, which involves Spoofax [28] and Prolog, in Sect. 4. Further tool support is being developed by the PLANCOMPS project.

Related Work. We discuss related work and alternative approaches in Sect. 5, then conclude and outline further work in Sect. 6. This paper is an extended and improved version of a MODULARITY '14 conference paper [13].

2   Component-Based Semantics

In this section, we first explain the general concepts underlying *fundamental constructs* (*funcons*), giving some simple examples. We then consider how to specify translations from programming languages to funcons. Finally, we recall MSOS (a modular variant of SOS) and show how we use it to specify, once and for all, the static and dynamic semantics of each funcon as a highly reusable component of language specifications.

2.1   Funcon Notation

As mentioned in Sect. 1.2, many funcons correspond closely to simplified programming language constructs. However, each funcon has fixed syntax and semantics. For example, executing the funcon term written **assign**(E_1, E_2) always has the effect of evaluating the funcon term E_1 to a variable, E_2 to a value (in any order, possibly with interleaving), then assigning the value to the variable; its static semantics requires the type of E_1 to be that of a variable for storing values of the type of E_2. In contrast, a language construct written '$E_1 = E_2$' may be interpreted as an assignment or as an equality test, depending on the language, and the details of the interpretation may differ (e.g., regarding the possibility of coercions, composite variables, or failure). In a logic programming language, '$E_1 = E_2$' is interpreted as unification, which differs more fundamentally.

Sorts and Signatures. We can introduce a notion of well-formedness for funcon terms, based on sorts and signatures. The *signature* of a funcon determines its name, how many arguments it takes (if any), the sort of each argument, and the sort of the result. In our approach signatures provide also a form of *strictness annotation*, relying on a notion of *lifting*, introduced below. We consider a funcon term to be *well-sorted* when each of its argument terms (if any) is well-sorted and is of the sort required by its lifted signature.

We distinguish between *value sorts* and *computation sorts*. The pre-defined value sorts include *booleans* (the values **false** and **true**), *ints* (the unbounded integers), *unit* (the single value **null**), *ids* (identifiers), and *variables* (imperative variables). Generic pre-defined value sorts include *lists*(X) (finite lists of values of sort X) and *maps*(X, Y) (finite maps from values of sort X to values of sort Y). New value sorts (such as *records* and *vectors*) can be defined using algebraic data types, instantiation of generic sorts, and subsort inclusion.

Values for us are intrinsically *independent* of the computational context in which they occur. For any value sort X, *computes*(X) is the computation sort of funcon terms which, whenever their executions terminate normally, compute values of sort X. The following computation sorts reflect fundamental conceptual distinctions commonly found in programming languages.

- The sort of *expressions* (*exprs*) is for funcons that compute arbitrary *values*, possibly with side-effects.
- The sort of *declarations* (*decls*) is for funcons that compute *environments*, which are maps from identifiers to values.
- The sort of *commands* (*comms*) is for funcons that are executed for their effects, computing always the same **null** value.

The computation sorts *exprs*, *decls* and *comms* abbreviate instances of *computes*(X); if needed, further sort abbreviations could be introduced. Importantly, the *effects* of computations of sort *computes*(X) are completely unconstrained: they may include abrupt termination, assignment, spawning concurrent processes, communication, synchronisation, etc. Note that a computation sort *computes*(X) always includes the value sort X as a subsort, since we regard values as terminated computations.

Table 1 shows the signatures of some funcons. The funcons **if-true** (conditional choice), **scope** (local binding), **seq** (sequencing) and **supply** (value-passing) are polymorphic: the sort variable X in a signature may be instantiated (uniformly) with any value sort.

Lifting. Value sorts in signatures can always be *lifted* to computation sorts. For example, consider the value operation **not**(*booleans*) : *booleans*. By lifting the signature to **not**(*exprs*) : *exprs* we can use **not** as a funcon, applying it to any expression E. The value of **not**(E) is computed by first computing the value of E, then (provided that this is a value of sort *booleans*) applying the unlifted **not** operation. The same principle applies to funcons with a single value sort argument, such as **assigned-value**: its lifted signature is **assigned-value**(*exprs*) : *exprs*,

Table 1. Some funcon sorts and signatures

Funcon sorts

    comms = *computes*(*unit*)
     decls = *computes*(*environments*)
     exprs = *computes*(*values*)

Funcon signatures

$$\textbf{assign}(\textit{variables}, \textit{values}) : \textit{comms}$$
$$\textbf{assigned-value}(\textit{variables}) : \textit{exprs}$$
$$\textbf{bind-value}(\textit{ids}, \textit{values}) : \textit{decls}$$
$$\textbf{bound-value}(\textit{ids}) : \textit{exprs}$$
$$\textbf{effect}(\textit{values}) : \textit{comms}$$
$$\textbf{given} : \textit{exprs}$$
$$\textbf{if-true}(\textit{booleans}, \textit{computes}(X), \textit{computes}(X)) : \textit{computes}(X)$$
$$\textbf{scope}(\textit{environments}, \textit{computes}(X)) : \textit{computes}(X)$$
$$\textbf{seq}(\textit{unit}, \textit{computes}(X)) : \textit{computes}(X)$$
$$\textbf{supply}(\textit{values}, \textit{computes}(X)) : \textit{computes}(X)$$
$$\textbf{while-true}(\textit{exprs}, \textit{comms}) : \textit{comms}$$

---

and the computation of the argument value is followed by applying the original funcon to it. For funcons such as **if-true** and **scope**, which have one or more further arguments with explicit computation sorts, the computation of those argument(s) depends on the funcon itself. An extreme case of this is **while-true**(E, C), where the computations E and C generally need to be repeated, depending on the values computed by E.

When we lift value operations and funcons (such as **assign**) with two or more value sort arguments, those argument values may be computed in any order, allowing also interleaving of side-effects. We can use the funcons **supply** and **given** to insist on a particular order of funcon argument evaluation. For example, **supply**$(E_2, \textbf{assign}(E_1, \textbf{given}))$ always evaluates E_2 before E_1. The funcon **given** refers to the value computed by the first argument of the closest-enclosing **supply**.

Although lifting of value operations to funcons is reminiscent of functional programming, the argument computations themselves need not be purely functional: they may throw exceptions, assign to variables, spawn concurrent processes, or even diverge, and their interleaving may give rise to nondeterminism. In Sect. 2.3, we shall see how MSOS allows us to specify the interleaving of computations without making any assumptions at all about their possible effects.

Well-Typedness. The lifted signatures of funcons and value operations determine a set of well-sorted funcon terms for each sort. However, the well-sortedness of a funcon term is independent of its context, and it does not exclude terms whose computation leads to the *value* of an argument not being of the required sort. For example, consider **if-true**(E, C_1, C_2), which is well-sorted whenever E is of sort *exprs* and C_1, C_2 are both of sort *comms*: after evaluating E, the computation gets stuck unless the value of E is true or false. In contrast, **if-true**(E, C_1, C_2) is *well-typed* in a particular context only if E is guaranteed to compute a Boolean value whenever it terminates normally. The well-typedness of funcon terms is required by their static semantics, which is considered in Sect. 2.4.

2.2   Language Semantics

We next consider how to specify a translation from a programming language to funcons. Each funcon has not only dynamic semantics (as illustrated in Sect. 2.3) but also static semantics (see Sect. 2.4), so a single translation of complete programs to funcon terms determines both the static and dynamic semantics of the programs.

The starting point for specifying a translation to funcons is a context-free grammar for the abstract syntax of the source language. We define functions mapping abstract syntax trees generated by the grammar to terms of the appropriate computation or value sorts. The functions are compositional: the translation of a composite language construct is a combination of the translations of its components. We specify the translation functions inductively, by equations (much as in denotational semantics).

The following examples illustrate how to specify the translation of some simple language constructs to funcons. Their main purpose is to show the form of the equations used to define the translation functions. Section 3 provides excerpts from a component-based semantics for a complete language, demonstrating how our approach scales up, and how to translate some less straightforward language constructs to funcons.

Expressions. Let *exp* be the nonterminal symbol for expressions in some programming language. We specify that the function *expr*$[\![\_]\!]$ translates abstract syntax trees generated by *exp* to funcon terms of sort *exprs* thus:

$$expr[\![\_ : exp]\!] : exprs$$

Note that language constructs are always inside $[\![\cdots]\!]$, and funcons outside, so clashes of notation between them are insignificant. Let the meta-variable E, optionally subscripted and/or primed, range over abstract syntax trees generated by *exp*.

Recall the conditional expressions specified in SOS in Sect. 1. When their conditions are Boolean-valued, the intended semantics of these expressions correspond exactly to the semantics of the funcon **if-true** (lifted from *booleans* to *exprs* in its first argument), so we can specify their translation very simply indeed:

$$expr[\![\,E_1\,?\,E_2:E_3\,]\!] = \textbf{if-true}(expr[\![\,E_1\,]\!], expr[\![\,E_2\,]\!], expr[\![\,E_3\,]\!]) \qquad (10)$$

The variant where E_1 is a numerical expression can be specified by inserting the appropriate value operations to compute **true** when the value of E_1 is non-zero, and **false** otherwise:

$$expr[\![\,E_1\,?\,E_2:E_3\,]\!] = \textbf{if-true}(\textbf{not}(\textbf{equal}(expr[\![\,E_1\,]\!],0)), \qquad (11)$$
$$expr[\![\,E_2\,]\!], expr[\![\,E_3\,]\!])$$

Notice that the well-sortedness of the terms in the above equation comes from lifting the value operations **not** and **equal** to the computation sort *exprs*. Lifting also allows the following straightforward translation of equality test expressions.

$$expr[\![\,E_1 == E_2\,]\!] = \textbf{equal}(expr[\![\,E_1\,]\!], expr[\![\,E_2\,]\!]) \qquad (12)$$

To specify left-to-right evaluation of '$E_1 == E_2$', we can use the funcons **supply** and **given**, as follows.

$$expr[\![\,E_1 == E_2\,]\!] = \ \textbf{supply}(expr[\![\,E_1\,]\!], \textbf{equal}(\textbf{given}, expr[\![\,E_2\,]\!])) \qquad (13)$$

When identifiers I in expressions can refer only to (imperative) variables, we can translate them as follows:

$$expr[\![\,I\,]\!] = \textbf{assigned-value}(\textbf{bound-value}(id[\![\,I\,]\!])) \qquad (14)$$

Here $id[\![\,\_\,]\!]$ translates identifiers in a language to elements of our pre-defined value sort *ids*. The funcon **assigned-value** requires its argument to compute a variable, and gives the value currently assigned to that variable. When identifiers might also refer to other sorts of values, we use a funcon (not illustrated here) that gives the same result as **assigned-value** when the value of its argument is a variable, and otherwise simply returns the value.

Statements. Let *stm* be the nonterminal symbol for statements S in some programming language. The corresponding sort of funcons is *comms* (commands), so we use the following translation function.

$$comm[\![\,\_:stm\,]\!] : comms$$

An assignment statement '$I = E$; ' corresponds to a straightforward combination of the **assign** and **bound-value** funcons:

$$comm[\![\,I = E\,;\,]\!] = \textbf{assign}(\textbf{bound-value}(id[\![\,I\,]\!]), expr[\![\,E\,]\!]) \qquad (15)$$

The following translation of assignment *expressions* illustrates repeated use of a previously computed value, which is first assigned, then returned as the result:

$$expr[\![\,I = E\,]\!] = \textbf{supply}(expr[\![\,E\,]\!], \ \textbf{seq}(\textbf{assign}(\textbf{bound-value}(id[\![\,I\,]\!]), \textbf{given}),$$
$$\textbf{given})) \qquad (16)$$

The combination of assignment expressions and the following expression statements (which discard the value of E) allows the specification of assignment *statements* in (15) to be derived.

$$comm [\![E \, ; \,]\!] = \textbf{effect}(expr [\![E]\!]) \tag{17}$$

Our translation of if-else statements uses the same polymorphic **if-true** funcon as that of conditional expressions above:

$$comm [\![\, \texttt{if} \, (\, E \,) \, S_1 \, \texttt{else} \, S_2 \,]\!] = \textbf{if-true}(expr [\![E]\!], comm [\![S_1]\!], comm [\![S_2]\!]) \tag{18}$$

For if-then statements, we can exploit the usual 'desugaring', which we specify by the following equation.

$$comm [\![\, \texttt{if} \, (\, E \,) \, S \,]\!] = comm [\![\, \texttt{if} \, (\, E \,) \, S \, \texttt{else} \, \{ \, \} \,]\!] \tag{19}$$

Provided that we do not introduce circularity between such equations, they give the effect of translating a language to a kernel sublanguage, followed by translation of the kernel constructs to funcons. When the grammar of the kernel is of particular interest, we could exhibit it, and separate the specification of desugaring from the specification of the translation of the kernel to funcons.

The translation of the empty statement '{ }' used above is just as simple as one might expect:

$$comm [\![\, \{ \, \} \,]\!] = \textbf{null} \tag{20}$$

While-statements with Boolean conditions correspond exactly to our **while-true** funcon (without any lifting, since the computations of both the expression E and the statement S may need to be repeated):

$$comm [\![\, \texttt{while} \, (\, E \,) \, S \,]\!] = \textbf{while-true}(expr [\![E]\!], comm [\![S]\!]) \tag{21}$$

Our final illustrative example of specifying translations demonstrates a technique used frequently in our CAML LIGHT case study in Sect. 3. Statement sequences may consist of more than two statements, but our **seq** funcon for sequencing commands takes only two arguments. In the following equation, we use '$\cdots$' *formally* as a meta-variable ranging over *stm** (possibly-empty sequences of statements).

$$comm [\![S_1 \, S_2 \, \cdots]\!] = \textbf{seq}(comm [\![S_1]\!], comm [\![S_2 \, \cdots]\!]) \tag{22}$$

To translate a sequence of just two statements, '$S_1 \, S_2 \, \cdots$' matches '$\cdots$' with the empty sequence, and we can then regard '$S_2 \, \cdots$' as a single statement, whose translation is specified by our other equations. To translate a sequence of three or more statements, '$S_1 \, S_2 \, \cdots$' matches '$\cdots$' with a non-empty sequence, and we can use the above equation recursively to translate '$S_2 \, \cdots$'. For instance, the above equations translate a sequence of the form '$S_1 \, S_2 \, S_3$' to a funcon term $\textbf{seq}(C_1, \textbf{seq}(C_2, C_3))$, where each C_i is the translation of the single statement S_i.

We give many further examples of specifying translations from language constructs to funcons in Sect. 3.

2.3   Dynamic Semantics of Funcon Notation

The preceding subsections illustrate how we use sorts and signatures to specify the syntax of funcon notation, and how we specify translation functions that map programs to funcon terms. We now explain and illustrate how to specify the dynamic semantics of funcons, once and for all, using a modular form of operational semantics; Sect. 2.4 does the same for their static semantics.

Modular SOS (MSOS). Modular SOS [42] is a simple variant of structural operational semantics (SOS) [56]. It allows a particularly high degree of reuse without any need for reformulation. The specification of each language construct in MSOS is independent of the features of the other constructs included in the language. This is achieved by incorporating all auxiliary entities used in transition formulae (environments, stores, etc.) in *labels* (L) on transitions. Thus transition formulae for expressions are always of the form $E \xrightarrow{L} E'$ (and similarly for other sorts of language constructs).

The MSOS notation for labels ensures automatic propagation of all *unmentioned* auxiliary entities between the premise(s) and conclusion of each rule. For this to work, the labels on adjacent steps of a computation are required to be *composable*, and a set of *unobservable* labels is distinguished.[2] This allows the following MSOS rules for the dynamic semantics of conditional expressions '$E_1 ? E_2 : E_3$' to be used both for imperative and for purely functional languages, without any reformulation:

$$\frac{E_1 \xrightarrow{L} E_1'}{(E_1 ? E_2 : E_3) \xrightarrow{L} (E_1' ? E_2 : E_3)} \tag{23}$$

$$(\texttt{true} ? E_2 : E_3) \xrightarrow{\tau} E_2 \tag{24}$$

$$(\texttt{false} ? E_2 : E_3) \xrightarrow{\tau} E_3 \tag{25}$$

The variable τ varies over all *unobservable* labels, whereas L ranges over arbitrary labels. By not mentioning specific auxiliary entities, the rules assume neither their presence nor their absence, ensuring reusability – even when expression evaluation can throw exceptions or spawn concurrent processes. This also makes the rules significantly simpler, and easier to read (some conventional rules in the literature almost hurt ones eyes to look at!) and reduces the likelihood of making clerical mistakes when formulating them.

The MSOS rules for assignment expressions are as follows.

$$\frac{E \xrightarrow{L} E'}{(I = E) \xrightarrow{L} (I = E')} \tag{26}$$

$$(I = V) \xrightarrow{\rho, \sigma, \sigma' = \sigma[\rho(I) \mapsto V], \tau} V \tag{27}$$

---

[2] In fact labels in MSOS are the morphisms of a *category*, and the unobservable labels are identity morphisms, as explained in [42]. However, models of MSOS specifications correspond to ordinary labelled transition systems.

The notation used on the transition arrow in (27) above indicates that when assignment expressions are included in a language, the labels on transitions are to have at least an environment ρ and a pair of stores σ, σ'. The inclusion of τ in the label specifies that any further components must be unobservable, which is necessary to ensure that executing this simple assignment expression cannot have further effects (e.g., assigning to other variables, printing, or throwing an exception).[3]

If we include the above conditional expressions and assignment expressions in the same language, no changes at all are needed to their MSOS rules – in marked contrast to the weaving required in SOS, as illustrated in Sect. 1.

Implicitly-Modular SOS (I-MSOS) [49]. This combines the benefits of MSOS regarding modularity and reusability with the familiar notational style of ordinary SOS: auxiliary entities not actually mentioned in a rule are implicitly propagated between its premise(s) and conclusion, just as in MSOS, but *without* the notational burden of putting an explicit label on every transition relation.

All that is needed is to declare the notation used for the transition formulae being specified (which is in any case normal practice in SOS descriptions of programming languages, e.g. [54]), distinguishing any required auxiliary arguments from the syntactic source and target of transitions. Here, we do this by insisting on some notational conventions commonly followed in SOS:

- Environments ρ (and any other entities that are *preserved* by successive transitions) are written before a turnstile, e.g., $\mathsf{env}\,\rho \vdash \_ \to \_$.
- Stores σ (and any other entities that can be *updated* by transitions) are written after the syntactic source and target, e.g., $(\_, \mathsf{store}\,\sigma) \to (\_, \mathsf{store}\,\sigma')$.
- Signals ε (and any other entities *emitted* by transitions) are written as labels above transition symbols, e.g., $\_ \xrightarrow{\mathsf{exception}\,\varepsilon} \_$.

The entities are tagged with distinct markers (such as env, store and $\mathsf{exception}$) to ensure that they cannot be confused with other entities needed in the same position.

The I-MSOS rules for conditional expressions can be formulated *exactly* as the SOS rules (1)–(3) given in Sect. 1. The I-MSOS rules for assignment expressions are as follows.

$$\frac{E \to E'}{(I = E) \to (I = E')} \tag{28}$$

$$\mathsf{env}\,\rho \vdash (I = V, \mathsf{store}\,\sigma) \to (V, \mathsf{store}\,\sigma[\rho(I) \mapsto V]) \tag{29}$$

Notice that entities such as environments ρ and stores σ can (and should!) be omitted whenever a rule does not involve inspecting or updating them.

---

[3] For an assignment that might throw an exception, the corresponding MSOS rule would make explicit the conditions under which that occurs, and incorporate the exception flag in the label.

It is straightforward to generate MSOS rules directly from I-MSOS rules (and label categories from transition formulae declarations). The label patterns in a generated rule involve only those auxiliary entities explicitly mentioned in the original I-MSOS rule. The foundations of MSOS [42], together with its recently developed modular bisimulation theory and congruence format [11], provide correspondingly modular foundations for I-MSOS specifications.

I-MSOS Specifications of Funcons. The I-MSOS rules given below specify the dynamic semantics of all the funcons whose signatures are listed in Table 1 (page 138). In these rules, the (optionally subscripted or primed) meta-variables C range over *comms*, D over *decls*, E over *exprs*, V over *values*, and X over arbitrary computations (including their computed values).

When specifying the dynamic semantics of a funcon using small-step I-MSOS rules, the so-called 'congruence' rules for evaluation of any lifted arguments can be generated from the signature and left implicit, which dramatically improves the conciseness of our specifications. The elimination of the many tedious congruence rules that would be needed in small-step SOS specifications of funcons is a major advantage of our approach, and the resulting conciseness of small-step I-MSOS specifications is competitive with that of specifications using the popular framework of reduction semantics, based on evaluation contexts [19]. This feature of I-MSOS is closely related to (and was inspired by) the use of strictness annotations in the K framework [58].

The funcon **if-true**(V, X_1, X_2) is generic: X_1, X_2 can be of the same arbitrary computation sort (usually expressions or commands). Its first argument is generally lifted from *booleans* to *exprs*. Since the rule specifying the evaluation of the lifted argument is implied by the signature, only the following two rules need to be explicitly specified.

$$\textbf{if-true}(\textbf{true}, X_1, X_2) \rightarrow X_1 \tag{30}$$

$$\textbf{if-true}(\textbf{false}, X_1, X_2) \rightarrow X_2 \tag{31}$$

seq(C, X) is generic in its second argument, whereas its first argument is always a command (lifted from the value sort *unit* in the signature). The funcon first executes C. The value **null** is computed by all commands on normal termination, so all we need to specify is that when that has happened, the computation continues with X:

$$\textbf{seq}(\textbf{null}, X) \rightarrow X \tag{32}$$

effect(E) is the command funcon which evaluates the expression E and then discards the value. The argument is lifted to expressions from a value sort, so here again the rule specifying the evaluation of the argument is left implicit.

$$\textbf{effect}(V) \rightarrow \textbf{null} \tag{33}$$

while-true(E, C) involves repeated evaluation of the expression E, and repeated execution of the command C, so the signature cannot involve lifting from value sorts.

The execution of this funcon is specified simply by the obvious unfolding rule, exploiting the existence of the funcons **if-true** and **seq**.[4]

$$\textbf{while-true}(E, C) \rightarrow \textbf{if-true}(E, \textbf{seq}(C, \textbf{while-true}(E, C)), \textbf{null}) \qquad (34)$$

assign(E_1, E_2) is a command funcon that simply updates the imperative variable V_1 computed by E_1 to the value V_2 computed by E_2.

$$\frac{V_1 \in \textbf{dom}(\sigma)}{(\textbf{assign}(V_1, V_2), \textbf{store}\,\sigma) \rightarrow (\textbf{null}, \textbf{store}\,\sigma[V_1 \mapsto V_2])} \qquad (35)$$

Notice that the rules above for assignment mention stores σ but not environments ρ. It is characteristic that, in contrast to many language constructs, each funcon generally involves only one kind of auxiliary entity.

The assignment funcon is compatible with shared-memory access by concurrent threads: the steps specified above are atomic updates, and can be serialised.

The expression funcon **assigned-value**(E) inspects the value currently stored in the variable computed by E, without changing it.

$$(\textbf{assigned-value}(V), \textbf{store}\,\sigma) \rightarrow (\sigma(V), \textbf{store}\,\sigma) \qquad (36)$$

bind-value(I, E) is a declaration funcon used to compute the single-point environment that maps I to the value of E.

$$\textbf{bind-value}(I, V) \rightarrow \{I \mapsto V\} \qquad (37)$$

bound-value(I) is an expression funcon that inspects the value currently bound to the identifier I; the result is undefined (and the rule inapplicable, which would lead to a stuck computation) if I is not in the domain of the current environment ρ.

$$\textbf{env}\,\rho \vdash \textbf{bound-value}(I) \rightarrow \rho(I) \qquad (38)$$

scope(D, X) executes the declaration D to compute an environment ρ_1, then binds the identifiers in the domain of ρ_1 locally in the computation X, letting these bindings override the bindings represented by the current environment ρ. This funcon is lifted in its first argument, whereas the rule for the computation of its second argument has to be explicitly specified, since the environment is not merely propagated. Rule (40) applies only when V is a value, which is independent of the current context.

$$\frac{\textbf{env}\,(\rho_1/\rho) \vdash X \rightarrow X'}{\textbf{env}\,\rho \vdash \textbf{scope}(\rho_1, X) \rightarrow \textbf{scope}(\rho_1, X')} \qquad (39)$$

$$\textbf{scope}(\rho_1, V) \rightarrow V \qquad (40)$$

given is an expression which gives the value computed by the closest-enclosing **supply**. The rules specifying these funcons below are essentially simplified versions of the above rules for **bound-value** and **scope**, with **given** corresponding

---

[4] In small-step semantics, the use of auxiliary funcons for specifying **while-true** appears to be unavoidable.

to the value currently bound to a fixed pseudo-identifier, propagated by a corresponding auxiliary entity.

$$\text{given } V \vdash \textbf{given} \rightarrow V \tag{41}$$

$$\frac{\text{given } V \vdash X \rightarrow X'}{\text{given } \_ \vdash \textbf{supply}(V, X) \rightarrow \textbf{supply}(V, X')} \tag{42}$$

$$\textbf{supply}(V_1, V_2) \rightarrow V_2 \tag{43}$$

This concludes the specification of the dynamic semantics of all the funcons whose signatures are shown in Table 1. The rules have been validated indirectly: by generating Prolog clauses from them, then using those clauses to execute programs in various languages according to their translations to funcons, as described in Sect. 4.

Most of the funcons specified above are (re)used in the CAML LIGHT case study presented in Sect. 3, together with some more advanced funcons involving abstractions, patterns and exceptions. Before that, let us see how to specify the static semantics of funcons.

2.4   Static Semantics of Funcon Notation

For a program in some programming language, its static semantics represents analysis that is supposed to be done on the (parsed) program text before running the program. In many languages, the scopes of identifier bindings are determined by the structure of the program, and the required analysis checks that there are no unbound occurrences. Such languages may also be statically typed, i.e., the type of values potentially computed by each expression in the program can be determined, and checked to be consistent with the type of values required by the context of the expression. When the types of identifiers are not given explicitly in the program, the analysis needs to infer them. The outcome of the analysis of an entire program is either its type, or an indication that some part of it is not well-typed.

Running a program usually involves executing only certain parts of it, in a particular order, possibly with iteration, procedure activation, abrupt termination, etc. Small-step (I-M)SOS is particularly well-suited to specifying the dynamic semantics of such programs. In contrast, static analysis of a program generally involves the analysis of each of its parts just once, in no particular order, to carry out all the required checks; this motivates the use of the big-step style of (I-M)SOS for specifying static semantics [27].

The static semantics of a language is specified by a *typing relation* between expressions E, types T, and *typing contexts* Γ (mapping identifiers to their types), conventionally written '$\Gamma \vdash E : T$'; further arguments of the typing relation (e.g., store types, type variable assignments) may be introduced, if needed. We can informally read the relation as saying that expression E has type T in context Γ. When the typing relation is *sound* in relation to evaluation, this means that E can only compute a value of type T when the environment can be typed by Γ. An environment ρ is typed by Γ whenever Γ maps each identifier I in the domain of ρ to the type of the value $\rho(I)$. The typing relation can be inductively specified using *typing rules* [54], which are similar in form to big-step SOS rules. Using I-MSOS, we can formulate our typing rules omitting auxiliary entities whenever they merely need to be propagated.

I-MSOS Specifications of Funcons. The I-MSOS rules given below specify the static semantics of all the funcons whose signatures are listed in Table 1 (page 138). The meta-variable T ranges over the value sort *types*, which provides notation for type constants and constructors independently of language syntax.

The funcon **if-true**(E, X_1, X_2) requires E to have type *booleans*, and X_1 and X_2 to have the same arbitrary type T, all in the same typing context Γ (which I-MSOS lets us leave implicit):

$$\frac{E : \textit{booleans} \qquad X_1 : T \qquad X_2 : T}{\textbf{if-true}(E, X_1, X_2) : T} \tag{44}$$

seq(C, X) requires C to be a well-typed command, which corresponds to it having the singleton type *unit*. The funcon then has the same type as X:

$$\frac{C : \textit{unit} \qquad X : T}{\textbf{seq}(C, X) : T} \tag{45}$$

effect(E) merely requires E to be a well-typed expression:

$$\frac{E : T}{\textbf{effect}(E) : \textit{unit}} \tag{46}$$

while-true(E, C) requires E to have type *booleans*:

$$\frac{E : \textit{booleans} \qquad C : \textit{unit}}{\textbf{while-true}(E, C) : \textit{unit}} \tag{47}$$

An imperative variable for storing values of a specific type T has the type *variables*(T). The funcon command **assign**(E_1, E_2) requires the types of E_1 and E_2 to match accordingly:

$$\frac{E_1 : \textit{variables}(T) \qquad E_2 : T}{\textbf{assign}(E_1, E_2) : \textit{unit}} \tag{48}$$

assigned-value(E) allows E to have any variable type:

$$\frac{E : \textit{variables}(T)}{\textbf{assigned-value}(E) : T} \tag{49}$$

For languages where identifiers might be bound to constant values as well as to variables, whether to use **assigned-value** or not depends on the type of the identifier. Assuming that the types of identifiers are statically determined, the static semantics of funcons could subsequently eliminate irrelevant alternatives.[5]

bind-value(I, E) is a declaration, and its type is the single-point typing context that maps I to the type of E:

$$\frac{E : T}{\textbf{bind-value}(I, E) : \{I \mapsto T\}} \tag{50}$$

bound-value(I) has the type determined by the current typing context Γ (which I-MSOS allowed us to leave implicit in all the above rules). If I is not in the domain of Γ, $\Gamma(I)$ is undefined, and the rule cannot be applied.

$$\text{env } \Gamma \vdash \textbf{bound-value}(I) : \Gamma(I) \tag{51}$$

scope(D, X) adjusts the typing context used for X to account for the local bindings computed by D:

$$\frac{\text{env } \Gamma \vdash D : \Gamma_1 \qquad \text{env } (\Gamma_1 / \Gamma) \vdash X : T}{\text{env } \Gamma \vdash \textbf{scope}(D, X) : T} \tag{52}$$

It is important here that we require environments to map identifiers to *values* (not computations), and for our values to be context-free. These requirements suffice to ensure that the typeability of a dynamic environment is preserved by overriding. Consequently, given this typing rule for **scope**, the corresponding dynamic rules (39), (40) are safe with respect to type preservation.

The static semantics of **given** and **supply** is related to that of **bound-value** and **scope** in the same way as their dynamic semantics. It involves the introduction of a read-only entity that shows the type of value provided by **supply**.

$$\text{given } T \vdash \textbf{given} : T \tag{53}$$

$$\frac{\text{given } T_1 \vdash E : T \qquad \text{given } T \vdash X : T'}{\text{given } T_1 \vdash \textbf{supply}(E, X) : T'} \tag{54}$$

This concludes the specification of the static semantics of all the funcons whose signatures are shown in Table 1. Under these static semantics, each dynamic rule is safe from the point of view of type preservation. Therefore, the typing rules for the funcons that we have considered in this section are sound in relation to their dynamic semantics: when a funcon term has type T in a typing context Γ, the values it computes on normal termination in an environment typed by Γ are always of type T.

3   An Illustrative Case Study: CAML LIGHT

CAML LIGHT descends from CAML, a predecessor of the language OCAML, and is similar to the core of STANDARD ML [38]. It has first-class functions, assignable

---

[5] Static semantics sometimes requires such so-called partial evaluation.

state, exception handling mechanisms, and pattern matching. It is statically typed, and supports algebraic data types and polymorphism.

The syntax and semantics of CAML LIGHT are specified in its reference manual [32]. It contains a formal context-free grammar of 'concrete abstract syntax': this generates CAML LIGHT programs, but disambiguation details are abstracted away. However, the explanation it gives of the intended semantics of CAML LIGHT programs is completely informal.

In this section, after introducing the syntax of CAML LIGHT, we illustrate our approach by presenting excerpts from a component-based semantics of the language. Section 3.1 gives an overview of the required values and funcons; Sect. 3.2 gives examples of specifying the translation of CAML LIGHT into combinations of funcons; Sect. 3.3 specifies the dynamic semantics of the funcons; Sect. 3.4 specifies their static semantics; and Sect. 3.5 specifies the translation of CAML LIGHT constructs that involve funcons which only have static significance. The complete specification of the translation of CAML LIGHT to funcons is provided in the Appendix, and the sources of the full specifications can be found online [12].

CAML LIGHT is a language built around *expressions* which compute values, including numbers, strings, function abstractions, tuples and lists. Commands (or statements) are not a separate syntactic category, but rather expressions that compute a particular null value, written (). Expressions are given a type, which includes ground types (e.g. int), tuple types (e.g. int*int) and function types (e.g. int->int). Commands and () have type unit.

Some example CAML LIGHT programs can be found in Table 2. First, we see a recursively defined Fibonacci function fib. The function is defined using the function constructor, introducing a closed function abstraction. Identifiers may be bound to particular values within an expression using let bindings, and recursive functions using the let rec construct. Formal arguments can also appear as parameters before the '=', as in the definitions of append and insertion_sort.

As well as expressions, values and types, CAML LIGHT supports matching values against *patterns* which bind identifiers. This is demonstrated in the append example, where the first argument zs is matched against two patterns: the empty list [], and the list-constructor pattern x::xs, which binds x to the head and xs to the tail of a nonempty list.

CAML LIGHT also supports imperative behaviour, as can be seen in the insertion_sort example, acting on an array. Arrays are mutable: their content may be updated. A single assignable reference cell is constructed using ref, and it may be accessed using explicit dereferencing '!' and updated using ':='. In this example we also see two different looping constructs.

An extract of the CAML LIGHT reference grammar [32] is given in Table 3.

3.1   Further Funcon Notation

In Sect. 2, we introduced some basic funcons for commands, declarations and expressions. We next consider the further funcons used in our CAML LIGHT case study, involving abstractions, patterns and exception handling. They are listed

Table 2. Some example CAML LIGHT programs

```
let rec fib = function n ->
  if n < 2 then n else fib(n-1) + fib(n-2) ;;

let rec append zs ys =
  match zs with
  | []     -> ys
  | x::xs -> x :: (append xs ys) ;;

let insertion_sort a =
  for i = 1 to vect_length a - 1 do
    let val_i = a.(i) in
    let j = ref i in
    while !j > 0 & val_i < a.(!j - 1) do
      a.(!j) <- a.(!j - 1);
      j := !j - 1
    done;
    a.(!j) <- val_i
  done;;
```

---

in Table 4, with their signatures. We discuss their semantics informally, focusing on dynamic semantics; see Sects. 3.3 and 3.4 for their formal specifications.

Abstractions. A value of sort *funcs* is an abstraction encapsulating an expression that computes a value which may depend on the value of an argument supplied by application. Dependence of the expression on the current environment may occur only when its execution is forced (by applying the abstraction) or when a closure is formed (by copying the current environment into the expression). Static scoping is obtained by computing the closure of each abstraction when it is created; application of abstractions otherwise gives dynamic scoping.

Abstractions A can be constructed using **patt-abs**(P, E), which abstracts an expression E over a pattern P. When no matching of the given value is needed, **abs**(E) allows E to refer to it using the funcon **given**. Abstractions can be turned into self-contained function closures using the **close** funcon, to ensure static scoping. Abstractions may be applied to argument values using the **apply** funcon. An application of the abstraction **prefer-over**(A_1, A_2) applies A_1 to the given argument value, applying A_2 only if that *fails*. (Failure is a kind of abrupt termination, considered in more detail in Sect. 3.3.)

Patterns. A value of sort *patts* is an abstraction encapsulating a declaration that computes an environment from a given value. An example pattern is **any**,

Table 3. An extract of the CAML LIGHT reference grammar [32], with EBNF replaced by $(\cdot)^*$, $(\cdot)^+$, $(\cdot)^?$ and the nonterminal *expr* renamed to *exp*

Lexical syntax

$$I : ident$$
$$Int : integer\text{-}literal$$
$$Float : float\text{-}literal$$
$$Char : char\text{-}literal$$
$$String : string\text{-}literal$$

Context-free syntax

$T : typexpr ::=$ ' *ident* | *typexpr* -> *typexpr* | *typexpr* (* *typexpr*)$^+$
      | *typeconstr* | *typexpr* *typeconstr*
      | (*typexpr* (, *typexpr*)*) *typeconstr*

$C : constant ::=$ *integer-literal* | *float-literal* | *char-literal* | *string-literal*
      | **false** | **true** | [] | ()

$P : pattern ::=$ *ident* | _ | *pattern* **as** *ident*
      | (*pattern*) | (*pattern* : *typexpr*)
      | *pattern*|*pattern* | *constant* | *pattern* (, *pattern*)$^+$
      | [] | [*pattern* (; *pattern*)*] | *pattern* :: *pattern*

$E : exp ::=$ *ident* | *constant* | (*exp*) | **begin** *exp* **end**
      | (*exp* : *typexpr*) | *exp* (, *exp*)$^+$
      | *exp* :: *exp* | [*exp* (; *exp*)*] | [| *exp* (; *exp*)* |]
      | *exp* *exp* | *prefix-op* *exp* | *exp* *infix-op* *exp*
      | **not** *exp* | *exp* & *exp* | *exp* **or** *exp*
      | *exp* . (*exp*) | *exp* . (*exp*) <- *exp*
      | **if** *exp* **then** *exp* (**else** *exp*)$^?$
      | **while** *exp* **do** *exp* **done**
      | **for** *ident* = *exp* (**to** | **downto**) *exp* **do** *exp* **done**
      | *exp* ; *exp*
      | **match** *exp* **with** *simple-matching*
      | **function** *simple-matching*
      | **try** *exp* **with** *simple-matching*
      | **let** (**rec**)$^?$ *let-binding* (**and** *let-binding*)* **in** *exp*

$SM : simple\text{-}matching ::=$ *pattern* -> *exp* (| *pattern* -> *exp*)*
$LB : let\text{-}binding ::=$ *pattern* = *exp*

Table 4. Funcon signatures (see also Table 1)

Abstraction sorts

> $funcs = abs(values, values)$
>
> $patts = abs(values, environments)$

Funcon and abstraction signatures

$$\textbf{abs}(exprs) : funcs$$
$$\textbf{any} : patts$$
$$\textbf{apply}(funcs, values) : exprs$$
$$\textbf{bind}(ids) : patts$$
$$\textbf{catch}(exprs, funcs) : exprs$$
$$\textbf{catch-else-rethrow}(exprs, funcs) : exprs$$
$$\textbf{close}(funcs) : exprs$$
$$\textbf{closure}(computes(X), environments) : computes(X)$$
$$\textbf{else}(computes(X), computes(X)) : computes(X)$$
$$\textbf{fail} : computes(X)$$
$$\textbf{match}(values, patts) : decls$$
$$\textbf{only}(values) : patts$$
$$\textbf{patt-abs}(patts, exprs) : funcs$$
$$\textbf{patt-union}(patts, patts) : patts$$
$$\textbf{prefer-over}(abs(X, Y), abs(X, Y)) : abs(X, Y)$$
$$\textbf{throw}(values) : computes(X)$$

---

which matches any value and produces no bindings, modelling the '_' wildcard in CAML LIGHT. The funcon **only** takes a value and matches just that value, again producing no bindings. The pattern **bind**(I) matches any value, and binds I to it. Compound patterns may be constructed out of more primitive patterns.

Exceptions. The computation **throw**(V) terminates abruptly, and so can be seen to compute a value of any sort, vacuously. The **catch** funcon handles abrupt termination of its first argument by applying a function to the thrown value. The **catch-else-rethrow** funcon abbreviates a variant on this: it rethrows the exception should it fail to be in the domain of the handler.

3.2   CAML LIGHT Semantics

We translate CAML LIGHT (abstract syntax trees) into funcon terms. The signatures of the translation functions are listed in Table 5. For CAML LIGHT, computed values include ground constants (integers, Booleans, strings, floats, chars) as well as records (maps, wrapped in a data constructor), variants for disjoint unions (a single value tagged with a constructor), tuples, and function abstractions.

Table 5. Translation function signatures

Semantics

$$id\,[\![\;\_\;:\,ident\,]\!]\,:\,ids$$
$$type\,[\![\;\_\;:\,typexpr\,]\!]\,:\,types$$
$$value\,[\![\;\_\;:\,constant\,]\!]\,:\,values$$
$$patt\,[\![\;\_\;:\,pattern\,]\!]\,:\,patts$$
$$expr\,[\![\;\_\;:\,exp\,]\!]\,:\,exprs$$
$$func\,[\![\;\_\;:\,simple\text{-}matching\,]\!]\,:\,funcs$$
$$decl\,[\![\;\_\;:\,let\text{-}binding\,]\!]\,:\,decls$$

We next show some of the equations specifying the translation of CAML LIGHT programs to funcon terms. We will first consider dynamic semantics, specifying a translation which captures the intended runtime behaviour. Often, this translation will also capture the static semantics correctly (since each funcon by design has a natural combination of dynamic and static semantics). When it does not, we need to add funcons to the translation to reflect the intended compile-time behaviour, as we illustrate in Sect. 3.5.

Conditional. CAML LIGHT's conditional construct on Booleans is translated straightforwardly into the **if-true** funcon we have already seen:

$$expr\,[\![\;\text{if } E_1 \text{ then } E_2 \text{ else } E_3\;]\!]\,= \tag{55}$$
$$\textbf{if-true}(expr\,[\![\,E_1\,]\!], expr\,[\![\,E_2\,]\!], expr\,[\![\,E_3\,]\!])$$

Here we are lifting the funcon **if-true** in the first argument to computations that *might* compute a Boolean, and similarly when lifting is applied to pure data operations, such as **not**. The static semantics of the translation of a complete program to funcons checks that the arguments are in fact of type *booleans*.

$$expr\,[\![\;\text{not } E\;]\!]\,=\textbf{not}(expr\,[\![\,E\,]\!]) \tag{56}$$

We also use the **if-true** funcon in the translation of other CAML LIGHT constructs, such as the conditional conjunction operator:

$$expr\,[\![\,E_1 \;\&\; E_2\,]\!]\,=\textbf{if-true}(expr\,[\![\,E_1\,]\!], expr\,[\![\,E_2\,]\!], \textbf{false}) \tag{57}$$

Sequencing. The sequencing construct of CAML LIGHT is translated as follows:

$$expr[\![\, E_1 \; ; \; E_2 \,]\!] = \mathbf{seq}(\mathbf{effect}(expr[\![\, E_1 \,]\!]), expr[\![\, E_2 \,]\!]) \tag{58}$$

Here, we explicitly discard the computed value of the first expression.

Pattern Matching. We translate CAML LIGHT's simple matching construct SM to a function abstraction using $func[\![\, \_ \,]\!]$. Our analysis of a match expression is as an application of such an abstraction to the matched expression, inserting **prefer-over** to take into account what happens when the pattern fails to match the given value:

$$expr[\![\, \mathtt{match}\, E\, \mathtt{with}\, SM \,]\!] = \tag{59}$$
$$\mathbf{apply}(\mathbf{prefer\text{-}over}(func[\![\, SM \,]\!], \mathbf{abs}(\mathbf{throw}(\mathbf{cl\text{-}match\text{-}failure}))),$$
$$expr[\![\, E \,]\!])$$

The funcon **cl-match-failure** is CAML LIGHT-specific, and is defined simply as a convenient abbreviation for the (translated) `Match_failure` constructor of CAML LIGHT's built in `exn` type.

Function Application. The funcon **apply** corresponds directly to CAML LIGHT's call-by-value function application:

$$expr[\![\, E_1\, E_2 \,]\!] = \mathbf{apply}(expr[\![\, E_1 \,]\!], expr[\![\, E_2 \,]\!]) \tag{60}$$

The signature of **apply** indicates that it should be applied to a function abstraction and an argument *value*; it is lifted here to computations. We would specify call-by-name semantics by forming a (parameterless closed) abstraction from the argument expression, to prevent its premature evaluation.

Function Abstraction. CAML LIGHT is a functional language, and we represent functions as abstraction values.

$$expr[\![\, \mathtt{function}\, SM \,]\!] = \tag{61}$$
$$\mathbf{prefer\text{-}over}(func[\![\, SM \,]\!], \mathbf{abs}(\mathbf{throw}(\mathbf{cl\text{-}match\text{-}failure})))$$

Simple Matchings. We will next see how $func[\![\, \_ \,]\!]$ translates simple matchings to abstractions. For a single body, the **patt-abs** funcon captures matchings accurately; sequences of simple matchings are combined using **prefer-over**. We use the **close** funcon to specify static bindings.

$$func[\![\, P\, \text{->}\, E \,]\!] = \mathbf{close}(\mathbf{patt\text{-}abs}(patt[\![\, P \,]\!], expr[\![\, E \,]\!])) \tag{62}$$

$$func[\![\, P\, \text{->}\, E \mid SM \,]\!] = \mathbf{prefer\text{-}over}(func[\![\, P\, \text{->}\, E \,]\!], func[\![\, SM \,]\!]) \tag{63}$$

Declarations. Local declarations are provided in CAML LIGHT by the 'let - in' construct, corresponding to the **scope** funcon:

$$expr[\![\text{ let } LB \text{ in } E]\!] = \textbf{scope}(decl[\![LB]\!], expr[\![E]\!]) \qquad (64)$$

Let-bindings are translated to declarations.

$$decl[\![P = E]\!] = \qquad\qquad\qquad\qquad\qquad\qquad (65)$$
$$\textbf{match}(expr[\![E]\!],$$
$$\textbf{prefer-over}(patt[\![P]\!], \textbf{abs}(\textbf{throw}(\textbf{cl-match-failure}))))$$

An identifier expression refers to its bound value.

$$expr[\![I]\!] = \textbf{bound-value}(id[\![I]\!]) \qquad (66)$$

The preceding two equations account for dynamic semantics. To accurately model CAML LIGHT's let-polymorphism, further details are required, which we outline in Sect. 3.5 (113).

Catching Exceptions. CAML LIGHT's try construct corresponds directly to the **catch-else-rethrow** funcon:

$$expr[\![\text{ try } E \text{ with } SM]\!] = \textbf{catch-else-rethrow}(expr[\![E]\!], func[\![SM]\!]) \qquad (67)$$

Also here, further details are required to capture CAML LIGHT's static semantics, see Sect. 3.5 (112).

Basic Patterns. We have notation corresponding directly to basic patterns.

$$patt[\![I]\!] = \textbf{bind}(id[\![I]\!]) \qquad\qquad (68)$$
$$patt[\![\_]\!] = \textbf{any} \qquad\qquad\qquad (69)$$
$$patt[\![C]\!] = \textbf{only}(value[\![C]\!]) \qquad\qquad (70)$$

Compound Data. CAML LIGHT expressions include tupling. We represent tuple values using the **tuple-empty** and binary **tuple-prefix** data constructors. These are lifted to computations in the usual way. We use a small auxiliary translation function $expr\text{-}tuple[\![\_]\!]$:

$$expr[\![E_1 , E_2 \cdots]\!] = expr\text{-}tuple[\![E_1 , E_2 \cdots]\!] \qquad (71)$$

$$expr\text{-}tuple[\![E]\!] = \textbf{tuple-prefix}(expr[\![E]\!], \textbf{tuple-empty}) \qquad (72)$$

$$expr\text{-}tuple[\![E_1 , E_2 \cdots]\!] = \textbf{tuple-prefix}(expr[\![E_1]\!], expr\text{-}tuple[\![E_2 \cdots]\!]) \qquad (73)$$

Compound Patterns. Patterns may also be combined using sequential choice, reusing the **prefer-over** funcon.

$$patt[\![\, P_1 \mid P_2\,]\!] = \textbf{prefer-over}(patt[\![\, P_1\,]\!], patt[\![\, P_2\,]\!]) \tag{74}$$

One may also bind an identifier to the value matched by a pattern:

$$patt[\![\, P \text{ as } I\,]\!] = \textbf{patt-union}(patt[\![\, P\,]\!], \textbf{bind}(id[\![\, I\,]\!])) \tag{75}$$

Built-In Operators. In CAML LIGHT, many built-in operators (e.g., assignment, dereferencing, allocation, and raising exceptions) are provided in the initial library as identifiers bound to functions (and may be rebound in programs). We reflect this by using the funcon **scope** to provide an initial environment to the translations of entire CAML LIGHT programs.

3.3   Dynamic Semantics of Further Funcon Notation

In Sect. 2.3 we explained and illustrated how to define the dynamic semantics of the simple funcons introduced in Sect. 2.1. We now define the dynamic semantics of the further funcons introduced in Sect. 3.1, which involve abstractions, patterns and exceptions. See Table 4 (page 152) for the signatures of these funcons.

Abstractions. An abstraction **abs**(X) is a value constructed from a computation X that may depend on a given argument value. The funcon **apply** takes a computed abstraction value **abs**(X) and an argument value V:

$$\textbf{apply}(\textbf{abs}(X), V) \rightarrow \textbf{supply}(V, X) \tag{76}$$

(The funcon **supply** was introduced in Sect. 2.) The **apply** funcon is lifted in both arguments.

When an abstraction **abs**(X) is applied, evaluation of **bound-value**(I) in X gives the value *currently* bound to I, which corresponds to dynamic scopes for non-local bindings. To specify static scoping, we use the **close** funcon, which takes an abstraction and returns a closure formed from it and the current environment.

$$\text{env } \rho \vdash \textbf{close}(\textbf{abs}(X)) \rightarrow \textbf{abs}(\textbf{closure}(X, \rho)) \tag{77}$$

The auxiliary funcon **closure** (not used when specifying translations) sets the current environment for any computation X:

$$\frac{\text{env } \rho \vdash X \rightarrow X'}{\text{env } \_ \vdash \textbf{closure}(X, \rho) \rightarrow \textbf{closure}(X', \rho)} \tag{78}$$

$$\textbf{closure}(V, \rho) \rightarrow V \tag{79}$$

Thus, whether a language is statically or dynamically scoped may be specified in its translation to funcons simply by the presence or absence of the **close** funcon when forming abstractions.

Patterns. A pattern can be seen as a form of abstraction: while a function computes a value depending on a given value, a pattern computes an *environment* depending on a given value. Matching the value of an expression E to a pattern P computes an environment. It corresponds to the application of P to E:

$$\mathsf{match}(E, P) \rightarrow \mathsf{apply}(P, E) \tag{80}$$

The funcon $\mathsf{patt\text{-}abs}(P, X)$ is similar to $\mathsf{abs}(X)$, except that it takes also a pattern P that is matched against the given value to compute an environment. This allows nested abstractions to refer to arguments at different levels, using the identifiers bound by the respective patterns. The following rule defines the dynamic semantics of $\mathsf{patt\text{-}abs}$ using the abs constructor:

$$\mathsf{patt\text{-}abs}(P, X) \rightarrow \mathsf{abs}(\mathsf{scope}(\mathsf{match}(\mathsf{given}, P), X)) \tag{81}$$

Patterns may be constructed in various ways. For example, the pattern $\mathsf{bind}(I)$ matches any value and binds the identifier I to it:

$$\mathsf{bind}(I) \rightarrow \mathsf{abs}(\mathsf{bind\text{-}value}(I, \mathsf{given})) \tag{82}$$

The wildcard pattern any also matches any value, but computes the empty environment:

$$\mathsf{any} \rightarrow \mathsf{abs}(\emptyset) \tag{83}$$

Other patterns do not match all values. An extreme example is the pattern $\mathsf{only}(V)$, matching just the single value V or executing the funcon fail, which is defined below (87).

$$\mathsf{only}(V) \rightarrow \mathsf{abs}(\mathsf{if\text{-}true}(\mathsf{equal}(\mathsf{given}, V), \emptyset, \mathsf{fail})) \tag{84}$$

The definition of the operation $\mathsf{prefer\text{-}over}$ on abstractions and (as a special case) on patterns involves the funcon else, which is defined below (88–90).

$$\mathsf{prefer\text{-}over}(\mathsf{abs}(X), \mathsf{abs}(Y)) \rightarrow \mathsf{abs}(\mathsf{else}(X, Y)) \tag{85}$$

For patterns, $\mathsf{prefer\text{-}over}$ corresponds to ordered *alternatives*, as found in CAML LIGHT.

Another way to combine two patterns, also found in CAML LIGHT, is *conjunctively*, requiring them both to match, and uniting their bindings. This corresponds to the funcon $\mathsf{patt\text{-}union}$:

$$\mathsf{patt\text{-}union}(\mathsf{abs}(X), \mathsf{abs}(Y)) \rightarrow \mathsf{abs}(\mathsf{map\text{-}union}(X, Y)) \tag{86}$$

Here, the data operation $\mathsf{map\text{-}union}$ is lifted to computations.

Failure and Back-Tracking. The funcon fail emits the signal 'failure true' and then makes a transition to the funcon stuck (which has no further transitions).

$$\mathsf{fail} \xrightarrow{\text{failure true}} \mathsf{stuck} \tag{87}$$

The funcon **else** allows recovery from failure. The signal 'failure **false**' indicates that the computation is proceeding normally, and is treated as unobservable.

$$\frac{X \xrightarrow{\text{failure false}} X'}{\textbf{else}(X,Y) \xrightarrow{\text{failure false}} \textbf{else}(X',Y)} \tag{88}$$

$$\frac{X \xrightarrow{\text{failure true}} X'}{\textbf{else}(X,Y) \xrightarrow{\text{failure false}} Y} \tag{89}$$

$$\textbf{else}(V,Y) \xrightarrow{\text{failure false}} V \tag{90}$$

Exceptions. We specify exception throwing and handling in a modular way using the emitted signals 'exception **some**(V)' and 'exception **none**' (the latter is unobservable).

$$\textbf{throw}(V) \xrightarrow{\text{exception some}(V)} \textbf{stuck} \tag{91}$$

If the first argument of the funcon **catch** signals an exception **some**(V), it applies its second argument (an abstraction) to V.

$$\frac{X \xrightarrow{\text{exception none}} X'}{\textbf{catch}(X,Y) \xrightarrow{\text{exception none}} \textbf{catch}(X',Y)} \tag{92}$$

$$\frac{X \xrightarrow{\text{exception some}(V)} X'}{\textbf{catch}(X,Y) \xrightarrow{\text{exception none}} \textbf{apply}(Y,V)} \tag{93}$$

$$\textbf{catch}(V,Y) \xrightarrow{\text{exception none}} V \tag{94}$$

The following funcon abbreviates a useful variant of **catch**: exceptions are propagated when the application of the abstraction to them fails.

$$\textbf{catch-else-rethrow}(E,A) \rightarrow \tag{95}$$
$$\textbf{catch}(E, \textbf{prefer-over}(A, \textbf{abs}(\textbf{throw}(\textbf{given}))))$$

For funcons whose I-MSOS rules do not mention the exception entity, exceptions are implicitly propagated to the closest enclosing funcon that can handle them. When the translation of a program to funcons involves **throw**, it needs to be enclosed in **catch**, to ensure that (otherwise-)unhandled exceptions cause abrupt termination.

3.4   Static Semantics of Further Funcon Notation

In Sect. 2.4 we explained and illustrated how to define the static semantics of the simple funcons introduced in Sect. 2.1. We now define the static semantics of the further funcons introduced in Sect. 3.1, complementing the dynamic semantics defined in Sect. 3.3. See Table 4 (page 152) for the signatures of these funcons.

Abstractions. As mentioned in Sect. 3.3, an abstraction $\mathbf{abs}(X)$ has dynamic scopes for its non-local bindings. When the abstraction is applied, the computation X is forced, and these bindings have to be provided by the context of the application.[6] The type of $\mathbf{abs}(X)$ is of the form $abs(\Gamma, T_1, T_2)$, and reflects the potential dependence of X not only on the argument value supplied by $\mathbf{apply}$, but also on the bindings available at application time. Abstractions are themselves values, so their types are specified independently of the current context in the following rule:

$$\frac{\text{env}\,\Gamma, \text{given}\,T_1 \vdash X : T_2}{\text{env}\,\_, \text{given}\,\_ \vdash \mathbf{abs}(X) : abs(\Gamma, T_1, T_2)} \tag{96}$$

Notice that an abstraction can have many types; in particular, when X does not refer to the given value at all, the argument type T_1 is arbitrary, and when X does not refer to non-local bindings, Γ is arbitrary, so it can be the empty context $\emptyset$.

The abstraction computed by the expression $\mathbf{close}(\mathbf{abs}(X))$ is closed, having static scopes for non-local bindings. More generally, a well-typed expression $\mathbf{close}(E)$ has a type of the form $abs(\emptyset, T_1, T_2)$ in a context that provides all required non-local bindings for the abstraction computed by E.[7]

$$\frac{\text{env}\,\Gamma \vdash E : abs(\Gamma_1, T_1, T_2) \qquad \Gamma_1 \subseteq \Gamma}{\text{env}\,\Gamma \vdash \mathbf{close}(E) : abs(\emptyset, T_1, T_2)} \tag{97}$$

Combining rules (96) and (97) we obtain a derived rule corresponding to the usual typing rule for abstractions with static scopes:

$$\frac{\text{env}\,\Gamma, \text{given}\,T_1 \vdash X : T_2}{\text{env}\,\Gamma, \text{given}\,\_ \vdash \mathbf{close}(\mathbf{abs}(X)) : abs(\emptyset, T_1, T_2)} \tag{98}$$

The typing rule for application specifies that the abstraction must be closed, but otherwise is the same as the usual rule for static bindings:

$$\frac{E_1 : abs(\emptyset, T_2, T) \qquad E_2 : T_2}{\mathbf{apply}(E_1, E_2) : T} \tag{99}$$

This approach to assigning static types to dynamically scoped abstractions is similar to the handling of implicit parameters proposed in [34]. However, while they extend statically scoped lambda calculus with implicit variables, we introduce types of dynamically scoped abstractions that can be specialised to statically scoped ones.

Patterns. A pattern is a *closed* abstraction that (when it matches a given value) computes an environment. The type of a pattern P is of the form $abs(\emptyset, T, \Gamma)$,

---

[6] In effect, non-local bindings correspond to implicit parameters.

[7] The notation $abs(T_1, T_2)$ for abstraction types in the conference version of this paper [13] abbreviates $abs(\emptyset, T_1, T_2)$.

where Γ determines the types of the identifiers bound when P is matched to a value of type T.

The typing rule for **match** is similar to that for **apply** (99):

$$\frac{E : T \qquad P : abs(\emptyset, T, \Gamma)}{\textbf{match}(E, P) : \Gamma} \tag{100}$$

The typing rule for **patt-abs**(P, X) is similar to that for **abs**(X) (96), except that the environment in which X is typed is updated with the type of the environment computed by P:

$$\frac{\text{env } \Gamma, \text{given } T \vdash P : abs(\emptyset, T_1, \Gamma_2) \qquad \text{env } (\Gamma_2/\Gamma_1), \text{given } T_1 \vdash X : T_2}{\text{env } \Gamma, \text{given } T \vdash \textbf{patt-abs}(P, X) : abs(\Gamma_1, T_1, T_2)} \tag{101}$$

The typing rules for patterns are as follows:

$$\textbf{bind}(I) : abs(\emptyset, T, \{I \mapsto T\}) \tag{102}$$

$$\textbf{any} : abs(\emptyset, T, \emptyset) \tag{103}$$

$$\frac{V : T}{\textbf{only}(V) : abs(\emptyset, T, \emptyset)} \tag{104}$$

$$\frac{P_1 : abs(\emptyset, T, \Gamma_1) \qquad P_2 : abs(\emptyset, T, \Gamma_2)}{\textbf{patt-union}(P_1, P_2) : abs(\emptyset, T, \textbf{map-union}(\Gamma_1, \Gamma_2))} \tag{105}$$

The funcon **prefer-over** is applicable to arbitrary abstractions, not just patterns, and so has a more general typing rule:

$$\frac{P_1 : abs(\Gamma_1, T_1, T_2) \qquad P_2 : abs(\Gamma_2, T_1, T_2) \qquad \Gamma_1 \subseteq \Gamma \qquad \Gamma_2 \subseteq \Gamma}{\textbf{prefer-over}(P_1, P_2) : abs(\Gamma, T_1, T_2)} \tag{106}$$

Failure and Back-Tracking. The funcon **fail** may have any type. The funcon **else** requires both its arguments to have the same type.

$$\textbf{fail} : T \tag{107}$$

$$\frac{X_1 : T \qquad X_2 : T}{\textbf{else}(X_1, X_2) : T} \tag{108}$$

Exceptions. The static semantics of the funcon **throw** allows it and its argument to have any type. The funcons **catch** and **catch-else-rethrow** check that the abstraction used to handle thrown exceptions computes values of the same type as normal termination.

$$\frac{E : T'}{\textbf{throw}(E) : T} \tag{109}$$

$$\frac{X : T \qquad E : abs(\emptyset, T', T)}{\textbf{catch}(X, E) : T} \tag{110}$$

$$\frac{X : T \qquad E : abs(\emptyset, T', T)}{\textbf{catch-else-rethrow}(X, E) : T} \tag{111}$$

3.5   CAML LIGHT Static Semantics

The translation specified in Sect. 3.2 appears to accurately reflect the dynamic semantics of CAML LIGHT programs. The funcons used in the translation also have static semantics, which provides a 'default' static semantics for the programs. In most cases, this agrees with the intended static semantics of CAML LIGHT – but not always. In the latter cases, we modify the translation by inserting additional funcons which affect the static semantics, but which leave the dynamic semantics unchanged. We consider some examples. The signatures of the extra funcons involved are shown in Table 6.

Table 6. Signatures of some funcons for adjusting static semantics

---

Funcon signatures

$$\textbf{generalise-decl}(\mathit{decls}) : \mathit{decls}$$
$$\textbf{instantiate-if-poly}(\mathit{exprs}) : \mathit{exprs}$$
$$\textbf{restrict-domain}(\mathit{abs}(X, Y), \mathit{types}) : \mathit{abs}(X, Y)$$

Catching Exceptions. The translation of $\text{try } E \text{ with } SM$ in Sect. 3.2 (67) allows any value to be thrown as an exception and caught by the handler. In Caml Light, however, the values that can be thrown and caught are restricted to those included in the type **exn**, so static semantics needs to check that $\mathit{func}[\![\, SM \,]\!]$ has type $\textbf{exn->} X$ for some X. This can be achieved using $\textbf{restrict-domain}(E, T)$, which checks that the type of E is that of an abstraction with argument type T, but otherwise (statically and dynamically) behaves just like E. The modified translation equation is:[8]

$$\mathit{expr}[\![\, \text{try } E \text{ with } SM \,]\!] = \qquad\qquad (112)$$
$$\textbf{catch-else-rethrow}(\mathit{expr}[\![\, E \,]\!],$$
$$\textbf{restrict-domain}(\mathit{func}[\![\, SM \,]\!], \textbf{bound-type}(\mathit{id}[\![\, \text{exn} \,]\!])))$$

Using Polymorphism. CAML LIGHT has polymorphism, where a type may be a type schema including universally quantified variables. The interpretation of identifier binding inspection using just the **bound-value** funcon (66) does not account for instantiation of polymorphic variables. We can rectify this as follows:

$$\mathit{expr}[\![\, I \,]\!] = \textbf{instantiate-if-poly}(\textbf{bound-value}(\mathit{id}[\![\, I \,]\!])) \qquad (113)$$

The funcon **instantiate-if-poly** takes all universally quantified type variables in the type of its argument, and allows them to be instantiated arbitrarily; it does not affect the dynamic semantics.

---

[8] When I is bound to a type, **bound-type**(I) corresponds to **bound-value**(I), but it is evaluated as part of static semantics.

Generating Polymorphism. Expressions with polymorphic types in CAML LIGHT arise from let definitions, where types are generalised as much as possible, up to a constraint regarding imperative behaviour known as *value-restriction* [60]. The appropriate funcon is **generalise-decl**, which finds all generalisable types in its argument environment and explicitly quantifies them, universally. Whether this generalisation should be applied is determined entirely by the outermost production of the right-hand side (E) of the let definition.

$$decl [\![P = E]\!] = \textbf{generalise-decl}(decl\text{-}mono [\![P = E]\!]) \qquad (114)$$
$$\text{if } E \text{ is generalisable}$$

$$decl [\![P = E]\!] = decl\text{-}mono [\![P = E]\!] \qquad (115)$$
$$\text{if } E \text{ is not generalisable}$$

The translation funcon $decl\text{-}mono [\![\_]\!]$ is the same as the version of $decl [\![\_]\!]$ specified in Sect. 3.2 (65) for dynamic semantics.

$$decl\text{-}mono [\![P = E]\!] = \qquad (116)$$
$$\textbf{match}(expr [\![E]\!],$$
$$\textbf{prefer-over}(patt [\![P]\!], \textbf{abs}(\textbf{throw}(\textbf{cl-match-failure}))))$$

3.6 The Full CAML LIGHT Case Study

There is not sufficient space here to present all of our component-based semantics of the CAML LIGHT language. The complete translation for the subset of CAML LIGHT presented in Table 3 is given in the Appendix. Our translation of the following further constructs, together with the specifications of all the required funcons, is available online [12].

Values: records, with and without mutable fields; variant values.
Patterns: variant patterns; record patterns.
Expressions: operations on variants and records; function abstractions with multiple-matching arguments.
Global definitions: type abbreviations; record types; variant types; exception definitions.
Top level: module implementations; the core library.

We have not yet given semantics for modules (interfaces, directives, and references to declarations qualified by module names).

This concludes the presentation of illustrative excerpts from our CAML LIGHT case study. Our confidence in the accuracy of the specifications of the translation and of the funcons used in it is based partly on the simplicity and perspicuity of the specifications, as illustrated above, partly on our tool support for validating them, which is described in the next section.

4   Tool Support

This section gives an overview of the tools we have used in connection with the case study presented in Sect. 3. These tools support parsing programs, translating programs to funcon terms, generating an interpreter from funcon specifications, and running programs on generated interpreters. They also support developing and browsing the specifications of funcons and languages.

The main technical requirement for such tools is to be consistent with the foundations of our specifications. Using the tools to run programs in some specified language (and comparing the results with running the same programs on some reference implementation) then tests the correctness of the language specification. With our component-based approach, the language specification consists of the equations for translating programs to funcons, together with the static and dynamic rules of the funcons used in the translation.

The PLANCOMPS project is currently developing integrated tools to support component-based language specification, but these are not yet ready for use in case studies. We have therefore used a combination of several existing tools to develop and test our specification of CAML LIGHT: SDF for parsing programs; ASF+SDF and Stratego for translating programs to funcons; Prolog for parsing I-MSOS specifications and generating Prolog code from them, and for executing funcon terms; and Spoofax for generating editors for our specification languages.

The rest of this section summarises what the various tools do, and illustrates the support they have provided for our specification of CAML LIGHT (CL). All our source code is available for download along with the CL specification.

4.1   Parsing Programs

The syntax of CL is defined in its reference manual [32] by a highly ambiguous context-free grammar in EBNF (see Table 3, page 151) together with some tables and informal comments regarding the intended disambiguation. We originally extracted the text of the grammar from the HTML version of the reference manual and converted it (semi-automatically) to SDF [61], which supports the specification of arbitrary context-free grammars.

We used the existing tool support for SDF to generate a scannerless GLR parser for CL, which was able to parse various test programs. To obtain a unique parse-tree for a program, however, expressions generally needed additional grouping parentheses. SDF supports several ways of specifying disambiguation, including relative priorities, left/right associativity, prefer/avoid annotations, and follow-restrictions. These allowed us to express most of the intended disambiguation without introducing auxiliary nonterminal symbols, albeit with some difficulty (e.g., we ended up using position-specific non-transitive priorities). A closer investigation by colleagues working on disambiguation techniques led to the quite surprising result that SDF's disambiguation mechanisms are actually inadequate to specify one particular feature of expression grouping that is required by CL [1]. Fortunately, it appears that CL programmers tend to insert grouping parentheses to avoid potential misinterpretation in such cases, so although we know that ambiguity could arise when using our parser, we have not found practical programs for which that happens.

One of the initial advantages of using SDF was its support by the ASF+SDF Meta-Environment [8], which provided an IDE with some pleasant features. However, ASF+SDF is no longer maintained or developed, so we recently switched to Spoofax [28] for generating a CL parser from our SDF grammar. Our Spoofax editor project for CL supports parsing of CL programs while editing them in Eclipse, and we use the Spoofax command-line interface when running test suites.

4.2   Translating Programs to Funcons

After parsing a CL program, we need to be able to translate it to funcons. ASF+SDF [8] allowed such translation rules to be specified as term rewriting equations, based on the CL syntax together with notation for translation functions, meta-variables, and funcons, all specified in SDF. When we switched from ASF+SDF to Spoofax, we started to use Stratego [62] for specifying term rewriting. Fortunately, it was possible to re-express our ASF+SDF equations quite naturally as Stratego rules, by exploiting its support for concrete syntax; see Fig. 1 for some examples.

```
to-funcons:
  I[ expr[: ~E1 or ~E2 :] ]I ->
  I[ if_true(expr[: ~E1 :], true, expr[: ~E2 :]) ]I
to-funcons:
  I[ expr[: if ~E1 then ~E2 :] ]I ->
  I[ expr[: if ~E1 then ~E2 else ( ) :] ]I
to-funcons:
  I[ expr[: if ~E1 then ~E2 else ~E3 :] ]I ->
  I[ if_true(expr[: ~E1 :], expr[: ~E2 :], expr[: ~E3 :] ) ]I
to-funcons:
  I[ expr[: while ~E1 do ~E2 done :] ]I ->
  I[ while_true(expr[: ~E1 :], effect(expr[: ~E2 :])) ]I
```

Fig. 1. Some Stratego rules for transforming CL to funcons

Figure 2 shows a funcon term resulting from pressing the 'Generation' button after parsing a CL program in the Spoofax editor. To obtain funcon terms in the format used by our Prolog-based tools, we invoke a pretty-printer generated from SDF3 templates for funcon signatures.

4.3   Translating I-MSOS Rules to Prolog

A notation called MSDF had previously been developed for specifying transition rules for funcons in connection with teaching operational semantics using MSOS

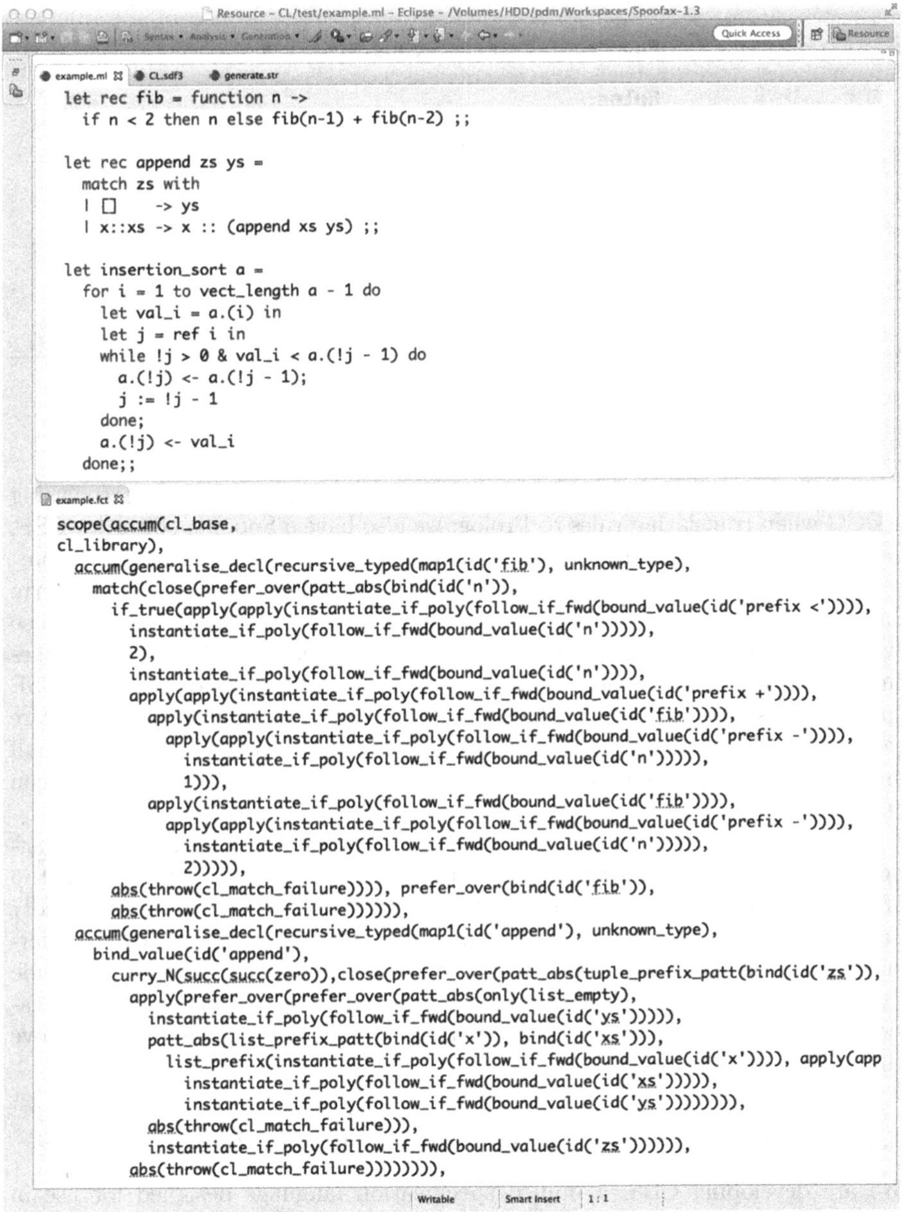

Fig. 2. A CL program and the generated funcon term

[44], along with a definite clause grammar (DCG) for parsing MSDF, and Prolog
code for transforming each MSDF rule to a Prolog clause (MSDF is used also in
the Maude MSOS Tool [10]). The PLANCOMPS project has developed a variant

```
Funcon if_true(booleans,X,X) : X

Rules:

if_true(true,X,Y) --> X

if_true(false,X,Y) --> Y

B : booleans, X : T, Y : T
------------------------------
      if_true(B,X,Y) : T
```

Fig. 3. A CSF specification

of MSDF called CSF for specifying I-MSOS rules for funcons. CSF is parsed using a DCG when translating rules to Prolog; we also have a Spoofax editor for CSF, based on an SDF grammar. Figure 3 shows an example of a CSF specification.

As with the original version of MSDF, we use a Prolog program to transform parsed CSF rules to Prolog clauses (supporting not only transitions but also typing assertions and equations) and to run funcon terms. A shell script invokes the Prolog program to generate Prolog code from our current collection of CSF specifications of funcons and values in a few seconds; further scripts run entire test suites. When all the generated clauses are loaded together with a small amount of fixed runtime code (mainly for MSOS label composition), funcon terms can be executed.

Directly interpreting small-step transition rules for funcons is inherently inefficient [3]: each step of running a program searches for a transition from the top of the entire program, and the term representing the program gets repeatedly unfolded in connection with recursive function calls. The number of Prolog inference steps is sometimes alarmingly high, but we have managed to execute a wide range of CL test programs. We intend to apply semantics-preserving transformation of small-step rules to so-called 'pretty-big-step' rules following [2] to remove this source of inefficiency.

4.4   A Component-Based Semantics Specification Language

We are developing CBS, a unified specification language designed for use in component-based semantics. CBS allows specification of abstract syntax grammars (essentially BNF with regular expressions), the signatures and equations for translation functions, and the signatures and rules for values and funcons, so it can replace our current combination of SDF, Stratego and CSF. Use of CBS should provide considerably greater notational consistency, and improve the readability of our specifications.

We have used Spoofax to create an editor for CBS, exploiting name resolution to check that all the notation used in a CBS project has been uniquely

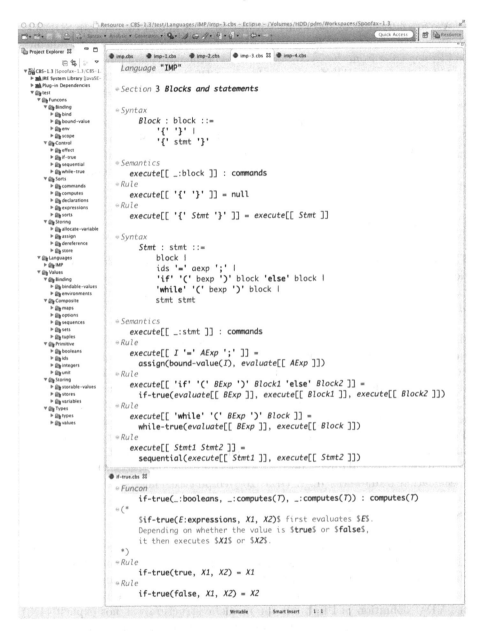

Fig. 4. CBS in use on IMP, a small imperative language

defined (possibly in a different file) and to hyperlink uses of funcons to their specifications. Figure 4 illustrates the use of the CBS editor to check the specification of a small imperative language for notational consistency in the presence of CBS specifications of the required funcons and values.

We are currently re-specifying CL in CBS. We intend to generate SDF and Stratego code from the CBS specification of the translation of CL to funcons, and Prolog rules from the CBS specifications of the individual funcons. We would also like to generate LATEX source code from CBS, to ensure consistency between examples provided in articles such as this, and the specifications that we have tested.

We expect our current case study of component-based semantics (C#) to be developed entirely in CBS, supported by tools running in Spoofax. Further tools currently being developed in the PLANCOMPS project are to integrate support for CBS with recent advances in GLL parser generation and disambiguation [26], aiming to provide a complete workbench for language specification.

5   Related Work

The component-based framework presented and illustrated in the previous sections was inspired by features of many previous frameworks. In this section, we mainly consider its relationship to semantic frameworks that have a high degree of modularity.

Algebraic Specification. Heering and Klint proposed in the early 1980 s to structure complete definitions of programming languages as libraries of reusable components [22]. This motivated the development of ASF+SDF [4], which provided strong support for modular structure in algebraic specifications. However, an ASF+SDF definition of a programming language did not, in general, permit the reuse of the individual language constructs in the definitions of other languages. The main hindrances to reuse in ASF+SDF were coarse modular structure (e.g., specifying all expression constructs in a single module), explicit propagation of auxiliary entities, and direct specification of language constructs. Other algebraic specification frameworks (e.g., OBJ [20]) emphasised finer modular structure, but still did not provide reusable components of language specifications. These issues are illustrated and discussed further in [48].

Monads. At the end of the 1980s, Moggi [39] introduced the use of monads and monad transformers in denotational semantics. (In fact Scott and Strachey had themselves used monadic notation for composition of store transformations in the early 1970s, and an example of a monad transformer can also be found in the VDM definition of PL/I, but the monadic structure was not explicit [47].) Monads avoid explicit propagation of auxiliary entities, and monad transformers are highly reusable components. Various monad transformers have been defined (e.g., see [35]) with operations that in many cases correspond to our funcons; monads can also make a clear distinction between sets T of values and sets of computations $M(T)$ of values in T.

One drawback of monad transformers with respect to modularity is that different orders of composition can lead to different semantics. For example, one order of composition of the state and exception monad transformers preserves the state when an exception is thrown, whereas the other restores it. In contrast, the semantics of our funcons is independent of the order in which they are added. The concept of monad transformers inspired the development of MSOS [42], the modular variant of SOS that we use to define funcons.

An alternative way of defining monads has been developed by Plotkin and Power [57] using Lawvere theories instead of monad transformers. Recently, Delaware et al. [14] presented modular monadic meta-theory, combining modular datatypes with monad transformers, focusing on modularisation of theorems and proofs. Both these frameworks assume some familiarity with Category Theory. In contrast, the foundations of our component-based framework involve MSOS, where labels happen to be morphisms of categories, but label composition can easily be explained without reference to Category Theory.

Abstract State Machines. Kutter and Pierantonio [30] proposed the Montages variant of abstract state machines (ASMs) with a separate module for each language construct. Reusability was limited partly by the tight coupling of components to concrete syntax.

Börger et al. [6,7] gave modular ASM semantics for JAVA and C#, identifying features shared by the two languages, but did not define components intended for wider reuse.

ASM specifications generally make widespread use of ad-hoc abbreviations for patterns of rules, and sometimes redefine these abbreviations when extending a described language. In our component-based approach, in contrast, the specifications of the funcons remain fixed, and it is only the specification of the translation to funcons that may need to change when extending the language.

Action Semantics. This framework combined features of denotational, operational and algebraic semantics. It was developed initially by Mosses and Watt [40,41,51]. The notation for actions used in action semantics can be regarded as a collection of funcons. Action notation supported specification of sequential and interleaved control flow, abrupt termination and its handling, scopes of bindings, imperative variables, asynchronous concurrent processes, and procedural abstractions, but the collection of actions was not extensible. Actions were relatively primitive, being less closely related to familiar programming constructs than funcons (e.g., conditional choice was specified using guards, and iteration by an 'unfolding'). Various algebraic laws allowed reasoning about action equivalence. Although action semantics was intended for specifying dynamic semantics, Doh and Schmidt [16] explored the possibility of using it also for static semantics.

The modular structure of specifications in action semantics was conventional, with separate sections for abstract syntax, auxiliary entities, and semantic equations. Doh and Mosses [15] proposed replacing it by a component-based structure, defining the abstract syntax and action semantics of each language construct in a separate module, foreshadowing the modular structure of funcon specifications (except that static semantics was not addressed).

Iversen and Mosses [24] introduced so-called Basic Abstract Syntax (BAS), which is a direct precursor of our current collection of funcons. They specified a translation from the Core of Standard ML to BAS, and gave action semantics for each BAS construct, with tool support using ASF+SDF [9]. However, having to deal with both BAS and action notation was a drawback. Mosses et al. [25, 43,45,46] reported on subsequent work that led to the present paper.

TinkerType. Levin and Pierce developed the TINKERTYPE system [33] to support reuse of conventional SOS specifications of individual language constructs. The idea was to have a variant of the specification of each construct for each combination of language features. To define a new language with reuse of a collection of previously specified constructs, TINKERTYPE could determine the union of the auxiliary entities needed for their individual specifications, and assemble the language definition from the corresponding variants. This approach alleviated some of the symptoms of poor reusability in SOS.

Ott. Another system supporting practical use of conventional SOS is OTT [59], which allows for specifications to be compiled to the languages of various theorem provers, including HOL (based on classical higher-order logic). OTT facilitates use of SOS, providing a metalanguage that supports variable binding and substitution; however, it does not provide support for reusable components.

Owens et al. [52,53] used OTT to specify a sublanguage of OCAML corresponding closely to CAML LIGHT. Owens [53] used the HOL code automatically generated from the language specification to prove a type soundness theorem. The dynamic semantics is formulated in terms of small-step rules, relying on congruence rules to specify order of evaluation. The approach departs from traditional SOS [56] in using substitution rather than environments; OTT requires binding occurrences of variables to be annotated as such in the abstract syntax. The need for renaming of bound value variables is avoided by not reducing under value variable binders, and by relying on the assumption that well-typed programs have no free value variables (i.e., they are context-independent). The static semantics uses De Brujin indices to represent type variables, and relies on substitution to deal with type variables in explicit type annotations. The use of labels to avoid explicit mention of the store is similar to MSOS. Some of the choices of techniques used in the specification are motivated by the HOL proofs – notably, their use of congruence rules instead of evaluation contexts, and of De Brujin indices.

The OCAML LIGHT specification is comparatively large: 173 rules for the static semantics and 137 rules for the dynamic semantics. It is interesting to observe that out of the 61 rules that are given for expression evaluation [52, Sect. 4.9], 18 are congruence rules, and 17 are exception propagation rules. Ultimately, little more than a third of the rules are reductions; these are the only ones which would need to be explicitly stated using an approach that takes full advantage of strictness annotations and of MSOS labels. For example, the OTT rules for evaluating if-else expressions are the following:

$$\frac{\vdash e_1 \xrightarrow{L} e_1'}{\vdash \textbf{if } e_1 \textbf{ then } e_2 \textbf{ else } e_3 \xrightarrow{L} \textbf{if } e_1' \textbf{ then } e_2 \textbf{ else } e_3} \text{ ifthenelse\_ctx}$$

$$\frac{}{\vdash \textbf{if } (\textbf{\%prim raise}) \ v \textbf{ then } e_1 \textbf{ else } e_2 \longrightarrow (\textbf{\%prim raise}) \ v} \text{ if\_raise}$$

$$\frac{}{\vdash \textbf{if true then } e_2 \textbf{ else } e_3 \longrightarrow e_2} \text{ ifthenelse\_true}$$

$$\frac{}{\vdash \textbf{if false then } e_2 \textbf{ else } e_3 \longrightarrow e_3} \text{ ifthenelse\_false}$$

The above specification can be compared to that for the **if-true** funcon (Fig. 3). In the OTT specification, the first rule (ifthenelse_ctx) is a congruence rule, and the second one (if_raise) is an exception propagation rule. Only the last two rules above are reduction rules, corresponding to our (30, 31). Note the use of the label L to thread the state in the first rule (as in MSOS), and the absence of environments (due to their use of substitution).

In the OTT typing rule below, E is a typing context, and σ^T is an assignment of types to type variables (needed in connection with polymorphism, to deal with explicit type annotations).

$$\frac{\sigma^T \& E \vdash e_1 : \textbf{bool} \qquad \sigma^T \& E \vdash e_2 : t \qquad \sigma^T \& E \vdash e_3 : t}{\sigma^T \& E \vdash \textbf{if } e_1 \textbf{ then } e_2 \textbf{ else } e_3 : t} \text{ ifthenelse}$$

This is similar to the corresponding static rule in our semantics (44). As a purely notational difference, we leave the typing context implicit, following the I-MSOS presentation style. The assignment to type variables is also left implicit in our treatment of polymorphism, see Sect. 3.5.

Evaluation Contexts. OTT supports also reduction semantics based on evaluation contexts. This framework is widely used for proving meta-theoretic results (e.g., type soundness).[9] The semantics of STANDARD ML presented in [21,31] uses an elaborative approach based on the translation of the source language to a type system (the *internal* language) and on a reduction semantics (relying on evaluation contexts), formalised and proved to be type sound in TWELF. Conciseness is achieved by defining the semantics on the internal language, rather than on the source one. However, the internal language is designed for the translation from a particular source (STANDARD ML in this case), and it is not particularly oriented toward extensibility and reuse.

The PLT REDEX tool [18] runs programs by interpreting their reduction semantics, and has been used to validate language specifications [29]. However,

---

[9] The lack of HOL support for evaluation contexts discouraged Owens from using them for his OCAML LIGHT case study [53].

it is unclear whether reduction semantics could be used to define reusable components whose specifications never need changing when combined – in particular, adding new features may require modification of the grammar for evaluation contexts.

Compared to a conventional small-step SOS, the specification of the same language by evaluation rules and the accompanying evaluation-context grammar is usually relatively concise. This is primarily because each congruence rule in the SOS corresponds to a single production of the evaluation context grammar; moreover, exception propagation is usually specified by inference rules in SOS, but by a succinct auxiliary evaluation context grammar in reduction semantics. However, our I-MSOS specifications of funcons avoid the need for many congruence rules, and exception propagation is implicit, which may well make our specifications even more concise than a corresponding reduction semantics.

Rewriting Logic and K. Competing approaches with a high degree of inherent modularity include Rewriting Logic Semantics [37] and the K framework [58]. Both frameworks have well-developed tool support, which allows not only execution of programs according to their semantics, but also model checking. K has been used to specify major programming languages such as C [17] and JAVA [5].

The lifting of funcon arguments from value sorts to computation sorts is closely related to (and was inspired by) strictness annotations in K. It appears possible to specify individual funcons independently in K, and to use the K Tools to translate programming languages to funcons [50], thereby incorporating our component-based approach directly in that framework.

6   Conclusions and Further Work

We regard our CAML LIGHT case study as significant evidence of the applicability and modularity of our component-based approach to semantics. The *key novel feature* is the introduction of an open-ended collection of fundamental constructs (funcons). The abstraction level of the funcons we have used to specify the semantics of CAML LIGHT appears to be optimal: if the funcons were closer to the language constructs, the translation of the language to funcons would have been a bit simpler, but the I-MSOS rules for the funcons would have been considerably more complicated; lower-level funcons (e.g., comparable to the combinators used in action semantics [40,41]) would have increased the size and decreased the perspicuity of the funcon terms used in the translation. Some of the funcons presented here do in fact correspond very closely to CAML LIGHT language constructs (e.g., eager function application and pattern-matching) but we regard that as a natural consequence of the clean design of this particular language, and unlikely to occur when specifying a language whose design is less principled.

CAML LIGHT is a real language, and we have successfully tested our semantics for it by generating funcon terms from programs, running them using Prolog code generated from the I-MSOS rules that define the funcons, then comparing the results with those given by running the same programs on the latest release of the

CAML LIGHT system (which is the *de facto* definition of the language). The test programs and funcon terms are available online [12] together with the generated Prolog code for each funcon. We have checked that our test programs exercise every translation equation, and that running them uses every applicable rule of every funcon, so we are reasonably confident in the accuracy of our specifications.

The work reported here is part of the PLANCOMPS project [55]. Apart from developing and refining the component-based approach to language specification, PLANCOMPS is developing a chain of tools specially engineered to support its practical use.

Ongoing and future case studies carried out by the PLANCOMPS project will test the reusability of our funcons. We are already reusing many of those introduced for specifying CAML LIGHT in a component-based semantics for C#. The main test will be to specify the corresponding JAVA constructs using essentially the same collection of funcons as for C#. We expect the approach to be equally applicable to domain-specific languages, where the benefits of reuse in connection with co-evolution of languages and their specifications could be especially significant.

We are quite happy with the perspicuity of our specifications. Lifting value arguments to computation sorts has eliminated the need to specify tedious 'congruence' rules in the small-step I-MSOS of funcons. The funcon names are reasonably suggestive, while not being too verbose, although there is surely room for improvement. When the PLANCOMPS project has completed its case studies, it intends to finalise the definitions of the funcons it has developed, and establish an open-access digital library of funcons and language specifications. Until then, the names and details of the funcons presented here should be regarded as tentative.

In conclusion, we consider our component-based approach to be a good example of modularity in the context of programming language semantics. We do not claim that any of the techniques we employ are directly applicable in software engineering, although component-based specifications might well provide a suitable basis for generating implementations of domain-specific languages.

Acknowledgments. Thanks to Erik Ernst and the anonymous referees for helpful comments and suggestions for improvement. The reported work was supported by EPSRC grant (EP/I032495/1) to Swansea University for the PLANCOMPS project.

Appendix

This appendix contains the translation equations for the subset of CAML LIGHT presented in Table 3, from which the illustrative examples in Sect. 3 are drawn. Our translation of the full CAML LIGHT language is available online [12].

Markup for formatting the equations given below was inserted manually in the Stratego rules used to translate CAML LIGHT programs to funcons. A few equations overlap; in Stratego we apply the more specific ones when possible.

Global names

$id[\![\ I\ ]\!] = \mathbf{id}('I')$

Type expressions

$type[\![\ (\ T\ )\ ]\!] = type[\![\ T\ ]\!]$

$type[\![\ I\ ]\!] = \mathbf{bound\text{-}type}(id[\![\ I\ ]\!])$

$type[\![\ T_1 \ \text{->}\ T_2\ ]\!] = \mathbf{abs}(\emptyset, type[\![\ T_1\ ]\!], type[\![\ T_2\ ]\!])$

$type[\![\ T\ I\ ]\!] = \mathbf{instantiate\text{-}type}(type[\![\ I\ ]\!], type\text{-}list[\![\ T\ ]\!])$

$type[\![\ {}'\ I\ ]\!] = \mathbf{typevar}('I')$

$type[\![\ T_1\ *\ T_2\ ]\!] = \mathbf{tuple\text{-}type2}(type[\![\ T_1\ ]\!], type[\![\ T_2\ ]\!])$

$type[\![\ T_1\ *\ T_2\ *\ T_3\ \cdots\ ]\!] = \mathbf{tuple\text{-}type\text{-}prefix}(type[\![\ T_1\ ]\!], type[\![\ T_2\ *\ T_3\ \cdots\ ]\!])$

$type[\![\ (T_1\ ,\ T_2\ \cdots)\ I\ ]\!] = \mathbf{instantiate\text{-}type}(type[\![\ I\ ]\!], type\text{-}list[\![\ T_1\ ,\ T_2\ \cdots\ ]\!])$

$type\text{-}list[\![\ T\ ]\!] = \mathbf{list1}(type[\![\ T\ ]\!])$

$type\text{-}list[\![\ T_1\ ,\ T_2\ \cdots\ ]\!] = \mathbf{list\text{-}prefix}(type[\![\ T_1\ ]\!], type\text{-}list[\![\ T_2\ \cdots\ ]\!])$

Constants

$value[\![\ Int\ ]\!] = Int$

$value[\![\ Float\ ]\!] = Float$

$value[\![\ Char\ ]\!] = \mathbf{char}(Char)$

$value[\![\ String\ ]\!] = String$

$value[\![\ \texttt{false}\ ]\!] = \mathbf{false}$

$value[\![\ \texttt{true}\ ]\!] = \mathbf{true}$

$value[\![\ \texttt{[ ]}\ ]\!] = \mathbf{list\text{-}empty}$

$value[\![\ \texttt{( )}\ ]\!] = \mathbf{null}$

Patterns

$patt[\![\ (\ P\ )\ ]\!] = patt[\![\ P\ ]\!]$

$patt[\![\ I\ ]\!] = \mathbf{bind}(id[\![\ I\ ]\!])$

$patt[\![\ \_\ ]\!] = \mathbf{any}$

$patt[\![\ P\ \texttt{as}\ I\ ]\!] = \mathbf{patt\text{-}union}(patt[\![\ P\ ]\!], \mathbf{bind}(id[\![\ I\ ]\!]))$

$patt[\![\ (\ P\ :\ T\ )\ ]\!] = \mathbf{patt\text{-}at\text{-}type}(patt[\![\ P\ ]\!], type[\![\ T\ ]\!])$

$patt[\![\ P_1\ |\ P_2\ ]\!] = \mathbf{patt\text{-}non\text{-}binding}(\mathbf{prefer\text{-}over}(patt[\![\ P_1\ ]\!], patt[\![\ P_2\ ]\!]))$

$patt[\![\ P_1\ ::\ P_2\ ]\!] = \mathbf{list\text{-}prefix\text{-}patt}(patt[\![\ P_1\ ]\!], patt[\![\ P_2\ ]\!])$

$patt[\![\ \texttt{[}\ P\ \texttt{]}\ ]\!] = patt[\![\ P\ ::\ \texttt{[ ]}\ ]\!]$

$patt[\![\ \texttt{[}\ P_1\ ;\ P_2\ \cdots\ \texttt{]}\ ]\!] = patt[\![\ P_1\ ::\ \texttt{[}\ P_2\ \cdots\ \texttt{]}\ ]\!]$

$patt[\![\ C\ ]\!] = \mathbf{only}(value[\![\ C\ ]\!])$

$patt[\![\ P_1\ ,\ P_2\ \cdots\ ]\!] = patt\text{-}tuple[\![\ P_1\ ,\ P_2\ \cdots\ ]\!]$

$patt\text{-}tuple[\![\ P\ ]\!] = \mathbf{tuple\text{-}prefix\text{-}patt}(patt[\![\ P\ ]\!], \mathbf{only}(\mathbf{tuple\text{-}empty}))$

$patt\text{-}tuple[\![\ P_1\ ,\ P_2\ \cdots\ ]\!] = \mathbf{tuple\text{-}prefix\text{-}patt}(patt[\![\ P_1\ ]\!], patt\text{-}tuple[\![\ P_2\ \cdots\ ]\!])$

Expressions

$expr[\![\ I\ ]\!] = $ **instantiate-if-poly**(**follow-if-fwd**(**bound-value**($id[\![\ I\ ]\!]$)))

$expr[\![\ C\ ]\!] = value[\![\ C\ ]\!]$

$expr[\![\ (\ E\ )\ ]\!] = expr[\![\ E\ ]\!]$

$expr[\![\ \texttt{begin}\ E\ \texttt{end}\ ]\!] = expr[\![\ E\ ]\!]$

$expr[\![\ (\ E\ :\ T\ )\ ]\!] = $ **typed**($expr[\![\ E\ ]\!], type[\![\ T\ ]\!]$)

$expr[\![\ E_1\ ,\ E_2\ \cdots\ ]\!] = expr\text{-}tuple[\![\ E_1\ ,\ E_2\ \cdots\ ]\!]$

$expr\text{-}tuple[\![\ E\ ]\!] = $ **tuple-prefix**($expr[\![\ E\ ]\!],$ **tuple-empty**)

$expr\text{-}tuple[\![\ E_1\ ,\ E_2\ \cdots\ ]\!] = $ **tuple-prefix**($expr[\![\ E_1\ ]\!], expr\text{-}tuple[\![\ E_2\ \cdots\ ]\!]$)

$expr[\![\ E_1\ ::\ E_2\ ]\!] = $ **list-prefix**($expr[\![\ E_1\ ]\!], expr[\![\ E_2\ ]\!]$)

$expr[\![\ [\ E\ ]\ ]\!] = expr[\![\ E\ ::\ [\ ]\ ]\!]$

$expr[\![\ [\ E_1\ ;\ E_2\ \cdots\ ]\ ]\!] = expr[\![\ E_1\ ::\ [\ E_2\ \cdots]\ ]\!]$

$expr[\![\ [|\ |]\ ]\!] = $ **vector-empty**

$expr[\![\ [|\ E\ |]\ ]\!] = $ **vector1**(**alloc**($expr[\![\ E\ ]\!]$))

$expr[\![\ [|\ E_1\ ;\ E_2\ \cdots\ |]\ ]\!] = $
    vector-append($expr[\![\ [|\ E_1\ |]\ ]\!], expr[\![\ [|\ E_2\ \cdots\ |]\ ]\!]$)

$expr[\![\ E_1\ E_2\ ]\!] = $ **apply**($expr[\![\ E_1\ ]\!], expr[\![\ E_2\ ]\!]$)

$expr[\![\ \texttt{-}\ E\ ]\!] = $ **int-negate**($expr[\![\ E\ ]\!]$)

$expr[\![\ \texttt{-.}\ E\ ]\!] = $ **float-negate**($expr[\![\ E\ ]\!]$)

$expr[\![\ \texttt{!}\ E\ ]\!] = expr[\![\ \texttt{prefix !}\ E\ ]\!]$

$expr[\![\ E_1\ \texttt{IO}\ E_2\ ]\!] = expr[\![\ \texttt{prefix}\ \texttt{IO}\ E_1\ E_2\ ]\!]$

$expr[\![\ E_1\ \texttt{.(}\ E_2\ \texttt{)}\ ]\!] = expr[\![\ \texttt{vect\_item}\ E_1\ E_2\ ]\!]$

$expr[\![\ E_1\ \texttt{.(}\ E_2\ \texttt{)}\ \texttt{<-}\ E_3\ ]\!] = expr[\![\ \texttt{vect\_assign}\ E_1\ E_2\ E_3\ ]\!]$

$expr[\![\ \texttt{not}\ E\ ]\!] = $ **not**($expr[\![\ E\ ]\!]$)

$expr[\![\ E_1\ \texttt{\&}\ E_2\ ]\!] = $ **if-true**($expr[\![\ E_1\ ]\!], expr[\![\ E_2\ ]\!],$ **false**)

$expr[\![\ E_1\ \texttt{or}\ E_2\ ]\!] = $ **if-true**($expr[\![\ E_1\ ]\!],$ **true**, $expr[\![\ E_2\ ]\!]$)

$expr[\![\ \texttt{if}\ E_1\ \texttt{then}\ E_2\ ]\!] = expr[\![\ \texttt{if}\ E_1\ \texttt{then}\ E_2\ \texttt{else (\ )}\ ]\!]$

$expr[\![\ \texttt{if}\ E_1\ \texttt{then}\ E_2\ \texttt{else}\ E_3\ ]\!] = $ **if-true**($expr[\![\ E_1\ ]\!], expr[\![\ E_2\ ]\!], expr[\![\ E_3\ ]\!]$)

$expr[\![\ \texttt{while}\ E_1\ \texttt{do}\ E_2\ \texttt{done}\ ]\!] = $ **while-true**($expr[\![\ E_1\ ]\!],$ **effect**($expr[\![\ E_2\ ]\!]$))

$expr[\![\ \texttt{for}\ I\ \texttt{=}\ E_1\ \texttt{to}\ E_2\ \texttt{do}\ E_3\ \texttt{done}\ ]\!] = $
    apply-to-each(**patt-abs**(**bind**($id[\![\ I\ ]\!]$), **effect**($expr[\![\ E_3\ ]\!]$)),
        int-closed-interval($expr[\![\ E_1\ ]\!], expr[\![\ E_2\ ]\!]$))

$expr[\![\ \texttt{for}\ I\ \texttt{=}\ E_1\ \texttt{downto}\ E_2\ \texttt{do}\ E_3\ \texttt{done}\ ]\!] = $
    apply-to-each(**patt-abs**(**bind**($id[\![\ I\ ]\!]$), **effect**($expr[\![\ E_3\ ]\!]$)),
        list-reverse(**int-closed-interval**($expr[\![\ E_2\ ]\!], expr[\![\ E_1\ ]\!]$)))

$expr[\![\ E_1\ ;\ E_2\ ]\!] = \textbf{seq}(\textbf{effect}(expr[\![\ E_1\ ]\!]), expr[\![\ E_2\ ]\!])$

$expr[\![\ \texttt{try}\ E\ \texttt{with}\ SM\ ]\!] =$
    $\textbf{catch-else-rethrow}(expr[\![\ E\ ]\!],$
        $\textbf{restrict-domain}(func[\![\ SM\ ]\!], \textbf{bound-type}(id[\![\ \texttt{exn}\ ]\!])))$

$expr[\![\ \texttt{let}\ VD\ \texttt{in}\ E\ ]\!] = \textbf{scope}(decl[\![\ VD\ ]\!], expr[\![\ E\ ]\!])$

$expr[\![\ \texttt{match}\ E\ \texttt{with}\ SM\ ]\!] =$
    $\textbf{apply}(\textbf{prefer-over}(func[\![\ SM\ ]\!], \textbf{abs}(\textbf{throw}(\textbf{cl-match-failure}))), expr[\![\ E\ ]\!])$

$expr[\![\ \texttt{function}\ SM\ ]\!] = \textbf{prefer-over}(func[\![\ SM\ ]\!], \textbf{abs}(\textbf{throw}(\textbf{cl-match-failure})))$

Pattern Matching

$func[\![\ P\ \texttt{->}\ E\ |\ SM\ ]\!] = \textbf{prefer-over}(func[\![\ P\ \texttt{->}\ E\ ]\!], func[\![\ SM\ ]\!])$

$func[\![\ P\ \texttt{->}\ E\ ]\!] = \textbf{close}(\textbf{patt-abs}(patt[\![\ P\ ]\!], expr[\![\ E\ ]\!]))$

Let Bindings

$decl[\![\ \texttt{rec}\ LB\ \cdots\ ]\!] =$
    $\textbf{generalise-decl}(\textbf{recursive-typed}(\textit{bound-ids}[\![\ LB\ \cdots\ ]\!], \textit{decl-mono}[\![\ LB\ \cdots\ ]\!]))$

$\textit{bound-ids}[\![\ LB_1\ \texttt{and}\ LB_2\ \cdots\ ]\!] =$
    $\textbf{map-union}(\textit{bound-ids}[\![\ LB_1\ ]\!], \textit{bound-ids}[\![\ LB_2\ \cdots\ ]\!])$

$\textit{bound-ids}[\![\ I\ \texttt{=}\ E\ ]\!] = \textbf{map1}(id[\![\ I\ ]\!], \textbf{unknown-type})$

$\textit{bound-ids}[\![\ (\ I\ :\ T\ )\ \texttt{=}\ E\ ]\!] = \textbf{map1}(id[\![\ I\ ]\!], type[\![\ T\ ]\!])$

$decl[\![\ LB_1\ \texttt{and}\ LB_2\ \cdots\ ]\!] = \textbf{map-union}(decl[\![\ LB_1\ ]\!], decl[\![\ LB_2\ \cdots\ ]\!])$

$decl[\![\ P\ \texttt{=}\ E\ ]\!] = \textbf{generalise-decl-if-true}(\textit{val-res}[\![\ E\ ]\!], \textit{decl-mono}[\![\ P\ \texttt{=}\ E\ ]\!])$

$\textit{decl-mono}[\![\ LB_1\ \texttt{and}\ LB_2\ \cdots\ ]\!] =$
    $\textbf{map-union}(\textit{decl-mono}[\![\ LB_1\ ]\!], \textit{decl-mono}[\![\ LB_2\ \cdots\ ]\!])$

$\textit{decl-mono}[\![\ P\ \texttt{=}\ E\ ]\!] =$
    $\textbf{match}(expr[\![\ E\ ]\!], \textbf{prefer-over}(patt[\![\ P\ ]\!], \textbf{abs}(\textbf{throw}(\textbf{cl-match-failure}))))$

$\textit{val-res}[\![\ \texttt{function}\ SM\ ]\!] = \textbf{true}$

$\textit{val-res}[\![\ C\ ]\!] = \textbf{true}$

$\textit{val-res}[\![\ I\ ]\!] = \textbf{true}$

$\textit{val-res}[\![\ \texttt{[| |]}\ ]\!] = \textbf{true}$

$\textit{val-res}[\![\ (E\ :\ T)\ ]\!] = \textit{val-res}[\![\ E\ ]\!]$

$\textit{val-res}[\![\ E_1\ ,\ E_2\ ]\!] = \textbf{and}(\textit{val-res}[\![\ E_1\ ]\!], \textit{val-res}[\![\ E_2\ ]\!])$

$\textit{val-res}[\![\ E_1\ ,\ E_2\ ,\ E_3\ \cdots\ ]\!] = \textbf{and}(\textit{val-res}[\![\ E_1\ ]\!], \textit{val-res}[\![\ E_2\ ,\ E_3\ \cdots\ ]\!])$

$\textit{val-res}[\![\ E_1\ \texttt{::}\ E_2\ ]\!] = \textbf{and}(\textit{val-res}[\![\ E_1\ ]\!], \textit{val-res}[\![\ E_2\ ]\!])$

$\textit{val-res}[\![\ [\ E\ ]\ ]\!] = \textit{val-res}[\![\ E\ ]\!]$

$\textit{val-res}[\![\ [\ E_1\ ;\ E_2\ \cdots\ ]\ ]\!] = \textbf{and}(\textit{val-res}[\![\ E_1\ ]\!], \textit{val-res}[\![\ [\ E_2\ \cdots\ ]\ ]\!])$

$\textit{val-res}[\![\ E\ ]\!] = \textbf{false}$

References

1. Afroozeh, A., van den Brand, M., Johnstone, A., Scott, E., Vinju, J.: Safe specification of operator precedence rules. In: Erwig, M., Paige, R.F., Van Wyk, E. (eds.) SLE 2013. LNCS, vol. 8225, pp. 137–156. Springer, Heidelberg (2013)
2. Bach Poulsen, C., Mosses, P.D.: Deriving pretty-big-step semantics from small-step semantics. In: Shao, Z. (ed.) ESOP 2014 (ETAPS). LNCS, vol. 8410, pp. 270–289. Springer, Heidelberg (2014)
3. Poulsen, C.B., Mosses, P.D.: Generating Specialized Interpreters for Modular Structural Operational Semantics. In: Gupta, G., Peña, R. (eds.) LOPSTR 2013. LNCS, vol. 8901, pp. 220–236. Springer, Heidelberg (2014)
4. Bergstra, J.A., Heering, J., Klint, P. (eds.): Algebraic Specification. ACM Press/Addison-Wesley, Reading (1989)
5. Bogdănaş, D., Roşu, G.: K-Java: a complete semantics of Java. In: POPL 2015. ACM (2015)
6. Börger, E., Fruja, N.G., Gervasi, V., Stärk, R.F.: A high-level modular definition of the semantics of C#. Theor. Comput. Sci. **336**(2–3), 235–284 (2005)
7. Börger, E., Stärk, R.F.: Exploiting abstraction for specification reuse: the Java/C# case study. In: de Boer, F.S., Bonsangue, M.M., Graf, S., de Roever, W.-P. (eds.) FMCO 2003. LNCS, vol. 3188, pp. 42–76. Springer, Heidelberg (2004)
8. den van Brand, M.G.J., et al.: The ASF+SDF meta-environment: a component-based language development environment. In: Wilhelm, R. (ed.) CC 2001. LNCS, vol. 2027, pp. 365–370. Springer, Heidelberg (2001)
9. van den Brand, M.G.J., Iversen, J., Mosses, P.D.: An action environment. Sci. Comput. Program. **61**(3), 245–264 (2006)
10. Chalub, F., Braga, C.: Maude MSOS tool. https://github.com/fcbr/mmt. Accessed Jan 2015
11. Churchill, M., Mosses, P.D.: Modular bisimulation theory for computations and values. In: Pfenning, F. (ed.) FOSSACS 2013 (ETAPS 2013). LNCS, vol. 7794, pp. 97–112. Springer, Heidelberg (2013)
12. Churchill, M., Mosses, P.D., Sculthorpe, N., Torrini, P.: Reusable components of semantic specifications: additional material (2015). http://www.plancomps.org/taosd2015
13. Churchill, M., Mosses, P.D., Torrini, P.: Reusable components of semantic specifications. In: Modularity 2014, pp. 145–156. ACM (2014)
14. Delaware, B., Keuchel, S., Schrijvers, T., Oliveira, B.C.: Modular monadic metatheory. In: ICFP 2013, pp. 319–330. ACM (2013)
15. Doh, K.G., Mosses, P.D.: Composing programming languages by combining action-semantics modules. Sci. Comput. Program. **47**(1), 3–36 (2003)
16. Doh, K.G., Schmidt, D.A.: Action semantics-directed prototyping. Comput. Lang. **19**, 213–233 (1993)
17. Ellison, C., Roşu, G.: An executable formal semantics of C with applications. In: POPL 2012, pp. 533–544. ACM (2012)
18. Felleisen, M., Findler, R.B., Flatt, M.: Semantics Engineering with PLT Redex. MIT Press, Cambridge (2009)
19. Felleisen, M., Hieb, R.: The revised report on the syntactic theories of sequential control and state. Theor. Comput. Sci. **103**(2), 235–271 (1992)
20. Goguen, J.A., Malcolm, G.: Algebraic Semantics of Imperative Programs. MIT Press, Cambridge (1996)

21. Harper, R., Stone, C.: A type-theoretic interpretation of Standard ML. In: Plotkin, G.D., Stirling, C., Tofte, M. (eds.) Proof, Language and Interaction: Essays in Honour of Robin Milner. MIT Press, Cambridge (2000)
22. Heering, J., Klint, P.: Prehistory of the ASF+SDF system (1980–1984). In: ASF+SDF95, pp. 1–4. Technical report 9504, Programming Research Group, University of Amsterdam (1995)
23. Hudak, P., Hughes, J., Jones, S.P., Wadler, P.: A history of Haskell: being lazy with class. In: HOPL-III, pp. 1–55. ACM (2007)
24. Iversen, J., Mosses, P.D.: Constructive action semantics for Core ML. Softw. IEE Proc. **152**, 79–98 (2005). Special issue on Language Definitions and Tool Generation
25. Johnstone, A., Mosses, P.D., Scott, E.: An agile approach to language modelling and development. Innov. Syst. Softw. Eng. **6**(1–2), 145–153 (2010). Special issue for ICFEM workshop FM+AM'09
26. Johnstone, A., Scott, E.: Translator generation using ART. In: Malloy, B., Staab, S., van den Brand, M. (eds.) SLE 2010. LNCS, vol. 6563, pp. 306–315. Springer, Heidelberg (2011)
27. Kahn, G.: Natural semantics. In: Brandenburg, F.J., Vidal-Naquet, G., Wirsing, M. (eds.) STACS 87. LNCS, vol. 247, pp. 22–39. Springer, Heidelberg (1987)
28. Kats, L.C.L., Visser, E.: The Spoofax language workbench. In: SPLASH/OOPSLA Companion, pp. 237–238. ACM (2010)
29. Klein, C., et al.: Run your research: on the effectiveness of lightweight mechanization. In: POPL 2012, pp. 285–296. ACM (2012)
30. Kutter, P.W., Pierantonio, A.: Montages specifications of realistic programming languages. J. Univ. Comput. Sci. **3**(5), 416–442 (1997)
31. Lee, D.K., Crary, K., Harper, R.: Towards a mechanized metatheory of Standard ML. In: POPL 2007, pp. 173–184. ACM (2007)
32. Leroy, X.: Caml Light manual, December 1997. http://caml.inria.fr/pub/docs/manual-caml-light
33. Levin, M.Y., Pierce, B.C.: TinkerType: a language for playing with formal systems. J. Funct. Program. **13**(2), 295–316 (2003)
34. Lewis, J.R., Launchbury, J., Meijer, E., Shields, M.B.: Implicit parameters: dynamic scoping with static types. In: POPL 2000, pp. 108–118. ACM (2000)
35. Liang, S., Hudak, P., Jones, M.: Monad transformers and modular interpreters. In: POPL 1995, pp. 333–343 (1995)
36. McCarthy, J.: Towards a mathematical science of computation. In: Popplewell, C.M. (ed.) Information Processing 1962, pp. 21–28. North-Holland, Amsterdam (1962)
37. Meseguer, J., Roşu, G.: The rewriting logic semantics project: a progress report. In: Owe, O., Steffen, M., Telle, J.A. (eds.) FCT 2011. LNCS, vol. 6914, pp. 1–37. Springer, Heidelberg (2011)
38. Milner, R., Tofte, M., Macqueen, D.: The Definition of Standard ML. MIT Press, Cambridge (1997)
39. Moggi, E.: An abstract view of programming languages. Technical report ECS-LFCS-90-113, Edinburgh University (1989)
40. Mosses, P.D.: Action Semantics, Cambridge Tracts in Theoretical Computer Science, vol. 26. Cambridge University Press, Cambridge (1992)
41. Mosses, P.D.: Theory and practice of action semantics. In: Penczek, W., Szałas, A. (eds.) MFCS 1996. LNCS, vol. 1113, pp. 37–61. Springer, Heidelberg (1996)
42. Mosses, P.D.: Modular structural operational semantics. J. Log. Algebr. Program. **60–61**, 195–228 (2004)

43. Mosses, P.D.: A constructive approach to language definition. J. Univ. Comput. Sci. **11**(7), 1117–1134 (2005)

44. Mosses, P.D.: Teaching semantics of programming languages with Modular SOS. In: Teaching Formal Methods: Practice and Experience. Electronic Workshops in Computing. BCS (2006)

45. Mosses, P.D.: Component-based description of programming languages. In: Visions of Computer Science. Electronic Proceedings, pp. 275–286. BCS (2008)

46. Mosses, P.D.: Component-based semantics. In: SAVCBS 2009, pp. 3–10. ACM (2009)

47. Mosses, P.D.: VDM semantics of programming languages: combinators and monads. Form. Asp. Comput. **23**, 221–238 (2011)

48. Mosses, P.D.: Semantics of programming languages: using ASF+SDF. Sci. Comput. Program. **97**(1), 2–10 (2013). http://dx.doi.org/10.1016/j.scico.2013.11.038

49. Mosses, P.D., New, M.J.: Implicit propagation in structural operational semantics. In: SOS 2008. Electr. Notes Theor. Comput. Sci., vol. 229(4), pp. 49–66. Elsevier (2009)

50. Mosses, P.D., Vesely, F.: FunKons: component-based semantics in K. In: Escobar, S. (ed.) WRLA 2014. LNCS, vol. 8663, pp. 213–229. Springer, Heidelberg (2014)

51. Mosses, P.D., Watt, D.A.: The use of action semantics. In: Formal Description of Programming Concepts III, Proceedings of IFIP TC2 Working Conference, Gl. Avernæs, 1986, pp. 135–166. Elsevier (1987)

52. Owens, S., Peskine, G., Sewell, P.: A formal specification for OCaml: the core language. Technical report, University of Cambridge (2008)

53. Owens, S.: A sound semantics for OCaml light. In: Drossopoulou, S. (ed.) ESOP 2008. LNCS, vol. 4960, pp. 1–15. Springer, Heidelberg (2008)

54. Pierce, B.C.: Types and Programming Languages. MIT Press, Cambridge (2002)

55. PLANCOMPS: Programming language components and specifications (2011). http://www.plancomps.org

56. Plotkin, G.D.: A structural approach to operational semantics. J. Log. Algebr. Program. **60–61**, 17–139 (2004)

57. Plotkin, G.D., Power, A.J.: Computational effects and operations: an overview. In: Proceedings of Workshop on Domains VI. Electr. Notes Theor. Comput. Sci., vol. 73, pp. 149–163. Elsevier (2004)

58. Roşu, G., Şerbănuţă, T.F.: K overview and SIMPLE case study. Electr. Notes Theor. Comput. Sci. **304**, 3–56 (2014)

59. Sewell, P., Nardelli, F.Z., Owens, S., et al.: Ott: effective tool support for the working semanticist. J. Funct. Program. **20**, 71–122 (2010)

60. Tofte, M.: Type inference for polymorphic references. Inf. Comput. **89**(1), 1–34 (1990)

61. Visser, E.: Syntax Definition for Language Prototyping. Ph.D. thesis, University of Amsterdam (1997)

62. Visser, E.: Stratego: a language for program transformation based on rewriting strategies system description of Stratego 0.5. In: Middeldorp, A. (ed.) RTA 2001. LNCS, vol. 2051, pp. 357–361. Springer, Heidelberg (2001)

Probabilistic Model Checking
for Feature-Oriented Systems

Clemens Dubslaff$^{(\boxtimes)}$, Christel Baier, and Sascha Klüppelholz

Faculty of Computer Science, Technische Universität Dresden, Dresden, Germany
{dubslaff,baier,klueppelholz}@tcs.inf.tu-dresden.de

Abstract. Within *product lines*, collections of several related products
are defined through their commonalities in terms of features rather than
specifying them individually one-by-one. In this paper we present a compositional framework for modeling dynamic product lines by a state-
based formalism with both probabilistic and nondeterministic behaviors.
Rules for feature changes in products made during runtime are formalized by a coordination component imposing constraints on possible feature activations and deactivations. Our framework supports large-scaled
product lines described through multi-features, i.e., where products may
involve multiple instances of a feature.

To establish temporal properties for products in a product line, verification techniques have to face a combinatorial blow-up that arises
when reasoning about several feature combinations. This blow-up can be
avoided by family-based approaches exploiting common feature behaviors. We adapt such approaches to our framework, allowing for a quantitative analysis in terms of probabilistic model checking to reason, e.g.,
about energy and memory consumption, monetary costs, or the reliability
of products. Our framework can also be used to compute strategies how
to trigger feature changes for optimizing quantitative objectives using
probabilistic model-checking techniques.

We present a natural and conceptually simple translation of product lines into the input language of the prominent probabilistic model
checker PRISM and show feasibility of this translation within a case study
on an energy-aware server platform product line comprising thousands of
products. To cope with the arising complexity, we follow the family-based
analysis scheme and apply symbolic methods for a compact state-space
representation.

1 Introduction

The concept of *product lines* is widely used in the development and marketing of
modern hardware and software. In a product line, customers can purchase a base

A preliminary version of this paper appeared at Modularity'14 [23].

The authors are supported by the DFG through the collaborative research cen-
tre HAEC (SFB 912), the cluster of excellence cfAED, Deutsche Telekom Stiftung,
the ESF young researcher groups IMData (100098198) and SREX (100111037), the
Graduiertenkolleg QuantLA (1763), the DFG/NWO-project ROCKS, and the EU-
FP-7 grant MEALS (295261).

© Springer-Verlag Berlin Heidelberg 2015
S. Chiba et al. (Eds.): Transactions on AOSD XII, LNCS 8989, pp. 180–220, 2015.
DOI: 10.1007/978-3-662-46734-3_5

system extendible and customizable with functionalities, also called *features*. Following the definition for product lines in the software domain (also called *software product lines*), a product line can also be understood as the collection of all features itself and rules how the features can be combined into products [14]. The rules for the composition of features are typically provided using *feature diagrams* [7,35], where the features and their hierarchical structure are given by a tree-like structure. For describing large product lines supporting several instances of features, feature diagrams with *multi-features* come into place, where cardinality ranges are annotated to features indicating how many of them can be instantiated towards a valid feature combination [18].

Feature combinations are often assumed to be static, i.e., some realizable feature combination is fixed when the product is purchased and is never changed afterwards. However, this does not faithfully reflect adaptations of modern products during their lifetime. For instance, when in-app purchases are placed or when a free trial version of a software product expires, features are activated or deactivated during runtime of the system. Similarly, components of a hardware system might be upgraded to more powerful or energy-efficient ones or are necessarily replaced due to a hardware failure. In all these situations, the products change but still belong to the same product line. Such product lines capable of modeling adaptations after deployment are called *dynamic product lines* [29], for which the design of specification formalisms is an active and emerging field in product line engineering [19,22,31,45].

Verification of Product Lines. To meet requirements in safety-critical parts of the features or to guarantee overall quality (in particular within features that are used in many or most of the products of the product line) verification is of utter interest. Verification is even more important for dynamic product lines, where side-effects arising from dynamic feature changes are difficult to predict in the development phase of a product. Model checking [5,11] is a fully automatic verification technique for establishing temporal properties of systems (e.g., safety or liveness properties). Indeed, model checking has been already successfully applied to integrate features in components and to detect feature interactions [43]. However, the typical task for reasoning about static product lines is to solve the so-called *featured model-checking problem*:

> Compute the set of all valid feature combinations C such that some given temporal requirement φ holds for the products corresponding to C.

This is in contrast to the classical model-checking problem that amounts to prove that φ holds for some fixed system, e.g., one specific product obtained from a feature combination. The naive approach for solving the featured model-checking problem is to verify the products in the product line one-by-one after their deployment. However, already within static product lines, this approach certainly suffers from an exponential blow-up in the number of different valid feature combinations. To tackle this potential combinatorial blow-up, family-based approaches are very successful, checking all products in a product line at once rather than one-by-one [53]. In [12,13], the concept of *featured transition systems* has been introduced to encode the operational behaviors of all products in a product line into a single model. The transitions in featured transition systems are annotated by feature combinations: a transition can only be fired if it is labeled by the feature combination corresponding to the product deployed. Symbolic techniques [39] describe states and transitions of an operational model as sets with common properties rather than listing them one-by-one. Such techniques can be used for solving the featured model-checking problem for product lines represented by featured transition systems efficiently for both linear-time [13] and branching-time properties [12]. An extension of featured transition systems that introduces guarded transitions for switches between valid feature combinations was presented by Cordy et al. [16] allowing for dynamic adaptions of feature combinations during the lifetime of a product. Besides purely functional temporal requirements, the quality of (software) products crucially depends on quantitative properties. Measurement-based approaches for reasoning about feature-oriented software have been studied intensively, see, e.g., [41, 50,51]. In contrast, probabilistic model-checking techniques were studied only recently [28,52], relying on probabilistic operational models based on discrete-time Markov chains and probabilistic computation tree logic. For instance, Ghezzi and Sharifloo analyzed parametric sequence diagrams using the probabilistic model-checking tool PARAM [28].

A Compositional Framework for Feature-Oriented Systems. In this paper, we present a *compositional framework* to model dynamic product lines which allows for the automated *quantitative system analysis* using probabilistic model checking [5]. Our approach allows for easily specifying large-scaled product lines with thousands of products described through feature diagrams with multi-features.

Markov chains, the purely probabilistic model used in most approaches of probabilistic product-line analysis [28,52], are less adequate for the compositional design with parallel components than operational models supporting both, nondeterministic and probabilistic choices (see, e.g., [48]). A *Markov decision process (MDP)* is such a formalism, extending labelled transition systems by internal probabilistic choices taken after resolving nondeterminism between actions of the system. Our framework for dynamic product lines presented in this paper relies on MDPs with annotated costs [44]. In particular, it consists of

(1) feature modules: MDP-like models for the feature-dependent operational behavior of the components and their interactions,
(2) a parallel operator: feature-aware composing feature modules to represent the parallel execution of independent actions by interleaving and supporting communication between the feature modules,
(3) a feature controller: an MDP-like model for the potential dynamic switches of feature combinations, and
(4) a join operator: yielding a standard MDP model of the complete dynamic product line represented by feature modules and a feature controller.

A product line naturally induces a compositional structure over features, where a feature or a collection thereof corresponds to a component. In our framework, these components are called feature modules (1). Feature modules are composed using a parallel operator (2), which combines the operational behaviors of all features represented by the feature modules into another feature module. We only allow for composing compatible feature modules, i.e., feature modules which represent the operational behavior of different features. Thus, different implementations or versions of the same feature need either to be modeled as distinct features excluding each other or cannot be combined in our framework. Feature activation and deactivation at runtime is described through a feature controller (3), which is a state-based model controlling valid changes in the feature combinations. As within feature modules, choices between feature combinations can be probabilistic (e.g., on the basis of statistical information on feature combinations and their adaptations over time) or nondeterministic (e.g., if feature changes rely on internal choices of the controller or are triggered from outside by an unknown or unpredictable environment) and combinations thereof.

The semantics of a feature module under a given feature controller is defined as a parallel composition synchronizing over common feature annotations (4), providing an elegant formalization of the feature module's behavior within the dynamic product line represented by the feature controller. Note that our approach separates between computation and coordination [27,42,47], which allows for specifying features in the context of various different dynamic product lines. Feature-oriented extensions of programming languages and specialized composition operators such as *superimposition* are an orthogonal approach [1,2,36]. However, the effect of superimposition could also be encoded into our framework, e.g., using techniques proposed by Plath and Ryan [43].

Quantitative Analysis and Strategy Synthesis. Fortunately, the semantics of feature modules under feature controllers yields an MDP. Thus, our approach permits to apply standard but sophisticated probabilistic model-checking techniques to reason about quantitative properties. This is in contrast to existing (also nonprobabilistic) approaches, which require model-checking algorithms specialized for product lines. Within our approach, quantitative queries such as "minimize the energy consumption until reaching a target state" can be answered. Whereas for static product lines, one aims to solve the featured model-checking problem, we introduce the so-called *strategy synthesis problem* for dynamic product lines. This problem amounts to find an optimal strategy to resolve the nondeterminism between feature combination switches in the feature controller [23]. The strategy includes the initial step of the dynamic product line by selecting an initial feature combination, which suffices to solve the featured model-checking problem. Our approach thus additionally provides the possibility to reason over worst-case and best-case scenarios concerning feature changes during runtime.

Implementation and Case Study. Models of product lines have to face a combinatorial blow-up in the number of features. When modeling dynamic product lines, the number of possible feature changes during runtime yield an additional combinatorial blow-up. However, symbolic representations of models including all the behaviors in a product line can avoid these blow-ups [12]. In this paper, we extend our compositional framework for dynamic product lines [23] towards feature modules and controllers with variables, such that it nicely fits with guarded-command languages such as the input language of the symbolic probabilistic model checker PRISM [34]. PRISM uses multi-terminal binary decision diagrams for the symbolic encoding of the probabilistic model to obtain a compact representation. To demonstrate the usability of PRISM within our framework, we carried out a case study based on a real-case server-platform scenario, where several variants of a server can be endowed with different kinds of network interface cards. This product line can be equipped with an energy-aware network driver, similarly as done for the EBOND device [30]. Network cards with different performance characteristics are then bonded or switched off according to energy-saving algorithms which, e.g., take usage of the varying bandwidth requirements during day and night time. The arising energy-aware server system product line, which we call ESERVER, can be subject of several quantitative requirements, e.g., on the energy consumption of the products in the product line. We illustrate how PRISM can be used to solve the strategy synthesis problem w.r.t. to such requirements for ESERVER and can provide strategies how to equip a server used in different environments. In particular, we show that symbolic methods applied to dynamic product lines such as ESERVER clearly outperform explicit ones.

Outline. The paper starts with a brief summary on the foundations of product lines, feature models, relevant principles of MDPs and their quantitative analysis. The compositional framework for specifying dynamic product lines by means of feature modules and feature controllers is presented in Sect. 3. Section 4 is devoted to the encoding of our framework into guarded-command languages, such as the input language of the probabilistic model-checking tool PRISM. Our case study follows in Sect. 5, where we use PRISM and the encoding of our framework to discuss the scalability of our approach towards product lines with thousands of products and the influence of symbolic representations. The paper ends with some concluding remarks in Sect. 6.

2   Preliminaries

Before we recall the standard concepts for product lines, probabilistic models and their quantitative analysis, we introduce notations for Boolean and linear expressions to provide intuitive symbolic representations for sets.

Boolean Expressions. The powerset of a set X is denoted by 2^X. For convenience, we sometimes use symbolic notations based on Boolean expressions for the elements of 2^X, i.e., the subsets of X. Let $\mathbb{B}(X)$ denote the set of all Boolean expressions ρ built over Boolean variables $x \in X$ as atoms and the usual connectives of propositional logic (negation $\neg$, conjunction $\wedge$, etc.). The satisfaction relation $\models \subseteq 2^X \times \mathbb{B}(X)$ is defined in the obvious way. For instance, if $X = \{x_1, x_2, x_3\}$ and $\rho = x_1 \wedge \neg x_2$, then $Y \models \rho$ iff $Y = \{x_1\}$ or $Y = \{x_1, x_3\}$. To specify binary relations on 2^X symbolically, we use Boolean expressions $\rho \in \mathbb{B}(X \cup X')$, where X' is the set consisting of pairwise distinct, fresh copies of the elements of X. Then, the relation $R_\rho \subseteq 2^X \times 2^X$ is given by:

$$(Y, Z) \in R_\rho \;\; \text{iff} \;\; Y \cup \{z' : z \in Z\} \models \rho$$

As an example, the Boolean expression $\rho = (x_1 \vee x_3') \wedge \neg x_2$ represents the relation R_ρ consisting of all pairs $(Y, Z) \in 2^X \times 2^X$, where (1) $x_1 \in Y$ or $x_3 \in Z$ and (2) $x_2 \notin Y$. For $Y \subseteq X$, we use $Y = Y'$ as a shortform notation for the Boolean expression $\bigwedge_{y \in Y} y \leftrightarrow y'$.

Linear Constraints. The symbolic notations for subsets of X using Boolean expressions can be extended towards sets of functions $f \colon X \to \mathbb{N}$, i.e., elements of $\mathbb{N}^X$ which we define through *linear constraints* γ of the form

$$a_1 x_1 + a_2 x_2 + \ldots + a_n x_n \;\; \bowtie \;\; \theta,$$

where $a_i \in \mathbb{Z}$, $x_i \in X$ for all $i = 1, 2, \ldots, n$, $\bowtie \in \{<, \leq, =, \geq, >\}$ and $\theta \in \mathbb{Z}$. A function $f \in \mathbb{N}^X$ fulfills such a linear constraint γ as above if $a_1 f(x_1) + a_2 f(x_2) + \ldots + a_n f(x_n) \bowtie \theta$. We then write $f \models \gamma$. The set of all linear constraints over X is denoted by $\mathbb{C}(X)$, while the set of Boolean expressions over linear constraints is $\mathbb{BC}(X) = \mathbb{B}(\mathbb{C}(X))$. With these ingredients, the definitions stated above for subsets of variables X take over, e.g., to the satisfaction relation $\models \subseteq \mathbb{N}^X \times \mathbb{BC}(X)$. Note that this is indeed an extension of Boolean expressions over X: for $f \in \mathbb{N}^X$, let $C_f \subseteq X$ denote the *support* of f, i.e., $C_f = \{x \in X : f(x) \geq 1\}$. Then for any Boolean expression $\rho \in \mathbb{B}(X)$, replacing all variables x by the linear constraint $(x \geq 1) \in \mathbb{C}(X)$ yields $\hat{\rho} \in \mathbb{BC}(X)$, where for all $f \in \mathbb{N}^X$

$$f \models \hat{\rho} \;\; \text{iff} \;\; C_f \models \rho$$

Due to this, we also allow for mixed Boolean expressions in $\mathbb{B}(\mathbb{C}(X) \cup X)$, simply also denoted by $\mathbb{BC}(X)$. For instance, with $X = \{x_1, x_2\}$ the mixed expression

$$\rho \;\; = \;\; x_1 \wedge (2 \cdot x_1 + x_2 \leq 4)$$

defines exactly four functions $f \in \mathbb{N}^X$ where $f \models \rho$ is described through the pairs $(x_1, x_2) \in \{(1, 0), (1, 1), (1, 2), (2, 0)\}$. Similar as for Boolean expressions without linear constraints, a binary relation on $\mathbb{N}^X$ can be defined via an expression $\rho \in \mathbb{BC}(X \cup X')$, where X' is the set consisting of pairwise distinct, fresh copies of the elements of X. Then, the relation $R_\rho \subseteq \mathbb{N}^X \times \mathbb{N}^X$ is given by:

$$(f, g) \in R_\rho \;\; \text{iff} \;\; h \models \rho,$$

where $h \in \mathbb{N}^{X \cup X'}$ is defined by $h(x) = f(x)$ and $h(x') = g(x)$ for all $x \in X$. We also use $Y = Y'$ as a shortform notation of the expression $\bigwedge_{y \in Y} (y = y')$.

2.1   Feature Models

A *product line* is a collection of products, which have commonalities w.r.t. assets called *features* [14]. We discuss here a variant of product lines which allows for *multi-features*, i.e., a feature can appear in a product within multiple instances [18]. Let F denote the finite set of all such (multi-)features of a product line. A *feature combination* is a function f assigning to each feature $x \in F$ the cardinality $f(x)$. We say that $f \in \mathbb{N}^F$ is *valid* if there is a corresponding product in the product line consisting of exactly $f(x)$ instances of the features $x \in F$. A product line can hence be formalized in terms of a *feature signature* $(F, \mathcal{V})$, where $\mathcal{V} \subseteq \mathbb{N}^F$ is the set of valid feature combinations. A feature signature $(F, \mathcal{V})$ is *Boolean*, if $\mathcal{V} \subseteq \{0, 1\}^F$, i.e., there is at most one instance of each feature in a valid feature combination. *Feature diagrams* [35] provide a compact representation of feature signatures via a tree-like hierarchical structure (see, e.g., Fig. 1). Nodes in feature diagrams correspond to features of F. The nodes are annotated with integer ranges that restrict the number of instances built for the given feature [17,18]. The integer ranges are of the form $[l..u]$, where $l, u \in \mathbb{N}$ with $l \leq u$ standing for the lower and upper cardinality bound on the feature instances. Usually, range annotations $[1..1]$ are omitted in the feature diagrams, and instead of range annotations $[0..1]$ (corresponding to optional features) a circle above the respective feature node is drawn. If the node for feature x' is a son of the node for feature x, then every instance of feature x' requires its corresponding instance of x. Several types of branchings from a node for feature x towards its sons $x'_1, \ldots, x'_n$ are possible. Standard branchings denote that all sons of x are instantiated according to their cardinality range (AND connective) and connected branchings indicate that exactly one son is required (XOR connective). Boolean expressions of linear constraints over F may be further annotated to describe, e.g., numerical dependencies between the number of instances of features. In this paper, we stick to this informal and rather intuitive description of multi-feature diagrams as it suffices for obtaining the feature signature and the hierarchical structure of features. We refer to [17,18] for a detailed discussion on the semantics of multi-feature diagrams.

Dynamic Product Lines. Usually, product lines are static in the sense that a valid feature combination is fixed prior of launching the product. Product lines allowing for activation and deactivation of features during runtime of the system are called *dynamic product lines*. The common approach towards dynamic product lines is to indicate disjoint sets of *dynamic features* D and *environment features* E, which respectively include features that can be activated or deactivated at runtime either by the system itself (features of D) or by the environment (features of E). Intuitively, an activation and deactivation of an environment feature may impose (de-)activations of dynamic features [16]. In [22] dynamic product lines are formalized using a generalization of feature diagrams where dashed nodes represent elements of $D \cup E$. When not restricted by further annotated constraints, each instance of such a dynamic feature can be activated and deactivated at any time. In the approach by [19], the possible (de-)activations of each feature are defined explicitly by a switching relation over (Boolean) feature combinations. We choose a similar approach towards our compositional framework, which is also capable of supporting multi-features and explained in Sect. 3.

Further Extensions. Costs for feature activations in dynamic product lines have been considered in [54]. Besides assigning ranges to features describing their number of instances, ranges can also be annotated to branchings in the feature diagram, generalizing Boolean connectives for the branchings. In our formalization using linear constraints, such *group cardinalities* allow for a compact representation of lower and upper bounds on the number of instances in sons of the feature diagram [17].

Example 1. As the running example of this paper, let us consider an energy-aware server product line ESERVER, which is inspired by the server-rack product line of a famous computer vendor and incorporates an energy-aware driver for bonding network cards as presented in [30]. This product line can be represented by a feature diagram as shown in Fig. 1.

Each node is identified with the underlined letter, i.e., the set of features is

$$F = \{e, R, T, L, A, P, o, \dot{F}, S, C, y, g, H, B, D, W, M, x, b, N, G, i\}.$$

The ESERVER product line consists of a server rack (R), which has at most ten slots (o) where up to ten network cards (N) can be plugged in. Each slot supports either a high-speed data transfer (F) or only a slow-speed transfer (S). Clearly, a fast 10 GBit network card (G) can only be used when plugged into a fast slot. Depending on the type of the rack, the number of slots and their kind is restricted according to the linear constraints over F provided at the bottom of the feature diagram. E.g., an advanced (A) ESERVER has at least 2 but at most 7 slots, where at most 2 of them are fast ones. Besides these hardware features, the ESERVER product line consists also of a software feature in terms of a driver coordinating the interplay of the heterogeneous network cards (C). The ESERVER incorporates EBOND [30]: depending on the selected switch policy (y), network cards can be activated for serving more bandwidth or deactivated for saving energy. Furthermore, the method how the requested bandwidth is distributed along the active cards is coordinated by the feature D. For instance, the round robin feature (b) may stand for the standard uniform distribution of bandwidth, whereas the weighted feature (W) refers to distributing bandwidth such that every card has the same workload.

Note that the network card feature (N) is a dynamic multi-feature, i.e., its cardinality may vary from 1 to 10 during runtime of the ESERVER system. However, the annotated constraints still need to be fulfilled, e.g., $N \leq o$ for ensuring that at most as many cards as slots available are plugged.

Obviously, this dynamic product line is large-scaled, dominated by the possible combinations of the multi-features representing slots and network cards. Taking the linear constraints on the card combinations into account, the ESERVER product line amounts to 17,544 valid feature combinations.

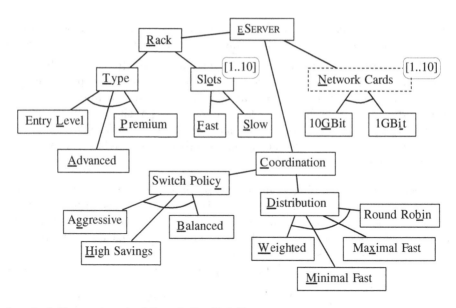

$$L \Rightarrow (o \le 2) \quad \wedge \quad A \Rightarrow (o \le 7 \wedge o \ge 2 \wedge F \le 2) \quad \wedge$$
$$P \Rightarrow (o \le 10 \wedge o \ge 6 \wedge F \le 8) \quad \wedge \quad (N \le o) \wedge (G \le F)$$

Fig. 1. Feature diagram of the dynamic ESERVER product line

2.2   Probabilistic Systems and Their Quantitative Analysis

The operational model used in this paper for modeling and analyzing the behavior of products in a dynamic product line is given in terms of *Markov decision processes (MDPs)* [44]. We deal here with MDPs where transitions are labeled with a cost value. MDPs with multiple cost functions of different types (e.g., for reasoning about energy and memory requirements and utility values) can be defined accordingly.

Distributions. Let S be a countable nonempty set. A *distribution over S* is a function $\sigma \colon S \to [0,1]$ with $\sum_{s \in S} \sigma(s) = 1$. The set $\{s \in S : \sigma(s) > 0\}$ is called the *support of σ* and is denoted by $supp(\sigma)$. $Distr(S)$ denotes the set of all distributions over S. Given $t \in S$, the *Dirac distribution $Dirac[t]$ of t over S* is defined by

$$Dirac[t](t) = 1 \quad \text{and} \quad Dirac[t](s) = 0 \text{ for all } s \in S \backslash \{t\}.$$

The *product* of two distributions $\sigma_1 \in Distr(S_1)$ and $\sigma_2 \in Distr(S_2)$ is defined as the distribution $\sigma_1 * \sigma_2 \in Distr(S_1 \times S_2)$, where $(\sigma_1 * \sigma_2)(s_1, s_2) = \sigma_1(s_1) \cdot \sigma_2(s_2)$ for all $s_1 \in S_1$ and $s_2 \in S_2$.

Markov Decision Processes. An MDP is a tuple

$$\mathcal{M} = (S, S^{init}, \mathsf{Moves}),$$

where S is a finite set of states, $S^{init} \subseteq S$ is the set of initial states and Moves $\subseteq$ $S \times \mathbb{N} \times Distr(S)$ specifies the possible moves of $\mathcal{M}$ and their costs. We require Moves to be finite and often write $s \xrightarrow{c} \sigma$ iff $(s, c, \sigma) \in$ Moves. Intuitively, the operational behavior of $\mathcal{M}$ is as follows. The computations of $\mathcal{M}$ start in some nondeterministically chosen initial state of S^{init}. If during $\mathcal{M}$'s computation the current state is s, one of the moves $s \xrightarrow{c} \sigma$ is selected nondeterministically first, before there is an internal probabilistic choice, selecting a successor state s' with probability $\sigma(s') > 0$. Value c specifies the cost for taking the move $s \xrightarrow{c} \sigma$.

Steps of $\mathcal{M}$, written in the form $s \xrightarrow{c}_p s'$, arise from moves $s \xrightarrow{c} \sigma$ resolving the probabilistic choice by plugging in some state s' with positive probability, i.e., $p = \sigma(s') > 0$. *Paths* in $\mathcal{M}$ are sequences of consecutive steps. In the following, we assume a finite path π having the form

$$\pi = s_0 \xrightarrow{c_1}_{p_1} s_1 \xrightarrow{c_2}_{p_2} s_2 \xrightarrow{c_3}_{p_3} \ldots \xrightarrow{c_n}_{p_n} s_n. \qquad (*)$$

We refer to the number n of steps as the length of π. If $0 \le k \le n$, we write $\pi \downarrow k$ for the prefix of π consisting of the first k steps (then, $\pi \downarrow k$ ends in state s_k). Given a finite path π, the probability $\Pr(\pi)$ is defined as the product of the probabilities in the steps of π and the accumulated costs $\mathrm{cost}(\pi)$ are defined as the sum of the costs of π's steps. Formally,

$$\Pr(\pi) = p_1 \cdot p_2 \cdot \ldots \cdot p_n \quad \text{and} \quad \mathrm{cost}(\pi) = c_1 + c_2 + \ldots + c_n.$$

State $s \in S$ is called *terminal* if there is no move $s \xrightarrow{c} \sigma$. A path is *maximal*, if it is either infinite or ends in a terminal state. The set of finite paths starting in some state of S^{init} is denoted by *FPaths*.

Schedulers and Probability Measure. Within MDPs, reasoning about probabilities requires the selection of an initial state and resolution of the nondeterministic choices between possible moves. The latter is formalized via *schedulers*, which take as input a finite path and decide which move to take next. For the purposes of this paper it suffices to consider deterministic, possibly history-dependent schedulers, i.e., partial functions

$$\mathfrak{S} \colon FPaths \to \mathbb{N} \times Distr(S),$$

where for all finite paths π as in $(*)$, $\mathfrak{S}(\pi)$ is undefined if π is maximal and otherwise $\mathfrak{S}(\pi) = (c, \sigma)$ for some $s_n \xrightarrow{c} \sigma$. An $\mathfrak{S}$-*path* is any path that arises when the nondeterministic choices in $\mathcal{M}$ are resolved by $\mathfrak{S}$. Thus, a finite path π is a $\mathfrak{S}$-path iff there are distributions $\sigma_1, \ldots, \sigma_n \in Distr(S)$ such that $\mathfrak{S}(\pi \downarrow k-1) = (c_k, \sigma_k)$ and $p_k = \sigma_k(s_k)$ for all $1 \le k \le n$. Infinite $\mathfrak{S}$-paths are defined accordingly.

Given a scheduler $\mathfrak{S}$ and some initial state $s \in S^{init}$, the behavior of $\mathcal{M}$ under $\mathfrak{S}$ and s is purely probabilistic and can be formalized by a tree-like infinite-state Markov chain $\mathcal{M}_s^{\mathfrak{S}}$ over the finite $\mathfrak{S}$-paths of $\mathcal{M}$ starting in s. Markov chains are MDPs that do not have any nondeterministic choices, i.e., where S^{init} is a singleton and $|\text{Moves}(s)| \le 1$ for all states $s \in S$. Using standard concepts, a probability measure $\mathbb{P}_s^{\mathfrak{S}}$ for measurable sets of maximal branches in the Markov chain $\mathcal{M}_s^{\mathfrak{S}}$ is defined and can be transferred to maximal $\mathfrak{S}$-paths in $\mathcal{M}$ starting in s. For further details we refer to standard text books such as [32,37,44].

Quantitative Properties. The concept of schedulers permits to talk about the probability of a measurable path property φ for paths starting in a fixed state s and respecting a given scheduler $\mathfrak{S}$. Typical examples for such a property φ are reachability conditions of the following type, where T and V are sets of states:

- reachability: $\varphi = \Diamond T$ denotes that eventually some state in T will be visited
- constrained reachability: $\varphi = V\,\mathcal{U}\,T$ imposes the same constraint as $\Diamond T$ with the side-condition that all states visited before reaching T belong to V.

For a worst-case analysis of a system modeled by an MDP $\mathcal{M}$, one ranges over all initial states and all schedulers (i.e., all possible resolutions of the nondeterminism) and considers the maximal or minimal probabilities for φ. If φ represents a desired path property, then $\mathbb{P}_s^{\min}(\varphi) = \inf_{\mathfrak{S}} \mathbb{P}_s^{\mathfrak{S}}(\varphi)$ is the probability for $\mathcal{M}$ satisfying φ that can be guaranteed even for the worst-case scenarios. Similarly, $\mathbb{P}_s^{\max}(\varphi) = \sup_{\mathfrak{S}} \mathbb{P}_s^{\mathfrak{S}}(\varphi)$ is the least upper bound that can be guaranteed for the likelihood of $\mathcal{M}$ to satisfy φ (best-case scenario).

One can also reason about bounds for expected costs of paths in $\mathcal{M}$. We consider here accumulated costs to reach a set $T \subseteq S$ of target states from a state $s \in S$. Formally, if $\mathfrak{S}$ is a scheduler such that $\mathbb{P}_s^{\mathfrak{S}}(\Diamond T) = 1$, then the *expected accumulated costs* for reaching T from s under $\mathfrak{S}$ are defined by

$$\mathbb{E}_s^{\mathfrak{S}}(\Diamond T) = \sum_{\pi} \text{cost}(\pi) \cdot \Pr(\pi),$$

where π as in $(*)$ ranges over all finite $\mathfrak{S}$-paths with $s_n \in T$, $s_0 = s$ and $\{s_0, \dots, s_{n-1}\} \cap T = \emptyset$. If $\mathbb{P}_s^{\mathfrak{S}}(\Diamond T) < 1$, i.e., with positive probability T will never be visited, then $\mathbb{E}_s^{\mathfrak{S}}(\Diamond T) = \infty$. Furthermore,

$$\mathbb{E}_s^{\min}(\Diamond T) = \inf_{\mathfrak{S}} \mathbb{E}_s^{\mathfrak{S}}(\Diamond T) \quad \text{and} \quad \mathbb{E}_s^{\max}(\Diamond T) = \sup_{\mathfrak{S}} \mathbb{E}_s^{\mathfrak{S}}(\Diamond T)$$

specify the greatest lower bound (least upper bound, respectively) for the expected accumulated costs reaching T from s in $\mathcal{M}$.

Quantitative Analysis. Several powerful probabilistic model-checking tools support the algorithmic quantitative analysis of MDPs against temporal specifications, such as the reachability properties stated above. But also for temporal properties such as formulas of linear temporal logic (LTL) or probabilistic computation-tree logic (PCTL) [6,8], there is a broad tool support. PCTL provides an elegant formalism to specify various temporal properties, reliability and resource conditions. In our case study, we will use the prominent probabilistic model checker PRISM [34] that offers a symbolic MDP-engine for PCTL, dealing with a compact internal representation of the MDP using multi-terminal binary decision diagrams [26]. For the purpose of the paper, the precise syntax and semantics of PCTL over MDPs is not relevant. It suffices to know that in PCTL, the (constrained) reachability properties above can be described and encapsulated with a probability or expectation operator. Probabilistic model-checking algorithms for PCTL then allow for computing minimizing and maximizing schedulers for probabilities (e.g., $\mathbb{P}_s^{\max}(\varphi)$) and expectations (e.g., $\mathbb{E}_s^{\min}(\Diamond T)$) up to an arbitrary precision [6,8,20,25]. For the computation of the latter we assume that $\mathbb{P}_s^{\min}(\Diamond T) = 1$.

3 Compositional Framework

A product line naturally induces a compositional structure where features correspond to modules composed, e.g., along the hierarchy provided by feature diagrams. Thus, it is rather natural to choose a compositional approach towards a modeling framework for dynamic product lines. We formalize feature implementations by so-called *feature modules* that might interact with each other and can depend on the presence of other features and their current own configurations. Dependencies between feature modules are represented in form of guarded transitions in the feature modules, which may impose constraints on the current feature combination and perform synchronized actions. The interplay of the feature modules can also be described by a single feature module, which arises from the feature implementations via parallel composition and hence only depends on the dynamic feature changes. Unlike other models for dynamic product lines, there is no explicit representation of the dynamic feature combination changes inside the feature modules. Instead, we implement a clear separation between computation and coordination as it is central for exogenous coordination languages [27,42,47]. In our approach, the dynamic activation and deactivation of features is represented in a separate module, called *feature controller*. This separation yields some advantages: feature modules can be replaced and reused for many scenarios that vary in constraints for switching feature combinations and that might even rely on different feature signatures.

We model both, feature modules and feature controllers, as MDP-like automata models with annotations for (possibly feature-dependent) interactions between modules and the controller. To reason about resource constraints, cost functions are attached to the transitions of both, the feature modules and the feature controller. Through parallel composition, the operational behavior of the complete dynamic product line has a standard MDP semantics. We show also that our approach towards dynamic product lines is more expressive than existing approaches by providing embeddings into our framework. The compositional framework we present here aims also to provide a link between abstract models for feature implementations and the guarded command languages supported by state-of-the art model checkers. This approach is orthogonal to the compositional approaches for product lines that have been proposed in the literature, presenting an algebra for the nonprobabilistic feature-oriented composition of modules that covers subtle implementation details (see, e.g., [2,33,40,43]).

3.1 Feature Modules

To keep the mathematical model simple, we put the emphasis on the compositional treatment of features and therefore present first a data-abstract lightweight formalism for the feature modules. In this setting, feature modules can be seen as labeled transition systems, where the transitions have guards that formalize feature-dependent behaviors and are annotated with probabilities and costs to model stochastic phenomena and resource constraints.

We start with the definition of a feature interface that declares which features are "implemented" by the given feature module (called *own features*) and on which *external features* the behavior of the module depends. In the following, we assume a given feature signature $(F, \mathcal{V})$, e.g., provided by a feature diagram, where $\mathcal{V} \subseteq \mathbb{N}^F$ is finite.

Definition 1 (Feature interface). *A feature interface* F *is a pair* $\langle \mathsf{OwnF}, \mathsf{ExtF} \rangle$ *consisting of two subsets* OwnF *and* ExtF *of* F *such that* $\mathsf{OwnF} \cap \mathsf{ExtF} = \varnothing$.

With abuse of notations, we often write F to also denote the set $\mathsf{OwnF} \cup \mathsf{ExtF}$ of features affected by the feature interface F. We now define feature modules as an MDP-like formalism according to a feature interface, where moves may depend on features of the feature interface and the change of own features can be triggered, e.g., by the environment. Note that we assume a feature module to incorporate all behaviors of the instances of the own features, i.e., its behavior depends on the cardinality of the instances of own features and its types, but cannot depend on the implementation of single instances.

Definition 2 (Feature module). *A tuple* $\mathsf{Mod} = (\mathsf{Loc}, \mathsf{Loc}^{init}, \mathsf{F}, \mathsf{Act}, \mathsf{Trans})$ *is called* feature module *when*

- Loc *is a countable set of locations,*
- $\mathsf{Loc}^{init} \subseteq \mathsf{Loc}$ *is the set of initial locations,*
- $\mathsf{F} = \langle \mathsf{OwnF}, \mathsf{ExtF} \rangle$ *is a feature interface,*
- Act *is a finite set of actions, and*
- $\mathsf{Trans} = \mathsf{TrAct} \cup \mathsf{TrSw}$ *is a finite transition relation.*

The operational behavior of Mod *specified by* Trans *is given by feature-guarded transitions that are either labeled by an action* (TrAct) *or by a switch event describing own feature changes* (TrSw)*. Formally:*

$$\mathsf{TrAct} \subseteq \mathsf{Loc} \times \mathbb{BC}(\mathsf{F}) \times \mathsf{Act} \times \mathbb{N} \times \mathit{Distr}(\mathsf{Loc})$$

$$\mathsf{TrSw} \subseteq \mathsf{Loc} \times \mathbb{BC}(\mathsf{F}) \times \mathbb{BC}(\mathsf{OwnF} \cup \mathsf{OwnF}') \times \mathbb{N} \times \mathit{Distr}(\mathsf{Loc})$$

Recall that $\mathbb{BC}(\cdot)$ *stands for the set of Boolean expressions over linear constraints on feature combinations.*

Let us go more into detail concerning the operational behavior of feature modules. Both types of transitions in Mod, action-labeled transitions and switch transitions, have the form $\theta = (\ell, \phi, \_, c, \lambda)$, where

- ℓ is a location, called *source location* of θ,
- $c \in \mathbb{N}$ specifies the cost[1] caused by executing θ,
- $\phi \in \mathbb{BC}(F)$ is a Boolean expression of linear constraints on feature combinations, called *feature guard*, and
- λ is a distribution over Loc specifying an internal choice that determines the probabilities for the successor locations.

For action-labeled transitions, the third component $\_$ is an action $\alpha \in \mathsf{Act}$ representing some computation of Mod, which will be enabled if the current feature combination fulfills the feature guard ϕ and not avoided by the interaction with other feature modules. For switch transitions, $\_$ is a Boolean expression $\rho \in \mathbb{BC}(\mathsf{OwnF} \cup \mathsf{OwnF}')$, enabling Mod to react or impose constraints on dynamic changes of features owned by Mod.

Note that we defined feature modules in a generic way, such that feature modules need not to be aware of the feature signature and realizable feature switches. This makes them reusable for different dynamic product lines.

3.2   Parallel Composition

We formalize the interactions of feature modules by introducing a parallel operator on feature modules. Thus, starting with separate feature modules for all features $f \in F$ one might generate feature modules that "implement" several features, and eventually obtain a feature model that describes the behavior of all "controllable" features of the product line. Additionally, there might be some features in the set of features F provided by an unknown environment, where no feature modules are given.

The parallel operator for two composable feature modules follows the style of parallel composition of probabilistic automata [48,49] using *synchronization* over shared actions (handshaking) and interleaving for all other actions. Let

$$\mathsf{Mod}_1 = (\mathsf{Loc}_1, \mathsf{Loc}_1^{init}, \mathsf{F}_1, \mathsf{Act}_1, \mathsf{Trans}_1)$$
$$\mathsf{Mod}_2 = (\mathsf{Loc}_2, \mathsf{Loc}_2^{init}, \mathsf{F}_2, \mathsf{Act}_2, \mathsf{Trans}_2),$$

where $\mathsf{F}_i = \langle \mathsf{OwnF}_i, \mathsf{ExtF}_i \rangle$ and $\mathsf{Trans}_i = \mathsf{TrAct}_i \cup \mathsf{TrSw}_i$ for $i = 1, 2$. Composability of Mod_1 and Mod_2 means that $\mathsf{OwnF}_1 \cap \mathsf{OwnF}_2 = \varnothing$. Own features of Mod_1 might be external for Mod_2 and vice versa, influencing each others behavior.

Definition 3 (Parallel composition). *The parallel composition of two composable feature modules* Mod_1 *and* Mod_2 *is defined as the feature module*

$$\mathsf{Mod}_1 \parallel \mathsf{Mod}_2 \;=\; (\mathsf{Loc}, \mathsf{Loc}^{init}, \mathsf{F}, \mathsf{Act}, \mathsf{Trans}),$$

---

[1] For simplicity, we deal here with a single cost value for each guarded transition. Feature modules with multiple cost values will be considered in the case study of Sect. 5 and can be defined accordingly.

$$\frac{\alpha \in \mathsf{Act}_1 \setminus \mathsf{Act}_2, \quad (\ell_1, \phi, \alpha, c, \lambda_1) \in \mathsf{TrAct}_1}{(\langle \ell_1, \ell_2 \rangle, \phi, \alpha, c, \lambda_1 * Dirac[\ell_2]) \in \mathsf{TrAct}} \qquad \frac{\alpha \in \mathsf{Act}_2 \setminus \mathsf{Act}_1, \quad (\ell_2, \phi, \alpha, c, \lambda_2) \in \mathsf{TrAct}_2}{(\langle \ell_1, \ell_2 \rangle, \phi, \alpha, c, Dirac[\ell_1] * \lambda_2) \in \mathsf{TrAct}}$$

$$\frac{\alpha \in \mathsf{Act}_1 \cap \mathsf{Act}_2, \quad (\ell_1, \phi_1, \alpha, c_1, \lambda_1) \in \mathsf{TrAct}_1, \quad (\ell_2, \phi_2, \alpha, c_2, \lambda_2) \in \mathsf{TrAct}_2}{(\langle \ell_1, \ell_2 \rangle, \phi_1 \wedge \phi_2, \alpha, c_1 + c_2, \lambda_1 * \lambda_2) \in \mathsf{TrAct}}$$

$$\frac{(\ell_1, \phi, \rho, c, \lambda_1) \in \mathsf{TrSw}_1}{(\langle \ell_1, \ell_2 \rangle, \phi, \rho \wedge \mathsf{OwnF}_2 = \mathsf{OwnF}_2', c, \lambda_1 * Dirac[\ell_2]) \in \mathsf{TrSw}}$$

$$\frac{(\ell_2, \phi, \rho, c, \lambda_2) \in \mathsf{TrSw}_2}{(\langle \ell_1, \ell_2 \rangle, \phi, \rho \wedge \mathsf{OwnF}_1 = \mathsf{OwnF}_1', c, Dirac[\ell_1] * \lambda_2) \in \mathsf{TrSw}}$$

$$\frac{(\ell_1, \phi_1, \rho_1, c_1, \lambda_1) \in \mathsf{TrSw}_1, \quad (\ell_2, \phi_2, \rho_2, c_2, \lambda_2) \in \mathsf{TrSw}_2}{(\langle \ell_1, \ell_2 \rangle, \phi_1 \wedge \phi_2, \rho_1 \wedge \rho_2, c_1 + c_2, \lambda_1 * \lambda_2) \in \mathsf{TrSw}}$$

Fig. 2. Rules for the parallel composition of feature modules

where the feature interface $\mathsf{F} = \langle \mathsf{OwnF}, \mathsf{ExtF} \rangle$,

$$\mathsf{Loc} = \mathsf{Loc}_1 \times \mathsf{Loc}_2 \qquad\qquad \mathsf{Loc}^{init} = \mathsf{Loc}_1^{init} \times \mathsf{Loc}_2^{init}$$
$$\mathsf{OwnF} = \mathsf{OwnF}_1 \cup \mathsf{OwnF}_2 \qquad\qquad \mathsf{ExtF} = (\mathsf{ExtF}_1 \cup \mathsf{ExtF}_2) \setminus \mathsf{OwnF}$$
$$\mathsf{Act} = \mathsf{Act}_1 \cup \mathsf{Act}_2 \qquad\qquad \mathsf{Trans} = \mathsf{TrAct} \cup \mathsf{TrSw}$$

and TrAct *and* TrSw *are defined by the rules shown in Fig. 2.*

Obviously, $\mathsf{Mod}_1 \parallel \mathsf{Mod}_2$ is again a feature module. In contrast to the (nonprobabilistic) superimposition approach for composing modules [36,43], the parallel operator $\parallel$ is commutative and associative. More precisely, if Mod_i for $i \in \{1, 2, 3\}$ are pairwise composable feature modules, then:

$$\mathsf{Mod}_1 \parallel \mathsf{Mod}_2 = \mathsf{Mod}_2 \parallel \mathsf{Mod}_1$$
$$(\mathsf{Mod}_1 \parallel \mathsf{Mod}_2) \parallel \mathsf{Mod}_3 = \mathsf{Mod}_1 \parallel (\mathsf{Mod}_2 \parallel \mathsf{Mod}_3)$$

For the parallel composition of feature modules with multiple cost functions, one has to declare which cost functions are combined. This can be achieved by dealing with types of cost functions (e.g., energy, money, memory requirements) and accumulating costs of the same type.

3.3   Feature Controller

We now turn to feature controllers, which specify the rules for the possible changes of feature combinations during runtime of the system. We start with purely nondeterministic controllers (Definition 4) switching feature combinations similar to [19]. Then, we extend the purely nondeterministic controllers by assigning probabilities to the feature switch events (Definition 5).

Definition 4. *A simple feature controller is a tuple*

$$\mathsf{Con} \; = \; (\mathcal{V}, \mathcal{V}^{init}, \mathsf{SwRel}),$$

where $\mathcal{V}^{init} \subseteq \mathcal{V}$ is the set of initial feature combinations and $\mathsf{SwRel} \subseteq \mathcal{V} \times \mathbb{N} \times \mathcal{V}$ is a relation, called (feature) switch relation, that formalizes the possible dynamic changes of the feature combinations and their cost. We refer to elements in SwRel as switch events *and require that $(f, d_1, f'), (f, d_2, f') \in \mathsf{SwRel}$ implies $d_1 = d_2$.*

If there are several switch events $(f, d_1, f_1), (f, d_2, f_2), \ldots$ that are enabled for the feature combination f, then the choice which switch event fires is made nondeterministically. This is adequate, e.g., to represent user activities such as upgrades or downgrades of a software product or to express environmental influences.

Although our focus is on dynamic product lines, static product lines can easily be modeled using the simple feature controller $\mathsf{Con}_{\mathsf{static}} = (\mathcal{V}, \mathcal{V}, \varnothing)$. The concept of simple feature controllers also covers the approach of [16,22], where dynamic product lines are represented by Boolean feature signatures $(F, \mathcal{V})$ extended with disjoint sets of dynamic features $D \subseteq F$ and environment features $E \subseteq F$. The features in $D \cup E$ can be activated or deactivated at any time, while the modes of all other features remain unchanged. This dynamic behavior of the feature combinations is formalized using the controller

$$\mathsf{Con}_{D,E} \; = \; (\mathcal{V}, \mathcal{V}, \mathsf{SwRel}_{D,E}),$$

where $\mathsf{SwRel}_{D,E}$ is defined for all $f, g \in \mathcal{V}$, omitting cost values of switch events for better readability:

$$(f, g) \in \mathsf{SwRel}_{D,E} \quad \text{iff} \quad \varnothing \neq \{x \in F : f(x) + g(x) = 1\} \subseteq D \cup E.$$

There might also be switch events where statistical data on the frequency of uncontrollable feature switch events is at hand. For instance, the deactivation of features that are damaged due to rare environmental events (electrical power outage, extreme hotness, etc.) might be better modeled probabilistically instead of nondeterministically. This leads to the more general concept of *probabilistic feature controllers*, where switch events are pairs (f, d, γ) consisting of a feature combination f, a cost value $d \in \mathbb{N}$ and a distribution γ over $\mathcal{V}$. Thus, probabilistic feature controllers can be seen as MDPs with switch events as moves.

Definition 5 (Controller). *A probabilistic feature controller, briefly called controller, is a tuple $\mathsf{Con} = (\mathcal{V}, \mathcal{V}^{init}, \mathsf{SwRel})$ as in Definition 4, but where*

$$\mathsf{SwRel} \; \subseteq \; \mathcal{V} \times \mathbb{N} \times Distr(\mathcal{V})$$

is finite and $(f, d_1, \gamma), (f, d_2, \gamma) \in \mathsf{SwRel}$ implies $d_1 = d_2$.

Clearly, each simple feature controller Con can be seen as a (probabilistic feature) controller. For this, we just have to identify each switch event (f, d, g) with $(f, d, Dirac[g])$.

3.4   MDP-Semantics

The semantics of a feature module Mod under some controller Con is given in terms of an MDP. If Mod stands for the parallel composition of all modules that implement the features of a given product line and the controller Con specifies the dynamic adaptions of the feature combinations, then the arising MDP formalizes the operational behaviors of the product line where the feature switches are resolved according to the rules specified by the controller. In what follows, we fix a feature module and a controller

$$\mathsf{Mod} = (\mathsf{Loc}, \mathsf{Loc}^{init}, \mathsf{F}, \mathsf{Act}, \mathsf{Trans})$$
$$\mathsf{Con} = (\mathcal{V}, \mathcal{V}^{init}, \mathsf{SwRel})$$

as in Definitions 2 and 5, where $\mathsf{F} \subseteq F$. Intuitively, an action-labeled transition $(\ell, \phi, \alpha, c, \lambda)$ of Mod is a possible behavior of Mod in location ℓ, provided that the current state f of the controller Con (which is simply the current feature combination) meets the guard ϕ. Switch events of the controller can be performed independently from Mod if they do not affect the own features of Mod, whereas if they affect at least one feature in OwnF, the changes of the mode have to be executed synchronously. Thus, feature modules can trigger or prevent switch events by offering or refusing the required interactions with the feature controller. This allows, e.g., to model that system upgrades may be only permitted when all internal actions of the feature modules are completed.

Definition 6 (Semantics of feature modules). *Let* Mod *and* Con *be as before. The behavior of* Mod *under the controller* Con *is formalized by the MDP*

$$\mathsf{Mod} \bowtie \mathsf{Con} = (S, S^{init}, \mathsf{Moves}),$$

where $S = \mathsf{Loc} \times \mathcal{V}$, $S^{init} = \mathsf{Loc}^{init} \times \mathcal{V}^{init}$ *and where* Moves *is defined by the rules in Fig. 3. Recall that* $\rho \in \mathbb{BC}(\mathsf{OwnF} \cup \mathsf{OwnF}')$ *is regarded as a Boolean expression on linear constraints over* $F \cup F'$ *specifying a binary relation* $R_\rho \subseteq \mathbb{N}^F \times \mathbb{N}^F$.

Due to the MDP semantics of feature modules under a controller, standard probabilistic model-checking techniques for the quantitative analysis can be directly

$$\frac{(\ell, \phi, \alpha, c, \lambda) \in \mathsf{TrAct}, \quad f \models \phi}{(\langle \ell, f \rangle, c, \lambda * Dirac[f]) \in \mathsf{Moves}}$$

$$\frac{(\ell, \phi, \rho, c, \lambda) \in \mathsf{TrSw}, \quad f \models \phi, \quad f \xrightarrow{d} \gamma, \quad \exists g \in supp(\gamma), x \in \mathsf{OwnF}.f(x) \neq g(x), \quad \forall g \in supp(\gamma).(f, g) \in R_\rho}{(\langle \ell, f \rangle, c + d, \lambda * \gamma) \in \mathsf{Moves}}$$

$$\frac{f \xrightarrow{d} \gamma, \quad \forall g \in supp(\gamma), x \in \mathsf{OwnF}.f(x) = g(x)}{(\langle \ell, f \rangle, d, Dirac[\ell] * \gamma) \in \mathsf{Moves}}$$

Fig. 3. Rules for the moves in the MDP Mod $\bowtie$ Con

applied. This includes properties involving feature combinations, since these are encoded into the states of the arising MDP.

3.5 Remarks on Our Framework

In this section, we briefly discuss how the basic formalisms of our framework can be refined for more specific applications.

Handling Switch Events. Within the presented formalism the switch events appear as nondeterministic choices and require interactions between the controller and all modules that provide implementations for the affected features. Employing the standard semantics of MDPs, where one of the enabled moves is selected nondeterministically, this rules out the possibility to express that certain switch events might be unpreventable. However, such unpreventable switch events can be included into our framework, refining the concept of feature controllers by explicitly specifying which switch events must be taken whenever they are enabled in the controller. This could modeled by adding an extra transition relation for *urgent* switch events or prioritizing switches.

Instead of urgency or priorities, one might also keep the presented syntax of feature modules and controllers, but refine the MDP-semantics by adding *fairness conditions* that rule out computations where enabled switch events are postponed ad infinitum. Also here, we can benefit from standard techniques to treat fairness assumptions within PCTL properties developed for MDPs [6].

Another option for refining the nondeterministic choices in the controller is the distinction between switch events that are indeed controllable by the controller and those that are triggered by the environment. This naturally leads to a game-based view of the MDP for the composite system.

Feature Controller as Feature Module. To emphasize the feature-oriented aspects of our framework, we used a different syntax for controllers and feature modules. Nevertheless, controllers can be viewed as special feature modules when we discard the concept of switch events and switch transitions and rephrase them as action-labeled transitions. To transform controllers syntactically to feature modules, we have to add the trivial guard "true" and introduce names for all switch events. When turning the switch transitions of the feature modules into action-labeled transitions, matching names must be introduced to align the parallel operators $\parallel$ and $\bowtie$. Note that in the constructed feature modules, all features are external and the controller locations coincide with feature combinations. However, the framework can easily be extended supporting also own operational behavior of the controllers by adding locations to the feature combinations. Furthermore, since controllers are then a special kind of feature modules, different feature controllers may be composed, enabling to specify the rules for switching features provided by different stakeholder perspectives, e.g., restrictions on feature combination switches imposed by the vendor of the product line, the operator of the system, or the user.

Multi-features as Multiple Features. We assumed that a multi-feature includes all the behaviors of the instances of the feature, i.e., the instances do not have a distinguishable characteristics. However, annotating each feature and its actions with the number of its instantiation makes multi-features explicit, breaking the symmetry between the multi-features. One consequence for feature models is that multi-feature diagrams then have the same expressiveness as simple feature diagrams. Concerning our framework, every instance of each multi-feature then requires its own implementation in terms of a feature module.

Superimposition. Feature modules and feature controllers might serve as a starting point for a low-level implementation of features in a top-down design process. Vice versa, feature modules may also be extracted from "real" implementations using appropriate abstraction techniques. Prominent composition operators for feature-oriented software such as superimposition [2,36,43] are only supported implicitly in our framework by representing the effect of superimposition by means of feature guards and synchronization actions.

4   Variables and Guarded-Command Languages

So far, we presented a lightweight data-abstract formalism for feature modules with abstract action and location names. This simplified the presentation of the mathematical model. From the theoretical point of view, feature modules in the sense of Definition 2 are powerful enough to encode systems where the modules operate on variables with finite domains. Even communication over shared variables can be mimicked by dealing with handshaking and local copies of shared variables. In practice, however, the explicit use of assignments for variables and guards for the transitions that impose constraints for local and shared variables is desirable; not only to avoid unreadable encodings, but also for performance reasons of the algorithmic analysis. The concept of variables can also help to generate more compact representations of the MDP-semantics for product lines according to our compositional framework, using, e.g., symbolic representations with linear constraints over variables. Furthermore, feature modules with variables could also provide operators that mimic the concept of superimposition [43]. The formal definition of an extension of *feature modules by variables* is rather technical, but fairly standard. However, such extended feature modules directly yield a translation into guarded-command languages, which makes our framework useful for the application of model-checking tools, such as PRISM [34].

4.1   Feature Modules with Variables

Let use suppose that *Var* is a finite set of typed variables, where the types are assumed to be finite as well (e.g., Boolean variables or integers with some fixed number of digits). We denote furthermore by $\mathcal{VAL}$ the set of valuation functions for the variables, i.e., type-consistent mappings that assign to each variable $x \in Var$ a value. In analogy to the symbolic representation of sets of integer-valued functions by Boolean expressions over linear constraints we introduced in the preliminaries, we can represent subsets of $\mathcal{VAL}$ by Boolean expressions, where the atoms are assertions on the values of the variables. Let $\mathbb{BC}(Var)$ denote the set of these Boolean expressions. Then, e.g., if x and y are variables with domain $\{0, 1, 2, 3\}$ and z a variable with domain $\{\text{red}, \text{green}, \text{blue}\}$, the Boolean expression $\phi = (x < y) \wedge (y > 2) \wedge (z \neq \text{green})$ represents all valuations $v \in \mathcal{VAL}$ with $v(x) < v(y) = 3$ and $v(z) \in \{\text{red}, \text{blue}\}$.

Interface. The interface of a feature module Mod now consists of a feature interface $\mathsf{F} = \langle \mathsf{OwnF}, \mathsf{ExtF} \rangle$ as in Definition 1 and a declaration which variables from Var are local and which ones are external. The local variables can appear in guards and can be modified by Mod, while the external variables can only appear in guards, but cannot be written by Mod. Instead, the external variables of Mod are supposed to be local for some other module. We denote these sets by OwnV and ExtV, write V for $\mathsf{OwnV} \cup \mathsf{ExtV}$ and extend the notion of composability of two feature modules by the natural requirement that there are no shared local variables.

Locations and Initial Condition. One can think of the variable valuations for the local variables to serve as locations in the module Mod. However, there is no need for an explicit reference to locations since all transitions will be described symbolically (see below). Instead of initial locations, we deal with an initial condition for the local variables.

Updates and Symbolic Transitions. Transitions in Mod might update the values of the local variables. The updates are given by sequences of assignments $x_1 := expr_1; \dots; x_n := expr_n$, where $x_1, \dots, x_n$ are pairwise distinct variables in OwnV and $expr_i$ are type-consistent expressions that refer to variables in V. We formalize the effect of the updates that might appear in Mod by functions $\mathsf{upd} : \mathcal{VAL} \rightarrow \mathcal{VAL}$ with $\mathsf{upd}(v)(y) = v(y)$ for all non-local variables $y \in Var \setminus \mathsf{OwnV}$.

Instead of explicit references to the variable valuations in the transitions, we use a symbolic approach based on symbolic transitions. Symbolic transitions represent sets of guarded transitions, possibly originating from multiple locations, and are of the following form

$$\theta = (guard, \phi, \_, c, prob\_upd),$$

where $guard \in \mathbb{BC}(\mathsf{V})$ is a variable guard imposing conditions on the local and external variables, and $\phi \in \mathbb{BC}(\mathsf{F})$ is a feature guard as before. The third and fourth component $\_$ and c are as in the data-abstract setting. That is, $\_$ stands for an action label $\alpha \in \mathsf{Act}$ or a Boolean expression $\rho \in \mathbb{BC}(\mathsf{OwnF} \cup \mathsf{OwnF}')$ for the switch events, while $c \in \mathbb{N}$ stands for the cost caused by taking transition θ. The last component $prob\_upd$ is a *probabilistic update*, i.e., a distribution over finitely many updates for variables in OwnV. These are written in the form

$$p_1 : \mathsf{upd}_1 + p_2 : \mathsf{upd}_2 + \dots + p_k : \mathsf{upd}_k,$$

where p_i are positive rational numbers with $p_1 + \dots + p_k = 1$ and the upd_i's are updates for the local variables. That is, p_i is the probability for update upd_i.

4.2 Data-Aware Parallel Composition

The extension of the parallel operator $\|$ for composable feature modules with variables is rather tedious, but straightforward. As stated above, composability requires that there are no common own features and no common local variables. The local variables of the composite module $\mathsf{Mod}_1 \| \mathsf{Mod}_2$ are the variables that are local for one module Mod_i, i.e., $\mathsf{OwnV} = \mathsf{OwnV}_1 \cup \mathsf{OwnV}_2$ and $\mathsf{ExtV} = (\mathsf{ExtV}_1 \cup \mathsf{ExtV}_2) \setminus \mathsf{OwnV}$. The feature interface of $\mathsf{Mod}_1 \| \mathsf{Mod}_2$ is defined as in the data-abstract setting. The initial variable condition of $\mathsf{Mod}_1 \| \mathsf{Mod}_2$ arises by the conjunction of the initial conditions for Mod_1 and Mod_2. Let us now turn to the transitions in $\mathsf{Mod}_1 \| \mathsf{Mod}_2$.

- All action-labeled symbolic transitions in Mod_1 or Mod_2 with some non-shared action α are also transitions in $\mathsf{Mod}_1 \| \mathsf{Mod}_2$.
- Action-labeled symbolic transitions

$$\theta_1 = (guard_1, \phi_1, \alpha, c_1, prob\_upd_1) \quad \in \mathsf{TrAct}_1$$
$$\theta_2 = (guard_2, \phi_2, \alpha, c_2, prob\_upd_2) \quad \in \mathsf{TrAct}_2$$

with a shared action $\alpha \in \mathsf{Act}_1 \cap \mathsf{Act}_2$ are combined into a symbolic transition of $\mathsf{Mod}_1 \| \mathsf{Mod}_2$:

$$\theta_1 \| \theta_2 = (guard, \phi, \alpha, c_1 + c_2, prob\_upd),$$

where $guard = guard_1 \wedge guard_2$, $\phi = \phi_1 \wedge \phi_2$ and $prob\_upd$ combines the probabilistic update functions $prob\_upd_1$ and $prob\_upd_2$. That is, if upd_i has probability p_i under distribution $prob\_upd_i$ for $i = 1, 2$, then the combined update that performs the assignments in upd_1 and upd_2 simultaneously has probability $p_1 \cdot p_2$ under $prob\_upd$.
- The adaption of the rules for switch transitions in $\mathsf{Mod}_1 \| \mathsf{Mod}_2$ can be obtained analogously as for action transitions and is omitted here.

4.3 Data-Aware MDP-Semantics

In the data-abstract setting, a reasonable MDP-semantics of a feature module Mod under controller $\mathsf{Con} = (\mathcal{V}, \mathcal{V}^{init}, \mathsf{SwRel})$ has been defined, no matter whether Mod is just a fragment of the product line and may interact with other modules or not. An analogous definition for the data-aware setting can be provided either for modules without external variables or by modelling the changes of the values of the external variables by nondeterministic choices.

Let us here consider the first case where we are given a module $\mathsf{Mod} = \mathsf{Mod}_1 \| \ldots \| \mathsf{Mod}_n$ that arises through the parallel composition of several modules such that all variables $x \in Var$ are local for some module Mod_i. Then, Mod has no external variables and $Var = \mathsf{OwnV} = \mathsf{V}$. Furthermore, OwnF is the set of all features of the given product line for which implementations are given, while ExtF stands for the set of features controlled by the environment. The MDP $\mathsf{Mod} \bowtie \mathsf{Con}$ has the state space $S = \mathcal{VAL} \times \mathcal{V}$. The initial states are the pairs

$\langle v, f \rangle$ where v satisfies the initial variable condition of Mod and $f \in \mathcal{V}^{init}$. The moves in Mod $\bowtie$ Con arise through rules that are analogous to the rules shown in Fig. 3 on page 18. More precisely, Moves is the smallest set of moves according to the following three cases, where $\langle v, f \rangle$ is an arbitrary state in Mod $\bowtie$ Con:

- An action-labeled transition $(guard, \phi, \alpha, c, prob\_upd)$ in Mod is enabled in state $\langle v, f \rangle$ if $f \models \phi$ and $v \models guard$. If $\mathsf{upd}_i(v) \neq \mathsf{upd}_j(v)$ for $i \neq j$, then:

$$(\langle v, f \rangle, c, \lambda * Dirac[f]) \in \mathsf{Moves},$$

  where $\lambda(\mathsf{upd}_i(v)) = p_i$ for $i = 1, \ldots, k$ and $\lambda(\hat{v}) = 0$ for all other valuation functions $\hat{v}$.
- If $f \overset{d}{\longrightarrow} \gamma$ is a switch transition in Con that does affect at most the features of the environment, i.e., $f(x) = g(x)$ for all $g \in supp(\gamma), x \in \mathsf{OwnF}$, then:

$$(\langle v, f \rangle, d, Dirac[\ell] * \gamma) \in \mathsf{Moves}$$

- Suppose that $(guard, \phi, \rho, c, prob\_upd)$ is a switch transition in Mod enabled in $\langle v, f \rangle$ and affecting own features, i.e., $f \models \phi$ and $v \models guard$ and there are $g \in supp(\gamma)$, $x \in \mathsf{OwnF}$ with $f(x) \neq g(x)$. Again, $\rho \in \mathbb{BC}(\mathsf{OwnF} \cup \mathsf{OwnF}')$ specifies a binary relation $R_\rho \subseteq \mathbb{N}^F \times \mathbb{N}^F$. If $(f, g) \in R_\rho$ for all $g \in supp(\gamma)$ then:

$$(\langle v, f \rangle, c + d, \lambda * \gamma) \in \mathsf{Moves},$$

where λ is defined as in the first (action-labeled) case.

5 Quantitative Feature Analysis

Within the compositional framework presented in the previous sections, let us assume that we are given feature modules $\mathsf{Mod}_1, \ldots, \mathsf{Mod}_n$ which stand for abstract models of certain features in F and a feature controller Con specifying the rules for feature combination changes. The feature set F might still contain other features where no implementations are given, which are external features controlled by the environment. Alternatively, one of the feature modules can formalize the interference of the feature implementations with a partially known environment, e.g., in form of stochastic assumptions on the workload, the frequency of user interactions, or reliability of components. Applying the compositional construction by putting feature modules in parallel and joining them with the feature controller, we obtain an MDP of the form

$$\mathcal{M} = (\mathsf{Mod}_1 \| \ldots \| \mathsf{Mod}_n) \bowtie \mathsf{Con}.$$

This MDP $\mathcal{M}$ formalizes the operational behavior of a dynamic product line and can now be used for a quantitative analysis. Whereas other family-based model-checking approaches for product lines require feature-adapted algorithms [12,13], the task of a quantitative analysis of dynamic product lines is thus reduced to standard algorithmic problems for MDPs and permits the use of generic probabilistic model-checking techniques.

5.1   The Strategy Synthesis Problem

A *quantitative worst-case analysis* in the MDP $\mathcal{M}$ that establishes least upper or greatest lower bounds for the probabilities of certain properties or for the expected accumulated costs as introduced in Sect. 2.2 can be carried out with standard probabilistic model-checking tools. These values provide guarantees on the probabilities under all potential resolutions of the nondeterministic choices in $\mathcal{M}$, possibly imposing some fairness constraints to ensure that continuously enabled dynamic adaptions of the feature combinations (switch events) cannot be superseded forever by action-labeled transitions of the feature modules.

In our framework, we separated the specifications of the potential dynamic adaptions of feature combinations (the controller) and the implementations of the features (the feature modules). Hence, although a worst-case analysis can give important insights in the correctness and quality of a product line, it appears natural to go one step further by asking for *optimal strategies* triggering switch events. Optimality can be understood with respect to queries like maximizing the probability for desired behaviors or minimizing the expected energy consumption while meeting given deadlines.

Several variants of this problem can be considered. The basic and most natural variant that we address here relies on the assumption that the nondeterminism in the MDP $\mathcal{M}$ for the composite system stands for decisions to be made by the controller, i.e., only the switch events appear nondeterministically, whereas the feature modules behave purely probabilistically (or deterministically) after joining them with the controller. More formally, we suppose that in each state s of $\mathcal{M}$, either there is a single enabled move representing some action-labeled transition of one or more feature modules or all enabled moves stand for switch events. Furthermore, we assume that features which are implemented as software or hardware components (usually the features not modeling the environment) act deterministically. In this case, an optimal strategy for the controller is just a scheduler for $\mathcal{M}$ that optimizes the quantitative measure of interest. The task that we address is the *strategy synthesis problem*, i.e., given $\mathcal{M}$ and some PCTL-query Φ as in Sect. 2.2, construct a scheduler $\mathfrak{S}$ for $\mathcal{M}$ that optimizes the solution of the query Φ. Indeed, the standard probabilistic model-checking algorithms for PCTL are applicable to solve the strategy synthesis problem. Note that if the feature controller represents a static behavior (see $\mathsf{Con}_{\mathsf{static}}$ in Sect. 3.3), the strategy synthesis problem coincides with the probabilistic version of the featured model-checking problem mentioned in the introduction, where the task amounts of computing all initial feature combinations such that the corresponding product satisfies Φ.

5.2   The ESERVER Product Line

In this section, we describe the ESERVER product line for which the feature model has been already introduced in the preliminaries (see Example 1). We modeled this dynamic product line following our framework, i.e., implementing feature modules and a feature controller.

Feature Modules. The feature diagram shown in Fig. 1 depicts the features of the ESERVER product line, including their hierarchical dependencies and cardinalities which restrict the valid feature combinations. We implemented each feature in a single feature module, where three basic feature modules arise through parallel composition: the rack (R), network cards (N), and coordination feature (C). The rack feature is the basic server hardware, where depending on its type multiple slots (o) for network cards can be chosen. Slots are either supporting a high or low bandwidth. The initial hardware configuration cannot be changed after deployment, except for the network cards feature, where during runtime the quantities of cards may increase (until the number of slots in the basic system is reached) or the type of the card can be changed upgrading from a slow 1 GBit to a fast 10 GBit network card. Clearly, a fast network card can only be used as such in a slot supporting high bandwidths. The rules for network card switches are formalized by the feature controller and will be described in the next section.

Besides these hardware features of the product line, the coordination feature stands for the software features. More precisely, it stands for the drivers which control the interplay between the hardware and the higher-level software layers. The distribution feature (D) manages how the requested bandwidth is distributed amongst the network cards in the system:

Round Robin stands for the standard distribution scheme, where a data package is served by the next network card having free capacities.
Weighted is like the round robin scheme, but weighs the fast cards according to their maximal bandwidth with a factor of 10 compared to the lower ones.
Maximal Fast first lets all fast network cards serve packages before a round robin distribution over all slow cards is performed.
Minimal Fast is as Maximal Fast with switched roles for fast and slow cards.

The switch policy feature (y) implements an energy-aware bonding of (heterogenous) network cards according to the EBOND principle [30] and exploits the different energy characteristics of the network cards to save energy. Individual network cards can be switched on at any time whenever more bandwidth is required and switched off otherwise. In [30], simulation-based techniques were used to show that within EBOND, energy savings up to 75 % can be achieved when the demand for bandwidth varies over time, e.g., between day and night time. In the ESERVER product line, we follow the energy-savings algorithms presented for EBOND, providing a switch policy how to activate and deactivate network cards during runtime:[2]

Aggressive stands for a policy where all those cards are switched off which have not been used within the last five minutes.
High Savings assumes 10 % higher bandwidth before switching off cards.

---

[2] Activation and deactivation of network cards should not be confused with changing the network cards feature by plugging or unplugging cards.

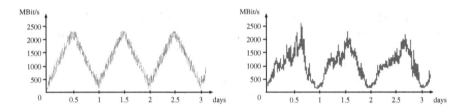

Fig. 4. Bandwidth feature (left) and real-world bandwidth behavior (right)

Balanced behaves as the high savings policy, but with an additional cool-down phase of 30 min after the activation of a network card in which network cards can only be activated but not deactivated.

Note that both, the distribution and switch policy feature, are chosen initially when the ESERVER is deployed and cannot be changed any further during runtime. Furthermore, all the features described by now behave deterministically, but depend on the environment modeled probabilistically.

Environment Features. For a quantitative analysis of ESERVER, we further incorporate environment features, which implement deterministic environment behavior such as time and statistical assumptions on the environment, e.g., the feature switch behavior or the requested bandwidth the server platform has to face. Feature switches are influenced by the environment, since replacing hardware clearly depends on the reliability of the technical staff of the server operator. We exemplified this influence by assuming that the technical staff requires at least five minutes after the need for a new network card has been discovered, and arrives with a probability of 90 % in each time interval of five minutes. The bandwidth is modeled via a noised zick-zag curve parameterized over a maximal bandwidth value the server has to expect. This curve follows the behavior of real-world server systems, where the same characteristics can be observed: during night time, bandwidth requirements are almost vanished, whereas in the mid day, the requested bandwidth peaks at a value which is almost constant over the days. In Fig. 4, a plot of our bandwidth model over three days is shown on the left, whereas a real-world example taken from [30] is shown on the right. In both cases, the peak for the requested bandwidth is about 2.4 GBit/s. Thanks to enhancing our framework by variables, these environmental parameters can easily be encoded as variables time and bandwidth.

Feature Controller. Rules for plugging new network cards or upgrading a slow network card to a fast one are implemented into a feature controller. These rules are a combination of restrictions provided by the vendor of the product line or the server operator. Whereas the vendor restricts feature switches only in the sense that the aimed product should not leave the product line, the server operator may require that money for new network cards should only be spent if the network card is needed for the ESERVER to operate faithfully, i.e., when the workload of the system is almost at the maximum of the available bandwidth. Furthermore,

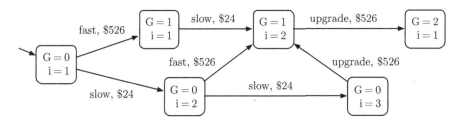

Fig. 5. Fragment of the ESERVER feature controller

we assume that network cards that are inactive do not consume any energy and the system operator does not allow for downgrading, i.e., unplugging a network card from the system. Figure 5 shows the fragment of the feature controller we implemented for ESERVER, where it is assumed that the initial product is an advanced server with two fast and one slow slot (similar to the professional ESERVER device presented in [23]) initially equipped with one slow network card only. The figure shows the quantity of the features for the network cards only, captured by pairs [$G = n$, $i = k$], which stand for n active 10 GBit features and k active 1 GBit network card features. There are three possible actions which can be performed by the feature controller: plugging a fresh 10 GBit card into the system (fast), replacing a 1 GBit card by a 10 GBit one (upgrade), and plugging a fresh 1 GBit card into the system (slow). New cards go along with monetary costs, i.e., a 10 GBit card costs \$526, whereas a 1 GBit card sells at \$24. These prices are taken from the vendors product line which inspired the ESERVER example. Not drawn in the figure are the constraints on the transitions, requiring, e.g., that the technical staff is present and that the current requested bandwidth justifies the need of changing the feature combination, both influenced by the environment feature. Expressing this more formally with variables and linear constraints on feature combinations, and assuming that the environment variable bandwidth is measured in GBit/s, each transition is in fact equipped with a guard

$$80\,\% \cdot (10 \cdot G + i) \; < \; \mathsf{bandwidth},$$

meaning that the workload of the network cards is higher than 80 % and hence, the system is under stress. This may lead to a point where the server may not be able to serve the bandwidth requested. The latter corresponds to a *service-level agreement (SLA) violation* in the terms by [30].

Energy Consumption and Monetary Costs. Quantitative properties of the ESERVER product line are incorporated through the annotation of costs, where we consider in particular the energy consumption of the network cards and monetary costs. For the latter, we annotated costs to the feature controller describing the money to be spent for plugging new cards. Furthermore, we annotate the initial costs for the system purchased, where the entry systems range from \$629 to \$1494, the advanced systems from \$1279 to \$1699 and the premium systems from \$2139 to \$9399. For requesting technical staff we assume costs of \$39.

The energy consumption of the network cards (we refer to an Intel Ethernet Server Adapter X520-T featuring an E76983 CPU as 10 GBit card and an Intel EXPI9301CTBLK network interface card with an E25869 CPU as 1 GBit card) highly depends on the workload. Detailed measurements for the cards mentioned above have been undertaken in [30] in the scope of EBOND. We approximate their results by linear functions, as suggested by the authors of [30]. The 10 GBit card consumes 7.88 W in the idle state and 8.10 W under full load. For the 1 GBit card, the power consumption rises linearly from 1.35 W until reaching a throughput of 540 MBit/s at 1.92 W, staying constantly at this energy consumption until the full load is reached. Thus, as one expects, the energy consumption of the fast card is higher than of the slower one. This yields potential for energy saving when controlling the utilization of the network cards, e.g., through different coordination features.

MDP-Semantics. Via parallel composition of the feature modules described above, including the environment features containing stochastic assumptions and joining them with the feature controller, we obtain the MDP semantics of the ESERVER product line:

$$\mathcal{M} = (\underbrace{\textsf{eServer} \parallel \textsf{Hardware} \parallel \textsf{Coord} \parallel}_{\text{ESERVER}} \underbrace{\textsf{Env}}_{\text{environment}}) \bowtie \textsf{Con}$$

Here, eServer stands for the basic server functionality, incorporating the interplay between software, hardware and environment, which are in turn implemented through the feature modules Hardware, Coord and Env. This interplay is managed in a cyclic manner through three phases: first, the hardware is allowed to be changed according to the rules by the feature controller Con, then the control is handed to Coord, activating and deactivating network cards according to its switching policy, before the environment takes over for five minutes, providing the model of the requested bandwidth from the users the server has to compete with. Each phase corresponds to a step in $\mathcal{M}$. Note that the feature modules given above are in fact feature modules which arise by parallel composition of feature modules standing for features in the feature diagram of the ESERVER product line. Coord arises by parallel composition of the modules belonging to the coordination feature, whereas Hardware arises by parallel composition of all the other feature modules except the environment features, which are implemented in the feature module Env.

5.3   Quantitative Analysis of the ESERVER Product Line

Besides solving the strategy synthesis problem for the ESERVER product line under certain assumptions on the environment regarding energy consumption and monetary costs (those characteristics rely on the ESERVER product line itself), we also consider the amount of time the server could not deliver the bandwidth requested by the users. This situation is called a *service-level agreement (SLA) violation* (according to [30]) and may happen either when the ESERVER is not appropriately equipped (the feature combination does not suffice) or when the requested bandwidth peaks and the coordination feature deactivated too many cards for saving energy. SLA violations also influence the money spent for the system during runtime. Besides the costs for purchasing the ESERVER, the costs for the technical staff and reconfiguration of features, we modeled costs for SLA violations that are rather expensive. Five minutes not serving the bandwidth requested costs \$200. It is clear that a customer then tries to avoid SLA violations by purchasing a device whose reliability guarantees the desired throughput functionality. On the other hand, a customer also tries to save initial costs when buying the device and to save energy during runtime using the advantages of the energy-saving switch policies.

This trade-off directly leads to the question how to choose the initial feature combination and when to reconfigure the system by feature switches. That is, solving the strategy synthesis problem for $\mathcal{M}$ regarding various quantitative objectives concerning, e.g., energy, money and SLA violations. Although our framework directly permits to consider arbitrary quantitative objectives which can be stated for standard MDPs, e.g., expressed within PCTL, we restrict ourselves to (constrained) reachability objectives in this case study. In particular, we consider here four different strategy synthesis problems for $\mathcal{M}$: maximizing the probability of not raising an SLA violation (i.e., reliability of the device), minimizing the expected energy consumption, money spent or time with SLA violations, respectively, all within a fixed time horizon:

$$\text{pmax} = \mathbb{P}^{\max}((\neg \textit{Violation}) \; \mathcal{U} \; T) \quad \text{emin} = \mathbb{E}^{\min}[\text{energy}](\Diamond T)$$
$$\text{mmin} = \mathbb{E}^{\min}[\text{money}](\Diamond T) \qquad \text{vmin} = \mathbb{E}^{\min}[\text{violation}](\Diamond T)$$

Here, the type of the expected minimal costs is annotated to the query (i.e., energy, money and violation for SLA violations). Furthermore, *Violation* stands for the set of states in $\mathcal{M}$ where an SLA violation occurred and T for the set of states in $\mathcal{M}$ where some fixed time horizon is reached. Using the compositional framework presented in Sect. 3 and its extension with variables (Sect. 4), we modeled a parameterized version of the ESERVER product line in the guarded-command input language of PRISM. Our model is parameterized in terms of the peak bandwidth during a day/night-cycle. Depending on this maximal bandwidth, different initial feature combinations and strategies for feature switches may provide different optimal solutions for pmax, emin, mmin, and vmin.

General Facts. For our case study we fixed certain model parameters. We chose a time horizon of the first day the deployed system is in operation ($T = 24$ h) and solved the strategy synthesis problem for maximal bandwidths ranging from 100 MBit/s to 16 GBit/s in steps of 100 MBit/s. For each of the quantitative objectives, we present four graphs, each showing one chart for each product configuration at the deployment of the ESERVER. The first three show the results for all entry level, advanced and premium ESERVER products, respectively. Charts with similar colors are representing similar multi-features, i.e., a similar number and types of slots and network cards. In all these graphs, the difference between the coordination features chosen can hardly be figured out, due to the large-scaled product line, which yields many overlapping charts. Hence, we spot on those advanced ESERVER products in the lower right graph which have one fast and two slow slots and are purchased with one 10 GBit card only. This gives rise to 12 possible charts, representing the feature combinations for the coordination feature: colors encode the distribution feature (black, red, green, blue for Round Robin, Weighted, Maximal Fast, and Minimal Fast features, respectively) and the line type stands for different switching policies (solid, dotted, dashed for Aggressive, High Savings, and Balanced, respectively).

Utility Analysis. We first look at pmax, i.e., the maximum probability of avoiding an SLA violation within the first day of usage, corresponding to a measure of reliability for an ESERVER product. In Fig. 6 it can be seen that when the maximal required bandwidth is below 1 GBit/s, SLA violations can almost surely be avoided within all kinds of servers. This is clear, since at least one card needs to be active in the server, such that at least a 1 GBit/s can be served at any time. When the initial feature combination is not sufficient to serve the maximal requested bandwidth, the maximal probability avoiding an SLA violation during one day drops significantly. This can be seen especially at bandwidths with 1, 2 or 10 GBit/s. In general, given the maximal bandwidth assumed to be requested by users, the best choice for an initial feature combination is the one corresponding to the topmost chart. The advanced products detailed in the last graph show that the chosen switching policy has a very similar influence on the results as determined in the original EBOND case studies [23, 30]. An aggressive strategy almost surely raises an SLA violation when turning 10 GBit/s, whereas plugging a new slow card and choosing a strategy with a higher bandwidth assumption still retains a possibility to circumvent an SLA violation until 11 GBit/s are reached. The distribution algorithms do not influence significantly this probability property and are almost indistinguishable.

Energy Analysis. When turning to the minimization of the expected energy consumption, i.e., computing emin for $\mathcal{M}$, it is clear that the best strategy is to never upgrade or buy new cards, keeping the energy costs as small as possible. Hence, the smallest configuration with only one slow card initially activated performs best with only 1.88 W of energy consumption for maximal bandwidths greater than 1 GBit/s (cf. Fig. 7). Configurations activating a fast card only in situations when the bandwidth is above 1 GBit/s range between the energy consumption of slow and fast cards until reaching 10 GBit/s. In between, the charts in Fig. 7 show mixed configurations, where mainly the switching policies influence the energy consumption. The aggressive policy requires least energy, followed by the high savings and the balanced one. This can also be seen in our example shown in the last graph, where until reaching 80 % workload of the initial fast card, the energy consumption equals the energy characteristics of the 10 GBit card. For higher bandwidths than 8 GBit/s, a new slow card can then be plugged and thus, the energy consumption can be reduced relying on the switching policy.

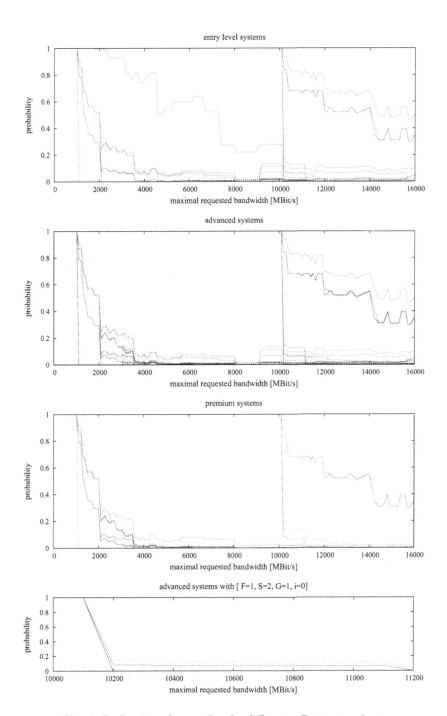

Fig. 6. Evaluation of pmax for the different ESERVER variants

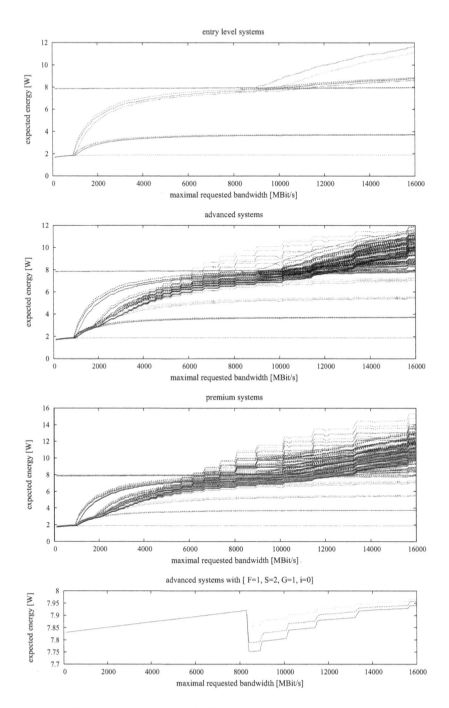

Fig. 7. Evaluation of emin for the different ESERVER variants

SLA Violation Analysis. When minimizing the expected number of SLA violations, i.e., computing vmin for $\mathcal{M}$, similar phenomena can be observed as within our utility analysis. The solution of the strategy synthesis problem yields a scheduler upgrading and plugging new and fast cards as soon as the feature controller permits it. However, as one can see in Fig. 8, choosing initial configurations with only slow slots, the expected percentage of time within an SLA violation increases significantly when the maximal required bandwidth exceeds the supported bandwidth of the server with the maximally equipped network cards. Especially for the entry level systems, one can easily distinguish between the systems having only one slot (raising SLA violations when the bandwidth exceeds 1 GBit/s or 10 GBit/s) and having two slots from which at least one is a slow slot (raising SLA violations at 2 GBit/s or 11 GBit/s). In the lower left, premium systems stay below 12 % of the time within an SLA violation if the bandwidth is below 6 GBit/s, which then may grow very fast. This is mainly due to the fact that a premium server system has at least six slots where cards can be plugged. When choosing the example configuration (see the last graph), the minimal expected percentage of time run with SLA violations with a maximal bandwidth of 11 GBit/s is quite low with at most 3 %. Note that as in EBOND case study, the balanced switching policy minimizes SLA violations always best, followed by the high savings and aggressive policy.

Monetary Analysis. Closely related to the SLA violation time analysis is the solution of the strategy synthesis problem which minimizes the money to be spent for the ESERVER system. Figure 9 shows the results for computing mmin for $\mathcal{M}$. Choosing a system with a fast 10 GBit network interface card does not yield additional costs after purchase, since SLA violations are very unlikely (see utility analysis for pmax). However, when purchasing only small configurations, expenses may exceed the costs for high equipped server products when facing higher bandwidths due to SLA violation fees to be paid. Thus, the customer may purchase a better performing but more expensive system if the maximal required bandwidth is high. However, as the first graph shows, it is a good strategy to buy an entry-level system with fast slots and upgrade cards on demand, facing only a few of SLA violations and resulting into low monetary costs.

5.4   Scalability and Statistical Evaluation

As the case study in the last section already illustrated, it is a challenging task to verify large-scaled product lines with thousands of feature combinations. However, using symbolic encodings for the model and information about the structure of the feature diagram, we managed to apply probabilistic model checking for a quantitative analysis. But even after we could reduce the size of the model encoding, we had to carefully choose the numerical methods to guarantee convergence of the approximation algorithms. In this section, we deal with the model and runtime characteristics of the ESERVER case study to show scalability of our approach towards model checking dynamic product lines which incorporate multi-features and hence are large-scaled.

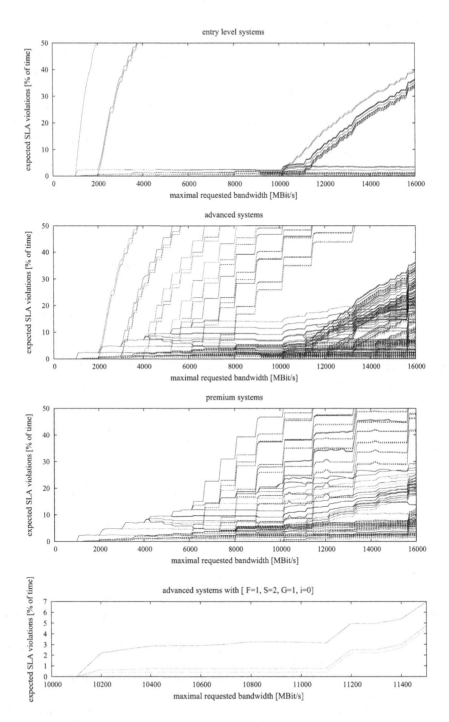

Fig. 8. Evaluation of vmin for the different ESERVER variants

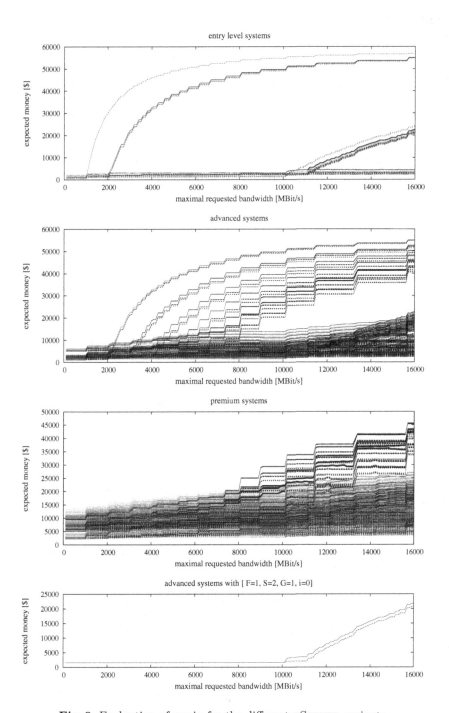

Fig. 9. Evaluation of mmin for the different ESERVER variants

Runtime Characteristics. The case study was carried out on an Intel Xeon X5650 @ 2.67 GHz with 384 GB of RAM and using the symbolic MTBDD engine of PRISM 4.1 with a precision of 10^{-5}. The logarithmically scaled Fig. 10 shows the time needed for model checking, the number of states in the model, and the memory consumption – each depending on the maximal bandwidth assumed in the environment feature. Note that the behaviors of all feature combinations and feature switches are encoded into one single model, such that the model-checking time includes the computation time of all the four properties of the case study and for all 17,544 initial feature combinations. The symbolic representation of the model allowed for a memory consumption of only a few MBytes in all cases. At 16 GBit/s we had to construct a system model of 465,950,960 states and 1,072,736,675 transitions.

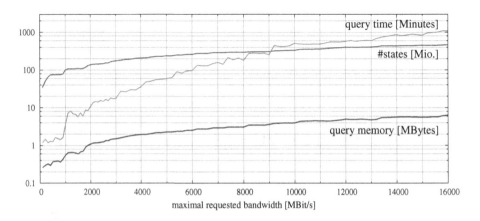

Fig. 10. Statistical evaluation of the experiments

Compact State-space Representation. Within models symbolically represented using multi-terminal binary decision diagrams (MTBDDs), states and transitions are encoded by a binary tree-like structure where branchings stand for decisions on variable valuations [26]. Traversing this tree-like diagram, the decisions are not made in an arbitrary fashion, but follow a given variable ordering. It is well-known that the size of such diagrams crucially depends on that variable ordering [9]. In our setting, the variables which appear in the MTBDD representation exactly correspond to the variables *Var* of the feature modules presented in Sect. 4, where we assume that also the locations of feature modules are encoded by variables. More formally, a variable ordering on *Var* is a partial order $\pi = (\textit{Var}, \leq)$, where if $x < y$, the variable x is decided prior to y in the MTBDD of the model. Given two sets of variables $A, B \in \textit{Var}$, we write $A \leq B$ iff for all $x \in A$, $y \in B$ we have $x \leq y$.

To optimize the size of the model representation of the large-scaled ESERVER product line $\mathcal{M}$, we investigated several variable orderings on *Var*. A good heuristic for variable orderings in MTBDDs is to first decide variables which are "most-influential", i.e., changed only at the beginning of an execution of the modeled system but influence the systems behavior significantly [38]. This directly fits to the product-line setting by placing variables of static features before the variables of dynamic features and to order variables of the same feature module close together. Also environment features and the base scheduling of interplay between hardware, software and environment can be assumed to change their behavior quite often and should be the greatest elements of an ordering. Keeping these facts in mind, we hence started with an intuitive variable ordering π_{start} defined using the modular structure of the product line:

$$Con \; < \; \underbrace{Hardware}_{T<o<N} \; < \; \underbrace{Coordination}_{D<y} \; < \; \underbrace{eServer}_{phase} \; < \; \underbrace{Env}_{bandwidth<time} \quad ,$$

where the sets stand for variables in Var contained in the respective feature modules, e.g., $Hardware$ contains all variables of the feature modules T, o and N incorporated in Hardware. phase is a variable encoding the three phases of ESERVER, i.e., whether the system is in a reconfiguration, coordination or environment phase. bandwidth and time are environment variables encoding the requested bandwidth and the time passed. Then, we applied sifting methods [46] for dynamically optimizing variable orderings, which revealed a variable ordering π_{opt}:

$$eServer \; < \; Con \; < \; Hardware \; < \; Coordination \; < \; Env.$$

For comparison reasons, we also defined variable orderings ρ_{start} and ρ_{opt}, which denote the reverse variable orderings of π_{start} and π_{opt}, respectively.

Table 1. Statistics of various variable orderings (maximal bandwidth $= 2.4\,\text{GBit/s}$)

Variable order	#states	#nodes	Memory [MB]	Query time [min]
π_{start}	145,984,112	116,381	2,337	17
ρ_{start}	"	168,043	3,275	72
π_{opt}	"	63,990	1,207	11
ρ_{opt}	"	175,467	9,253	237

Table 1 depicts the influence of these variable orderings on the performance of solving the strategy synthesis problem for $\mathcal{M}$ and the four queries pmax, emin, vmin and mmin under the assumption that the maximal requested bandwidth is 2.4 GBit/s. As it can be seen, optimizing the variable ordering has a strong impact on the nodes of the MTBDD required to encode the model and the time needed for the query computation. The complete case study presented in the last section has been carried out using the variable ordering π_{opt}. The computations would have taken more than one day each for maximal bandwidths greater than 5.4 GBit/s if we would have chosen the variable ordering ρ_{opt}.

Symbolic vs. Explicit Model Checking. It is well-known that an explicit engine is usually faster than a symbolic one when the model contains lots of different numeric values or available memory is not the restricting factor of the system setup. However, the operational model for product lines designed through multi-features contain lots of symmetric behaviors due to the several instances of multi-features and hence, symbolic methods outperform the explicit ones in our case study. Table 2 compares the characteristics solving the strategy synthesis problems for an ESERVER (again assuming 2.4 GBit/s maximal bandwidth) and the four queries of our case study using various engines. Besides the MTBDD engine used in the whole case study, we run the sparse and explicit engine of PRISM. Whereas the sparse engine constructs the model symbolically and then uses an explicit sparse matrix representation for solving queries, the explicit engine also constructs the model explicitly. This has a strong impact especially on memory consumption, peaking at over 240 GB within the explicit engine.

Table 2. Statistics of various PRISM engines (maximal bandwidth $= 2.4$ GBit/s)

Engine	All-in-one			One-by-one
	#states	Memory [MB]	Query time [min]	Query time [min]
MTBDD	145,984,112	1,207	11	3,112
sparse	"	11,167	224	3,156
explicit	"	241,991	432	802

All-in-one vs. One-by-one. Within our approach, all behaviors of the products in the dynamic product line are encoded into a single model, similar to the family-based approaches for product line analysis [53]. This allows to exploit the commonalities between the products, especially in combination with a symbolic representation of the model. However, we have shown in the last paragraph that explicit engines for probabilistic model checking do not perform well on large models due to memory constraints, such that checking every product in isolation and hence dividing the model into smaller parts might still yield a faster analysis method. Table 2 also depicts a comparison between the explicit and symbolic engines of PRISM used to analyze the 17,544 products of the ESERVER product line one-by-one when assuming a maximal bandwidth of 2.4 GBit/s. The largest model of a single product in the product line contains 120,575 states. Both, the MTBDD and sparse engine computations took more than two days. Although the explicit engine turned out to be the fastest engine for the one-by-one approach, it took more than 70 times longer than the all-in-one MTBDD-approach.

6   Conclusions

We presented a compositional modeling framework for dynamic product lines that relies on annotated versions of probabilistic automata. The implementation of features and the behavior of possibly unknown or only partially known implementations of external features are represented by feature modules, which are probabilistic automata with guards and special switch transitions for the feature changes. Constraints on the activation and deactivation of features during runtime of the system are imposed by feature controllers, probabilistic automata synchronizing with switch transitions of feature modules. Most of the family-based verification approaches for static and nonprobabilistic product lines use monolithic models including all behaviors of the products in the product line. Our approach with feature modules and controllers allows to generate such operational models in a compositional way.

Dynamic product lines modeled within our framework yield an MDP semantics, such that many problems for feature-oriented systems can be solved using standard algorithms. This includes model-checking problems for properties referring to feature combinations, which till now required specialized algorithms even in the nonprobabilistic setting [12]. We also presented a translation from our framework into guarded-command languages used, e.g., by the prominent probabilistic model checker PRISM. For a case study concerning an energy-aware server product line (called ESERVER), we used PRISM to solve the strategy synthesis problem that asks for strategies to trigger feature combination changes according to various quantitative properties. We also placed the focus on large-scaled product lines which contain thousands of valid feature combinations and can be described elegantly through multi-feature diagrams. For large-scaled ESERVER models, we compared different model-checking engines and showed that symbolic approaches clearly outperform explicit ones.

There are many other interesting variants of the strategy synthesis problem that are also solvable by known algorithms applicable to the MDP semantics of our framework. One might distinguish between switch events that are indeed controllable and those that cannot be enforced or prevented, but are triggered by the environment. In this case, the arising MDP can be seen as a stochastic game structure, where the controller and the environment are opponents and the task to generate an optimal strategy for the controller reduces to well-known game-based problems [10,15,21,24]. Similarly, one might take into account that also the feature modules can behave nondeterministically.

A challenge remaining for further work is to integrate our feature-oriented formalisms into model-checking tools to ease their use for software developers, enabling to integrate quantitative analyses into the workflow of product-line development. This includes the interpretation and compact output of the strategies solving the strategy synthesis problem, till now only internally computed by existing model-checking tools. Also investigations on feature-dependent multi-objectives are important in this context [4]. Such requirements would, e.g., enable to check whether the trade-off between energy consumption and the time without SLA violations is better for premium or advanced ESERVER variants [3].

References

1. Apel, S., Hutchins, D.: A calculus for uniform feature composition. ACM Trans. Program. Lang. Syst. **32**(5), 1–33 (2010)
2. Apel, S., Janda, F., Trujillo, S., Kästner, C.: Model superimposition in software product lines. In: Paige, R.F. (ed.) ICMT 2009. LNCS, vol. 5563, pp. 4–19. Springer, Heidelberg (2009)
3. Baier, C., Dubslaff, C., Klein, J., Klüppelholz, S., Wunderlich, S.: Probabilistic model checking for energy-utility analysis. In: van Breugel, F., Kashefi, E., Palamidessi, C., Rutten, J. (eds.) Horizons of the Mind. LNCS, vol. 8464, pp. 96–123. Springer, Heidelberg (2014)
4. Baier, C., Dubslaff, C., Klüppelholz, S., Daum, M., Klein, J., Märcker, S., Wunderlich, S.: Probabilistic model checking and non-standard multi-objective reasoning. In: Gnesi, S., Rensink, A. (eds.) FASE 2014 (ETAPS). LNCS, vol. 8411, pp. 1–16. Springer, Heidelberg (2014)
5. Baier, C., Katoen, J.-P.: Principles of Model Checking. The MIT Press, Cambridge (2008)
6. Baier, C., Kwiatkoswka, M.: Model checking for a probabilistic branching time logic with fairness. Distrib. Comput. **11**(3), 125–155 (1998)
7. Benavides, D., Segura, S., Ruiz-Cortés, A.: Automated analysis of feature models 20 years later: a literature review. Inf. Syst. **35**(6), 615–636 (2010)
8. Bianco, A., de Alfaro, L.: Model checking of probabilistic and nondeterministic systems. In: Thiagarajan, P.S. (ed.) FSTTCS 1995. LNCS, vol. 1026. Springer, Heidelberg (1995)
9. Bryant, R.E.: Graph-based algorithms for boolean function manipulation. IEEE Trans. Comput. **35**, 677–691 (1986)
10. Chatterjee, K., Jurdzinski, M., Henzinger, T.: Quantitative simple stochastic parity games. In: Proceedings of the 15th ACM-SIAM Symposium on Discrete algorithms (SODA), pp. 121–130. SIAM (2004)
11. Clarke, E.M., Emerson, E.A., Sistla, A.P.: Automatic verification of finite-state concurrent systems using temporal logic specifications. ACM Trans. Program. Lang. Syst. **8**, 244–263 (1986)
12. Classen, A., Heymans, P., Schobbens, P.-Y., Legay, A.: Symbolic model checking of software product lines. In: Proceedings of the 33rd Conference on Software Engineering (ICSE), pp. 321–330. ACM (2011)
13. Classen, A., Heymans, P., Schobbens, P.-Y., Legay, A., Raskin, J.-F.: Model checking lots of systems: efficient verification of temporal properties in software product lines. In: Proceedings of the 32rd Conference on Software Engineering (ICSE), pp. 335–344. ACM (2010)
14. Clements, P., Northrop, L.: Software Product Lines: Practices and Patterns. Addison-Wesley Professional, Reading (2001)
15. Condon, A.: The complexity of stochastic games. Inf. Comput. **96**(2), 203–224 (1992)
16. Cordy, M., Classen, A., Heymans, P., Legay, A., Schobbens, P.-Y.: Model checking adaptive software with featured transition systems. In: Cámara, J., de Lemos, R., Ghezzi, C., Lopes, A. (eds.) Assurances for Self-Adaptive Systems. LNCS, vol. 7740, pp. 1–29. Springer, Heidelberg (2013)
17. Cordy, M., Schobbens, P.-Y., Heymans, P., Legay, A.: Beyond boolean product-line model checking: dealing with feature attributes and multi-features. In: Proceedings of the 35rd Conference on Software Engineering (ICSE), pp. 472–481. IEEE Press (2013)

18. Czarnecki, K., Helsen, S., Eisenecker, U.W.: Formalizing cardinality-based feature models and their specialization. Softw. Process Improv. Pract. **10**(1), 7–29 (2005)
19. Damiani, F., Schaefer, I.: Dynamic delta-oriented programming. In: Proceedings of the 15th Software Product Line Conference (SPLC), vol. 2, pp. 34:1–34:8. ACM (2011)
20. de Alfaro, L.: Computing minimum and maximum reachability times in probabilistic systems. In: Baeten, J.C.M., Mauw, S. (eds.) CONCUR 1999. LNCS, vol. 1664, p. 66. Springer, Heidelberg (1999)
21. de Alfaro, L., Majumdar, R.: Quantitative solution of omega-regular games. J. Comput. Syst. Sci. **68**(2), 374–397 (2004)
22. Dinkelaker, T., Mitschke, R., Fetzer, K., Mezini, M.: A dynamic software product line approach using aspect models at runtime. In: Proceedings of the 1st Workshop on Composition and Variability (2010)
23. Dubslaff, C., Klüppelholz, S., Baier, C.: Probabilistic model checking for energy analysis in software product lines. In: Proceedings of the 13th Conference on Modularity (MODULARITY), pp. 169–180. ACM (2014)
24. Filar, J., Vrieze, K.: Competitive Markov Decision Processes. Springer, New York (1997)
25. Forejt, V., Kwiatkowska, M., Norman, G., Parker, D.: Automated verification techniques for probabilistic systems. In: Bernardo, M., Issarny, V. (eds.) SFM 2011. LNCS, vol. 6659, pp. 53–113. Springer, Heidelberg (2011)
26. Fujita, M., McGeer, P., Yang, J.-Y.: Multi-terminal binary decision diagrams: an efficient data structure for matrix representation. Formal Methods Syst. Des. **10** (2–3), 149–169 (1997)
27. Gelernter, D., Carriero, N.: Coordination languages and their significance. Commun. ACM **35**(2), 96–107 (1992)
28. Ghezzi, C., Sharifloo, A.M.: Model-based verification of quantitative non-functional properties for software product lines. Inf. Softw. Technol. **55**(3), 508–524 (2013)
29. Gomaa, H., Hussein, M.: Dynamic software reconfiguration in software product families. In: van der Linden, F.J. (ed.) PFE 2003. LNCS, vol. 3014, pp. 435–444. Springer, Heidelberg (2004)
30. Hähnel, M., Döbel, B., Völp, M., Härtig, H.: eBond: energy saving in heterogeneous R.A.I.N. In: Proceedings of the 4th Conference on Future Energy Systems (e-Energy), pp. 193–202. ACM, New York (2013)
31. Hallsteinsen, S., Hinchey, M., Park, S., Schmid, K.: Dynamic software product lines. IEEE Comput. **41**(4), 93–95 (2008)
32. Haverkort, B.: Performance of Computer Communication Systems: A Model-Based Approach. Wiley, New York (1998)
33. Hay, J.D., Atlee, J.M.: Composing features and resolving interactions. In: Proceedings of the 8th Symposium on Foundations of Software Engineering (SIGSOFT), pp. 110–119. ACM (2000)
34. Hinton, A., Kwiatkowska, M., Norman, G., Parker, D.: PRISM: a tool for automatic verification of probabilistic systems. In: Hermanns, H., Palsberg, J. (eds.) TACAS 2006. LNCS, vol. 3920, pp. 441–444. Springer, Heidelberg (2006)
35. Kang, K.C., Cohen, S.G., Hess, J.A., Novak, W.E., Peterson, A.S.: Feature-oriented domain analysis (FODA) feasibility study. Technical report CMU/SEI-90-TR-21, Carnegie-Mellon University, November 1990
36. Katz, S.: A superimposition control construct for distributed systems. ACM Trans. Program. Lang. Syst. **15**(2), 337–356 (1993)
37. Kulkarni, V.: Modeling and Analysis of Stochastic Systems. Chapman & Hall, London (1995)

38. Malik, S., Wang, A., Brayton, R., Sangiovanni-Vincentelli, A.: Logic verification using binary decision diagrams in a logic synthesis environment. In: Proceedings of the IEEE Conference on Computer-Aided Design (ICCAD), pp. 6–9 (1988)
39. McMillan, K.L.: Symbolic Model Checking. Kluwer Academic Publishers, Dordrecht (1993)
40. Millo, J.-V., Ramesh, S., Krishna, S.N., Narwane, G.K.: Compositional verification of software product lines. In: Johnsen, E.B., Petre, L. (eds.) IFM 2013. LNCS, vol. 7940, pp. 109–123. Springer, Heidelberg (2013)
41. Noorian, M., Bagheri, E., Du, W.: Non-functional properties in software product lines: a taxonomy for classification. In: Proceedings of the 24th Conference on Software Engineering & Knowledge Engineering (SEKE), pp. 663–667. Knowledge Systems Institute Graduate School (2012)
42. Papadopoulos, G.A., Arbab, F.: Coordination models and languages. Adv. Comput. **46**, 329–400 (1998)
43. Plath, M., Ryan, M.: Feature integration using a feature construct. Sci. Comput. Program. **41**(1), 53–84 (2001)
44. Puterman, M.: Markov Decision Processes: Discrete Stochastic Dynamic Programming. Wiley, New York (1994)
45. Rosenmüller, M., Siegmund, N., Apel, S., Saake, G.: Flexible feature binding in software product lines. Autom. Softw. Eng. **18**(2), 163–197 (2011)
46. Rudell, R.: Dynamic variable ordering for ordered binary decision diagrams. In: Proceedings of the IEEE/ACM Conference on Computer-Aided Design (ICCAD), pp. 42–47. IEEE Computer Society (1993)
47. Schneider, J.-G., Lumpe, M., Nierstrasz, O.: Agent coordination via scripting languages. In: Omicini, A., Zambonelli, F., Klusch, M., Tolksdorf, R. (eds.) Coordination of Internet Agents: Models, Technologies, and Applications, pp. 153–175. Springer, New York (2001)
48. Segala, R.: Modeling and verification of randomized distributed real-time systems. Ph.D. thesis, Massachusetts Institute of Technology (1995)
49. Segala, R., Lynch, N.A.: Probabilistic simulations for probabilistic processes. Nord. J. Comput. **2**(2), 250–273 (1995)
50. Siegmund, N., Rosenmüller, M., Kästner, C., Giarrusso, P.G., Apel, S., Kolesnikov, S.S.: Scalable prediction of non-functional properties in software product lines: footprint and memory consumption. Inf. Softw. Technol. **55**(3), 491–507 (2013)
51. Siegmund, N., Rosenmüller, M., Kuhlemann, M., Kästner, C., Saake, G.: Measuring non-functional properties in software product line for product derivation. In: Proceedings of the 15th Asia-Pacific Software Engineering Conference (APSEC), pp. 187–194. IEEE (2008)
52. Varshosaz, M., Khosravi, R.: Discrete time Markov chain families: modeling and verification of probabilistic software product lines. In: Proceedings of the 17th Software Product Line Conference Co-located Workshops, pp. 34–41. ACM (2013)
53. von Rhein, A., Apel, S., Kästner, C., Thüm, T., Schaefer, I.: The PLA model: on the combination of product-line analyses. In: Proceedings of the 7th Workshop on Variability Modelling of Software-intensive Systems (VaMoS), pp. 14:1–14:8. ACM (2013)
54. White, J., Dougherty, B., Schmidt, D.C., Benavides, D.: Automated reasoning for multi-step feature model configuration problems. In: Proceedings of the 13th Software Product Line Conference (SPLC), pp. 11–20. ACM (2009)

Author Index

Printed in the United States
By Bookmasters